# *The*
# AVERAGE
# AMERICAN

*The*

# AVERAGE
# AMERICAN

*The Extraordinary Search for
the Nation's Most Ordinary Citizen*

## KEVIN O'KEEFE

PublicAffairs
*New York*

Published in the United States by PublicAffairs™,
a member of the Perseus Books Group.

Book design by Jane Raese
Text set in 11-point Sabon

Library of Congress Cataloging-in-Publication Data
O'Keefe, Kevin.
The average American: the extraordinary search for the nation's most
ordinary citizen / Kevin O'Keefe.
p. cm.
ISBN-13: 978-1-58648-270-1
ISBN-10: 1-58648-270-X
1. United States—Description and travel. 2. National characteristics, American.
3. O'Keefe, Kevin—Travel—United States. I. Title.
E169.Z83O44 2005
305.8'00973—dc22
2005051338

First Edition

2 4 6 8 10 9 7 5 3 1

*To mom and dad*
*and Kathy*

# Contents

# A Note About You

*If* you *have ever lived* in any of the fifty states or Washington, D.C.—you were a candidate in the search for the nation's most ordinary person.

# Author's Note

*For nearly two decades,* my livelihood was predicated on a belief that I understood everyday consumers. For clients ranging from Crest toothpaste to *Maxim* magazine, I had worked on corporate marketing and public relations campaigns aimed at large national audiences. So when a prospective client accused me of not relating to the average American, I reacted with indignation: I had been raised in a middle-class Catholic family in a quiet New England village. My mother, the daughter of a public school teacher and a bookkeeper at an auto parts business, was a homemaker and secretary. My father, the son of a butcher and a mill worker, was a public school teacher and the manager of a summer 4-H camp. In a neighborhood that was ripe with tradition, I had engaged in all the activities American boys were supposed to—from playing baseball (which I loved—it was, of course, the National Pastime) to delivering newspapers (which I did not love, but it instilled in me that vaunted American work ethic). After college in the South and grad school in the Midwest, I had found success in the mass marketing field.

I had the common touch. Right?

On second thought, I wasn't quite sure. Simply because I followed contemporary trends to understand what resonated with certain everyday consumers, did that automatically mean I knew average Americans? By living and working in Chicago, Washington, Los Angeles, and New York City for most of my working life, immersed in the professional sports and entertainment business—even when I was on the road in the "rest" of America—was I hopelessly out of touch with the vast majority of my countrymen?

I began to track down some statistics about the typical American. They did not describe me. Some of the numbers were particularly revealing. I read that most Americans can be found in the state where they grew up; my four brothers still live in Connecticut, but I had bucked that norm many years ago. I read that the average American can expect to spend forty-eight hours per year shopping at the mall; I was forty-eight hours short of the mark.

I couldn't deny the pattern. For many years, I had avoided participating in the expected, the ordinary. From picnics to parenthood, from holidays to home buying, I had consciously rejected practices that could be considered typical. I had rented homes above my means and gravitated to creative urbanites and work with public figures. When producing, for instance, large charity events, I privately mocked the sheeplike behavior of many who attended. (I am, incidentally, not proud of this.) Probably for similar reasons, I had few close friends.

Whenever I had a choice between settling or struggling, I chose B. A, of course, stood for average.

The explanation was simple, really. I was scared of becoming ordinary.

The feelings triggered by my would-be client (who just happened, bizarrely, to be the quintessential irregular American, actor Marlon Brando, in need of a sales plan for a charity idea) came at a particularly disorienting time. My wife and I were still unpacking from our honeymoon.

Although I had long classified marriage as commonplace and decided that it was not for me, I'd recently been blindsided by love and made it to the altar—my first major A selection. As a result, I was happier than ever in my personal life.

Like an NFL receiver, I needed to face the fear of going across the middle. I marked a file with the words "Average American," told my wife why, and did a little more research.

But I didn't have the guts to continue.

Many months passed and I came across the file. An unfamiliar sheet—a page ripped from a museum program—was fastened inside. Written in pencil, in my wife's handwriting, was a Norman Rockwell quote.

"Commonplace never became tiresome," it read. "It is we who

become tired when we cease to be curious and appreciative. It is not a new scene which is needed, but a new viewpoint."

So, this was one of the blessings of marriage—the one you love the most telling you what you need to hear while guiding you toward the paths you are meant to explore.

Were other typical American traditions full of such value? I needed to know. I needed the numbers, the data, that would take me to the most ordinary American: the actual, living, breathing, in the flesh, coffee-with-milk-and-two-sugars, 2.3-kids, person.

If I could find the numbers, I could find the person, and if I could find the person, maybe I could find a piece of myself.

# One

# "ALL THAT IS GREAT, GOOD OR BEAUTIFUL"

*Candidates remaining: 281,421,906*

*My muse was not average.* A former opera composer and historian of love from Belgium, he was fond of wearing the type of high pompadour and low sideburns that Elvis—a century later—would make famous.

His name was Lambert Adolphe Jacques Quetelet, and he had died in 1874.

After surviving a childhood marked by poverty and tragedy—he was only seven when his dad died—Quetelet flirted with careers in music, poetry, journalism, and painting, then all but invented the field of social statistics. He created the first international statistics conference, and one of his breakthrough discoveries showed that human actions commonly reveal a pattern, known today as the bell curve, with the most average result charted in the peak position. Based on his belief that average was ideal, he formulated a new investigative tool for law enforcement—criminal profiling: Individuals became suspects if they deviated a certain degree from average models.

Quetelet (pronounced *kettle-ay*) understood that people who are viewed as atypical are often proven to be less so when actual social statistics are applied. For instance, Napoleon was—and still is— widely characterized as short simply because he was shorter than

1

most French *military* men, the people with whom he spent so much of his public time. Quetelet, whose transition into statistical work was shepherded by Napoleon's one-time minister of the interior, knew that among Frenchmen of his day, Napoleon was actually of ordinary height.

In 1827, Quetelet had a brainstorm. He believed that with a single idea, he could complete both the ultimate statistical study and the ultimate quest. He would set out to define the demographically average person, embarking on a search for the planet's consummate life form. "If an individual at any given epoch of society possessed all the qualities of the average man, he would represent all that is great, good or beautiful," Quetelet proclaimed.

Quetelet started his search by charting averages—for example, the median chest measurement among 5,738 Scottish soldiers. Eight years later, he had determined the average age, strength, and drunkenness of assorted Europeans, among other categories of data.

Quetelet's 1835 book on his research—later translated into English as *A Treatise on Man and the Development of His Faculties*—presented statistical charts for average individuals, using such measurements as height, weight, age, profession, and geographical region. From all his averages, Quetelet presented statistical profiles of average people, but there is no record of his ever identifying or even attempting to identify a specific average person.

Nonetheless, contemporary readers were captivated by his effort. Stephen Stigler wrote in his 1986 book *The History of Statistics* about the impact of Quetelet's study: "The average man was a fictional being in his creator's eye, but such was his appeal that he underwent a transformation, like Pinocchio or Pygmalion's statue, so that he still lives in headlines of our daily newspapers."

Today's headlines often characterize the average American not as great, good, or beautiful, but as fat, dumb, and ugly. However, the majority of Americans are of healthy weight, the nation's average intelligence score has continued to rise about four points every decade since nationwide IQ testing began in the 1920s, and scientific evidence shows that when it comes to facial beauty, we prefer averageness, even in strangers.

In recognition of Quetelet and John Q Public, and to separate fact from fiction, I began to fill a notebook, christened Mr. Q, with the most reputable statistics I could find about the average American.

On a misty day in December 2003, I headed with my new traveling companion to the headquarters of the U.S. Census Bureau.

*The* U.S. *Census,* held every ten years since 1790, was first conducted by Thomas Jefferson as secretary of state under President Washington. The national head count—taken by U.S. marshals on horseback—came in at 3.9 million people, although Jefferson told the president that the tally was probably some 100,000 people short.

The national census Quetelet created for Belgium in 1846 quickly became the international standard-bearer. Quetelet's careful data collection and statistical analysis so impressed Congressman James Garfield that the future president tracked down Quetelet to learn how to improve the U.S. Census.

Soon, the Census Bureau was an incubator for scientific advances, particularly those that had to do with efficient calculation. For the 1890 census, a bureau employer named Herman Hollerith invented the punch card, then left to launch a start-up company that later became International Business Machines, abbreviated by Hollerith as IBM. Separately, UNIVAC I, the world's first commercial computer, was created specifically to help process the 1950 census.

Today, the U.S. Census is not only the oldest continuing public census in the world, but the finest measurement of grand-scale human averageness. When I arrived at the Census Bureau, the 2000 census—or Census 2000, as its handlers prefer—had already generated more than 1.5 billion pages of data, enough to stretch from the earth to the moon. It included information on people living in more than 105 million occupied housing units (let's call them homes) on more than 8 million blocks. At a cost of nearly $10 billion, the U.S. Census had become the largest social science project in history. Although it doesn't measure fatness, dumbness, or ugliness, it serves as an important debunker to many other myths associated with the average American. Consider the notion that the most typical American is an adult in a traditional nuclear family—a married man or woman living with an opposite-sex spouse and offspring under eighteen years old. Census 2000 showed that the nuclear family now represents fewer than a quarter of all U.S. homes. Families consisting of a working dad, stay-at-home mom, and offspring make up only 7 percent of U.S. homes.

*Surrounded by a high security fence,* the Census Bureau headquarters in the Washington suburb of Suitland, Maryland, resembles a prison. Its flat and square main building—simply "Federal Office Building 3," according to the only sign out front—was slapped together in a few months as temporary World War II office space. Contaminated water, flooding, and electrical outages have long plagued the campus's four structures. When a supercomputer was installed in Office Building 4 in 1999, the floor couldn't hold it, freeing asbestos that had been idling for years.

Less than a half hour after I asked to speak with the nation's director of population analysis, I found myself in a small conference room sitting across from him. Dr. J. Gregory Robinson, a tall man with a slender face and a trim white mustache, wore a laminated photo ID clipped tidily to his shirt. On the wall behind me were three plaques, each proclaiming "100 Percent Goal Award, Population Division."

Census 2000 had created a snapshot of the 281,421,906 official residents of the fifty states and Washington, D.C., as determined in April 2000. However, because I was looking for the Average American, I knew I needed to apply to my search the most common definition of American: citizen of the United States. This immediately eliminated 7 percent of all U.S. residents. In California, 16 percent of the state's population was dismissed.

Greg Robinson enjoys numbers and people and, as a result, he enjoys his job. While in high school in Oak Ridge, Tennessee, he was elated when his parents gave him a slide rule as a graduation gift. Because he knows it will one day become a public document, his family's 2000 census form bears his inscription, "Hello, future generations!"

After two minutes of talking numbers with me, Robinson glanced at his watch.

It was time to confess: I wanted him to help me find the nation's most statistically average person. Robinson leaned back and smiled warmly. "This is a first," he said. "Go on."

In theory, my approach was simple. Ascertain which census demographics best distinguish people—age and educational level could be two—and secure the averages for each. Determine which American residents best matched all the criteria. To narrow this group to one individual, I would apply demographics from other reputable government agencies and public opinion firms. Together, these organizations provide the type of national information Quetelet would have died for: an absolutely stunning array of numbers, everything from how many one-way trips and pounds of trash the average American resident makes per day (four on both counts) to those who put an elbow on the table "at least once in a while" (86 percent, according to *American Demographics* in 2004) to those who believe in hell (70 percent, Gallup determined the same year).

I told Robinson about a 1964 episode of the CBS sitcom *The Munsters,* in which a national magazine tries to identify the "Average American Family." High jinks ensue after the magazine's computer statistics program goes on the fritz and mistakenly selects the Munsters. There's a lesson to be learned here, I said. If I was to declare someone the Average American, the Census Bureau would want me to get it right. We needed to go to the computer room, pronto.

Robinson slammed on the brakes. He said that the bureau's computer files cannot be connected in a way that would allow us to find the Americans who best hit the census averages. Plus, there is a privacy rule restricting bureau employees from sharing specific names or addresses of those counted by Census 2000. The penalty for violating this law is up to $5,000 and five years in prison. An individual's census information—the actual completed forms—can only be released after seventy-two years.

But I didn't come to Washington to find the most average American of 1930; nor could I wait until 2072. Without the bureau's collaboration, it seemed my search would be either incomplete or misguided.

Thankfully, Robinson wanted to help. In fact, he said he would be fine with someone calling him an average American, as he believes it signifies a kind of life balance overachievers do not have. "Those who are focused on work or themselves around the clock do so so that they can say they are above average," he said. "But I think they're missing life."

I told Robinson that I work long hours, have been called selfish, and unlike most Americans, was neither a parent nor a homeowner.

Nearby was a soft-cover book, with Robinson's name written in permanent ink across the top. "It's yours," he said, pushing it gently across the table. The publication was full of statistical averages and a kaleidoscope of maps from Census 2000. But no names or addresses of average Americans. No shortcut.

That was probably the point. How could I expect to conduct my search quickly and still understand average America?

It was time for my backup plan.

I had devised it after pondering my fear of being average. I had recognized that I was not so much afraid of hitting any average numbers as of being in the majority, which I had negatively interpreted to mean being dull.

I had also realized that the country I love has a constitution based on majoritarian democracy. It was Jefferson who championed "a common government, the fundamental principle of which is, that the will of the majority is to prevail." One Houghton Mifflin textbook defines Jefferson's brand of democracy as "a simple frugal government geared to the average citizen." Indeed, Jefferson started the Inauguration Day tradition of the president walking during the procession, and not riding in a carriage like the well-off, specifically to suggest that the regular American leads the nation.

A few years ago, in defense of a Supreme Court justice nominee not known for being a stellar intellect, a senator reportedly argued that at least one justice should be "average," as that would put him in the national majority. To this day, in the longest-standing democracy in the world, the average American, the ordinary American, is most commonly defined as someone in the nation's majority.

"The voice of the majority decides," Jefferson declared in 1800.

Fair enough. The Average American, the person I was searching for, didn't have to hit all averages but would instead fall within the majority. For example, it would not be as important that he have 12.7 years of education, the latest national average, which few residents would meet perfectly, than it would be that he have a high-school diploma, which most residents do.

Robinson said that continuing this approach could work. One by one, I could consistently apply majority statistics to the national population, until only one person met all of the majority numbers. If only one person in America is always in the majority, he certainly deserves to be the Average American.

I could sense that I would learn a lot about our nation by seeing it through the eyes of such an American. Indeed, majorities are not necessarily what they seem. Subconsciously, we dump all perceived conformists into the majority group, although such groups, say fraternity and sorority members as part of the nation's collegiate student body or union members as part of the blue-collar workforce, may not actually be in the majority. (These groups are not.) And although the news media churns out health and lifestyle stories, terrifying us with mad cow disease and human fingers found in restaurant food or thrilling us with low-carb diets and elective plastic surgery, the subjects involved rarely affect the majority of Americans. Indeed, a total of one American has died of mad cow disease, the found fingers do not add up to even half a hand (and at least one of the fingers was a hoax), the low-carb population topped out at around 10 percent, and fewer than 25 percent of Americans would even consider getting plastic surgery (and that statistic comes from the American Society for Aesthetic Plastic Surgery). And although

America is often described as NASCAR Nation, Gallup reported in 2005 that only three out of every ten Americans consider themselves fans of any form of auto racing (placing it below ice skating; Toe-Loop Nation, anyone?).

$Greg$ *Robinson reminded me* that the nation's demographics are constantly changing. Indeed, later that month, the Census Bureau would report that another U.S. resident dies every thirteen seconds, another is born every eight seconds, and one more immigrant arrives in the country every twenty-five seconds, giving America an increase of one person every twelve seconds. Because the Average American is a moving target, he can only be determined as average based on a specific period of time. Clearly, April 2000—the month on which Census 2000 is based—is the best starting point to use in identifying the Average American. Robinson mentioned that, like himself, most Americans—54.1 percent to be precise—have lived in the same home for at least the previous five years, in his mind an important symbol of stability in the life of a family man. He said that this is one of the reasons he sometimes sees himself as average.

I liked the way that Robinson mentioned this statistic. In collecting my criteria for the Average American, I could continue to rely on the guidance of other Americans, traveling the country with Mr. Q and talking with those who seemed average in some way, taking as criteria those categories they volunteered by words or actions as important in their lives. They would be responsible for leading me to the Average American.

After Robinson indicated that the five-year home criterion would most likely stay in the majority for at least five years, I made it a qualification for the Average American. For Joe or Jane Average— J. Average, I decided—five full years would certainly be enough time to cement his or her average status. I would wait until April 2005 to knock on the door of the Average American. Only those who stayed on the average American course during that span would be eligible. As Robinson likely knew, this would guarantee that the Average

American would be in the same home at the end of my search as he was when the Census 2000 numbers were applied.

With the citizen and home criteria, I had already eliminated more than 100 million Americans: I was ready to journey to pockets of average America, traveling primarily via rental car, always asking for "the most average mid-sized you've got." To make sure no one "performed" for me, I would not photograph or film anyone.

"You have an interesting odyssey ahead of you," Greg Robinson told me. "But you might find it hard to find the end of the road. Don't be disappointed. However far you go will be the farthest anyone has been."

In other words, go West, East, North, and South, young man, but don't expect a 100 Percent Goal Award. Given the uphill terrain that Robinson envisioned, the motto that Jefferson commissioned for our nation seemed like a battle cry. E Pluribus Unum. *Out of many, one.*

## *Two*

# "OBSCURITY IS FOREVER"

*Candidates remaining: fewer than 150 million*

*White bread is synonymous* with both obscurity and anonymity, which may explain the ad for Fleischmann's yeast that appeared in a 1920 issue of *Ladies Home Journal*. It features a drawing of a boy proudly holding a slice of plain bread on Halloween. The youngster is dressed as Napoleon and standing in front of a portrait of the emperor.

If anyone could appreciate Napoleon's most famous maxim— "Glory is fleeting, but obscurity is forever"—it is the ad's young illustrator, Norman Rockwell. He understood that, if carefully observed and drawn, an ordinary life could have an extraordinary shelf life. Indeed, the paintings Rockwell created over the next fifty-eight years for the *Saturday Evening Post* and other publications boosted the country's appreciation for average Americans like never before (or, probably, since).

In 1922, when Rockwell's images showed, for the most part, a sunny, wholesome nation, a mythical dark side of generic Americans was depicted by novelist Sinclair Lewis's George Follanbee Babbitt, a soulless, middle-aged real estate agent from suburban Ohio, who quickly became America's most visible and enduring common man. "Babbitt" is now part of the national lexicon.

But which everyday Joe is more plausible, the romanticized or the ridiculed version? By the late 1950s, one model—the loyal corporate cog—was a conflicted businessman in the complacent, dead-end postwar workplace, as depicted in *The Man in the Gray Flannel Suit* and *The Organization Man,* the respective titles of Sloan Wilson's 1955 novel and William Whyte's 1956 nonfiction study.

"They are the ones of our middle class who have left home, spiritually as well as physically, to take the vows of an organization life," Whyte wrote, mocking the Organization Man for being commonplace and conformist. "Only a few are top managers or ever will be." A recruiting film produced by one of the book's emblematic employers promises, "No geniuses here; just a bunch of average Americans working together." Novelist Kurt Vonnegut could relate. In his 1961 short story "Harrison Bergeron," he wrote about a grim future in which each American who is not "perfectly average" is persecuted for his exceptionality.

Our sanitized, more positive Everyman was most evident in national magazines and on network television. Unlike books and motion pictures, these media were dependent on mass advertisers, who demanded upbeat fare. The sponsors believed that when everyday surroundings were glorified, average Americans were more likely to purchase the goods and services that made up this environment. As a result, television, which had skyrocketed from being in 1 percent of U.S. homes in 1948 to being in more than 90 percent in 1961, had taken Rockwell's lead. Programs showed the Organization Man living the middle-class American Dream—cheerfully earning a paycheck to provide for his loving nuclear family. He was General Insurance Company manager Jim Anderson on *Father Knows Best* (1954–1963), corporate accountant Ward Cleaver on *Leave It to Beaver* (1957–1964), and other happy businessmen tricked out in their requisite business suits, fedoras, and briefcases.

In 1973, the year Rockwell donated his vast personal collection of paintings and drawings to a museum that had been named for him in Stockbridge, Massachusetts, millions of viewers tuned in to commercial-free television to watch a new kind of program. That January, *An American Family* debuted on PBS as a twelve-episode cinema vérité–style look at the Loud family of Santa Barbara, California. Famed anthropologist Margaret Mead called the primetime series "as significant as the invention of drama or the novel." But viewers who tuned in hoping for a glimpse of the American Dream were quickly disappointed. The Loud parents' divorce and other family breakdowns painted a troubled picture of contemporary American life.

At the start of the new millennium, while picking through the wreckage of the stock-market crash, U.S. broadcast networks turned to "reality series" as a practical business decision—to lower escalating production and talent costs. CBS's *Survivor* quickly showed that these serial dramas about unknown Americans could attract record ratings and prove extremely attractive to mainstream advertisers. Producers raced to develop shows that followed authentic Americans. But the participants were actually survivors of casting calls that advanced fame seekers, people with atypical aspirations, backgrounds, and personalities. The shows simply took their lead from other entertainment programming, which has always preferred one manipulated extreme or another over the undoctored ordinary.

Nonetheless, public tragedy—September 11—briefly inspired a genuine interest in everyday Americans. With its corporate workers and public servants recast as martyrs and heroes, New York City's future would include respectful montages of nameless Wall Street workers displayed at gritty downtown art houses, and the founding of the FDNY High School of Fire and Life Safety, with a sign there proclaiming, "Our greatest heroes are ordinary people."

Before long, the mainstream media returned to covering celebrities' "real life" activities with the urgency and seriousness of war correspondence, despite the fact that well-known entertainers are more stage-managed by handlers than ever before. Reality television did try changing the name of its genre to "unscripted series," but, like Banquo's ghost, writer credits still rolled.

The focus of this programming is generally not on those in the middle. As Alessandra Stanley wrote in the *New York Times* in January 2005, "Reality television is instructional in an atavistic way: the focus is less and less on the middle class and more on the wealthiest 1 percent at the top and the masses of striving people at the bottom." One harbinger of this trend: the man who was crowned America's first "Average Joe," on the NBC reality show of that name, was a single millionaire from Manhattan. Perhaps it was in the cards. In 2003, I went to a panel discussion to hear Craig Gilbert, the creator of *An American Family,* and he conceded that reality television has always been oxymoronic, even admitting that he cast the Louds in part because the dad "thought his family was the West Coast Kennedys."

Of course, to distinguish the most common among us from those above and below the norm, credible criteria—and many of them—must be applied. As Henry David Thoreau theorized during his nineteenth-century search for meaning and self-discovery in a cabin in northern Massachusetts, a "law of average" indicates that the more ways we observe someone, the more we are able to understand that person.

At Walden Pond, Thoreau experienced one manmade intrusion on his simple life: the nearby sounds of the Fitchburg Railroad, which he regarded as a roaring beast invading nature's calm. On a cold winter Tuesday in 1857, after he had completed his Walden experience, Thoreau hiked through the snow to the town of Fitchburg. He observed some of the townsfolk and decided that they were forsaking nature ("going only from house to shop and back to house again," he wrote) and holding too many possessions ("I see the crowd of materialists gathered together").

Instead of understanding such sociability and affluence to be the benefits of a tight-knit community and the realization of an American Dream, Thoreau, the quintessential loner, had a new community to illustrate his famous contention that "the mass of men lead lives of quiet desperation." The Fitchburg citizen became one of Thoreau's average Americans, a chaser of material possessions and other hollow pursuits.

But in positioning the Fitchburg citizen in this way, Thoreau never fully applied a scientific law of averages. To do so was not his style. An enormously talented, persuasive, and influential though impressionistic and moody writer, Thoreau never put the average American through a statistical test.

*It was a month after my visit* to the Census Bureau. I was well read on the subject of the average American and, with Mr. Q, well prepared to hit the road on my journey. Only I ran into one small problem: I didn't exactly know where to begin.

That evening, I received a call about the death of my Uncle Wally, a career firefighter who had been a citizen of Fitchburg his entire life.

Although I had hardly seen Wally since my school days, I had thought of him from time to time. Many years ago, as part of my need to differentiate myself from the majority of Americans, I was a contestant on a game show in Los Angeles, the one where the object is to match the fill-in-the-blank responses of six celebrities. I went o for 6 in the first round. During the break, a producer raced over and advised, "That was clever, but remember, we're trying to answer the way most people would. Next time, think of what the average guy would say." I did what I always had when asked to conjure up the image of such a man or to think of things the way "most people" would. I pictured Wally. The older of my two uncles was my default generic American. It wasn't so much my memories of his family-man image, his sturdy build, or his astronaut buzz cut. Instead, I was convinced that his impact was only within his hometown. Because I had long been focused on pursuing endeavors that at the least resonated on a regional level, this was not a compliment.

Wally had passed away one month shy of his seventy-seventh birthday. At the time, seventy-six-point-nine years was also the exact average American life-span. Wally's obituary noted that he had served in World War II, completed his formal education in high school, and raised three children. It was a typical profile of American men born in the 1920s.

Wally's hometown, settled on the Nashua River 50 miles northwest of Boston, was incorporated in 1764 and quickly grew as mills and factories sprouted up on the riverside to produce everything from paper to bicycles. Like the red, white, and blue signs that went up in 1970, proclaiming "Fitchburg: All-America City," most of the structures are now faded or gone. Still stately looking is a teacher's college, the city's largest employer. Many of the natives living at the nearby Sundial retirement center still refer to the college by its former name: Fitchburg Normal School.*

In some ways, Fitchburg is an especially accurate portrait of normal America. In both this city and the nation, according to Census 2000, 74 percent of the residents are adults, and the average household size is 2.6 people. In 1999, the full-time male worker in Fitchburg was earning a median annual income of $35,855, within $1,250 of his national counterpart. Among women, the average was $26,558, a mere $636 difference from the national average for females.

Because Fitchburg appears comfortably middle of the road, it seems appropriate that the city has been called the Finnish capital of America. Finland is well known for its nearly universal middle class, an environment that nonetheless contributed to its being placed at the top of the 2004 world competitiveness chart, which rewards those countries high in such measurements as technological innovation and the state of public institutions. (Over the past couple of years, Finland has also ranked first in the world in its citizens' honesty and reading skills.)

Wally was the son of Finnish parents. On a frigid January evening in a residential Fitchburg neighborhood, nearly a hundred people from Wally's life, many from the local Finnish community, walked past a gleaming white fire truck into a funeral home. Inside, two men in veterans' uniforms kneeled in front of the open casket to pay their respects. One rubbed away tears. When the room was more

*In the sixteenth century, the French took the Latin *norma,* meaning "model" or "standard," changed it to *normale,* and introduced it into their language to accompany *école,* meaning "school." In 1794, École Normale Supérieure opened in France as the country's first school for future teachers. The goal was for educators to learn and pass along the highest standards to generations of students. America adopted the idea and started its first normal school in 1839 in Lexington, Massachusetts. Unlike the French, Americans later adopted the world "normal"—from the Latin *normalis*—to mean "typical." Eventually, normal schools in the states simply became known as teacher colleges. But it was the presence of the original schools, and not any sense of ordinary, that gave Illinois' Normal, Pennsylvania's Normalville, and other such locales their names.

quiet, an officer from the firehouse stood in front and declared, "Wally cared. And he was manful."

From behind a wooden lectern, some of Wally's relatives took turns sharing stories about the importance Wally placed on family, faith, and community. One said Wally risked his life to protect his country and then again to protect his community.

I was much more moved than I thought I would be. I began to wonder whether a large chunk of my life had been squandered by not socializing with Americans, even relatives, who seemed too ordinary for my tastes. How much could I have learned if I had just spent a few weeks with Uncle Wally before he passed away?

*That evening when I was alone,* I pondered one way that Wally may have contributed to my search for the Average American. I thought about his closeness to others.

So many of those who spoke at Wally's wake, including some of his grandchildren, live in the Fitchburg area and have benefited from his everyday love and advice. Mr. Q noted that 60 percent of Americans live in the state in which they were born, a qualification I would require of J. Average.

I thought about the closeness of family. According to a 2003 Gallup study, 96 percent of Americans believe family is "extremely" or "very" important, a view that J. Average would need to hold. Nationwide, emphasis on close family ties may be strengthening every day. Consider the attitudes of Generation Y, the 73 million or so Americans born between 1977 and 1994. According to a 2004 *American Demographics* report, less than 30 percent from this group are "willing to sacrifice family time to 'get ahead.'"

I considered the closeness that comes from community. The only immediate way I could translate it into a criterion was that the Average American would need to be someone who is not only representative of the nation, but of his community. Indeed, someone who thoroughly fits a statistically average profile but lives in a ritzy neighborhood is conspicuous because he is unusual in his surroundings.

Unlike such communities as school, church, and Internet, which people can voluntarily choose to join, all Americans must live in *some* geographical community. Maybe this is why Quetelet used locality as a variable in constructing his average man. To identify the Average American, I had to identify the most average American community.

The importance of community in our lives is not a new concept. In the United States, the Supreme Court has even defined "just actions" as those considered to be so by "the average person in the community." In another case, the Court defined the ideal arbiter as "the average person, applying contemporary community standards." The justices did not define what they meant by "community." To help find the most average person in America, I needed to determine what best defines geographic community in America.

*In the morning breeze* at Wally's burial, I stood beside my parents in a large cemetery overlooking a McDonald's. Within the previous two years, they had buried both of my dad's parents on the same hill. My grandparents were married for seventy-seven years, longer than Wally had lived. I counted my blessings that I still had both my parents. I wanted to tell them that I would spend more quality time with them soon instead of the occasional holiday drop-ins that were my custom. But I knew I still had a lot to learn.

*Three*

# THE MIDDLE WAY

*Candidates remaining: fewer than 140 million*

*After its premiere in 1938,* Thornton Wilder's play *Our Town* won the Pulitzer Prize for its portrayal of routine life in a typical American community, Grover's Corners. At the author's direction, the play was performed on a threadbare stage, and, as first-night critic John Mason Brown of the *New York Evening Post* wrote, Wilder manages to "strip life down to its essentials, too." The last act opens on a windy hilltop cemetery with a man from out of town attending the burial of a relative he hasn't visited in years—the precise circumstances I had just left behind in Fitchburg.

The deceased locals in *Our Town,* now spirits talking about the meaning of life, agree that the everyday moments with everyday people are the greatest blessing. They describe with such warmth and fondness the act of looking directly into the faces of family members and fully absorbing and caring about what they are expressing. However, the spirits know all too well, few people realize the importance of such moments when alive. "To spend and waste time as though you had a million years," one of the deceased says. "Ignorance and blindness."

After spending some more time with family in Fitchburg, I had taken the main road north out of town, bound for Grover's Corners.

Although Wilder only imagined the location, the play's narrator says it is in New Hampshire, just across the Massachusetts line, that it has a Main Street, a hospital, a post office, a handful of Protestant churches, a proximity to Jaffrey, East Jaffrey, Peterborough, and Dublin, and that "Mount Monadnock is right here." That can describe only one place: Keene, New Hampshire, where Route 12 from Fitchburg hitches right and becomes Main Street.

In a small gift shop, I learned that Mount Monadnock is America's most-climbed mountain and that I had just stepped off the nation's widest Main Street. For forty dollars, I could buy a quilt bragging about this last fact. A pair of specially priced doodads proclaimed that Keene also boasts the world's largest annual collection of jack-o'-lanterns when, each October, more than 20,000 carved pumpkins are displayed on, again, The Widest Main Street in America.

This nation loves its destination superlatives. Magazine editors may seem the biggest beguilers, stuffing our newsstands with Best Places to Love, Work, Eat, Hike, and other lists that are most likely to resonate with their advertisers' demographic bases. But in proactively seeking and hyping such labels, government agencies are really, as they may say, *Ranked No. 1!* Cities and states inaccurately tout their professional sports teams that win North American titles as World Champions. Florida calls itself "The Sunshine State," but it is the sixth most sunny. In 1954, New Jersey began putting the motto "The Garden State" on its license plates to promote its farms, despite this claim by the governor at the time: "I do not believe that the average citizen of New Jersey regards his state as more peculiarly identifiable with gardening for farming than any of its other industries or occupations." And New Jersey does not lead the nation in farming or agricultural produce output. Since 1949, the nonprofit National Civic League has given "All-America City" honors to nearly 500 places that earn the award by exemplifying the "spirit of grassroots citizen involvement and collaborative problem-solving to address critical community issues." However, the distinction has been regularly promoted by winning towns and cities as a veritable Best Place prize. Since 1960, Keene is the only place in New Hampshire to have won the honor.

When it comes to such chest-thumping, even bottom-of-the-barrel recognition can suffice. In 2001, a story in the *Washington Post Magazine* named Battle Mountain, Nevada, "the armpit of America," the nation's worst town. Before long, on the interstate leading from Salt Lake City through northern Nevada, there was a large billboard, paid for by Battle Mountain's chamber of commerce, showing the exposed underarm of the Statue of Liberty and these giant words: *VOTED ARMPIT OF THE NATION, EXITS 229, 231, 233.* To further promote the recognition, the town held a two-week "Festival of the Pit."

Things are different where there's sameness.

In 1987, officials in Peoria, Illinois, paid a St. Louis PR firm $60,000 in an effort to combat the city's reputation as a bellwether of average America. "When all they say is, 'Will it play in Peoria?' and call us the most average of all average cities in the world, it really hurts," Jim Finch, vice president of Peoria's Economic Development Council, said when the campaign was launched.

Based on a few census criteria, a 1992 *American Demographics* survey of cities with more than 50,000 residents singled out Tulsa as the nation's most average place of that size. However, the self-proclaimed Space Capital of Oklahoma doesn't dare remind the public of its average distinction. Instead, in a lengthy overview of Tulsa prepared by the city's chamber of commerce, the city is promoted as having ranked "in the top 10 southern cities in *Southern Living* magazine." Some 250 miles south of Tulsa is another city that has been deemed representative of the nation. In 2001, *Advertising Age* listed the Wichita Falls, Texas, metropolitan area as the most average based on ethnic balance, household size, and median age. "Whatever you say about us, I don't know that I would say we're average," Wichita Falls mayor Jerry Lueck responded. "I think we're something else."

The town of Normal, Illinois, makes no noticeable attempt to capitalize on—or run from—its name. However, on the town's website, one does learn that it is "home to the first Steak 'n Shake restaurant in the world," and that on the top floor of its Watterson Towers, "you are at the highest point in Illinois between Chicago and St. Louis."

On his radio show about the fictional Minnesota town of Lake Wobegon, Garrison Keillor often reminds us that it is a wholesome place "where all the children are above average." But outside the United States—more specifically, in the district of Saanich in British Columbia—leaders believe that average is just what their children should be. In a report on its youth released in 2003, the district concluded, "Saanich is a picture of 'average Canada.'. . . Most importantly, being 'average' means we are a community where most young people are well balanced, pleasant people who contribute to the community in numerous ways."

Although some places celebrate their small-town lifestyle, they almost never describe it as being ordinary. The vast majority of American cities, towns, and other places were named generations ago, when the ideas of ordinariness and an unexceptional life were more acceptable. The once most popular city and place names in America—Fairview and Midway—connote averageness, but for years many such names have been replaced by others that appear bolder. This presumably is why Middletown, Ohio, became Prospect, and why Fairview, North Dakota, became Karnak, a name randomly plucked from the files of the Great Northern Railroad.

In Keene, I heard a radio spot in which then-governor John Rowland of Connecticut urged out-of-state listeners to "Get away from the ordinary" by visiting his state. Of course, the longest-lasting image of Connecticut—the hallmark Rowland must have been trying to counter—is of small-town New England, the *Our Town* feel. For the governor, who was later removed from office on ethics charges that landed him in a federal prison, maybe an ordinary life ended up looking pretty good.

*O*r *perhaps the advertising messages* are as cynical as that last thought. A national campaign for Wachovia promises to provide "Uncommon Wisdom." Another financial services company, E*Trade, urges us to "Challenge the Ordinary." Nissan wants us to "Escape the Ordinary," and Butterfinger to "Break Out of the Ordinary." The respective slogans for Corona and Red Hook Ale are "Miles Away from the Ordinary" and "Defy Ordinary." A Pepperidge Farms commercial concludes with the tagline "Never Have an Ordinary Day." (All of this from companies that want to handle your money or sell you cars, candy bars, beer, or, literally, white bread.) Universal Orlando Resort wants us to "Take a Vacation from the Ordinary."

We're left with a nation where, as far as I could determine, no location or national consumer-product company since the start of the millennium has been created as an homage to human averageness. Except one. In April 2000, at the height of the Internet boom, a wholesale food manager named Jim Baker and his wife, Judith, a temp agency employee, started a home-based online apparel and golf accessories enterprise named Average Joe and Average Jane Athletics Company. Although the Bakers still can't afford to quit their day jobs, they continue to operate the business. Their slogan, "Because Average Is Good Enough," appears boldly on many of the company's Average Joe Golfer products. A sales brochure is more emphatic, with "Average is Good Enough!" printed on the cover. Some items in the Average Jane Golfer line carry another slogan, "For the Plain Fun of It." The business is in the only city north of Massachusetts that has the same percentage of at-home workers as America: Keene.

I reached the precise address well past dinnertime. I found a modest house, white with green trim, with an American flag flapping in a bitter wind. Judith, a tall, middle-aged woman in slippers and a hefty mop of salt-and-pepper hair, answered my knock and expressed concern about my standing in the New Hampshire cold, the temperature in the single digits. Jim, also tall, mid-fifties at most, appeared from a side room and said hello. We had spoken by phone earlier.

"I must admit, when I found out the reason you were calling, I was taken aback," Judith said. "Your timing!" We were seated in a sunken living room with glasses of cranberry and orange juice before us. Over Jim's shoulder, wood carvings of moose and framed photos of five children were neatly arranged.

"I was drafting a letter to the editor," Judith continued.

"Oh, c'mon, no politics," Jim said, turning briefly to his wife. "Judith loves her politics. We have one rule when we're together, whether it's talking or listening to the news: no politics."

That month, Jim's rule was being broken again and again. Two weeks later, the nation's first Democratic presidential primary would be decided in New Hampshire, and hundreds of candidate placards were being hammered into front yards all over Keene.

"Well, I don't have to mention the specifics of the letter," Judith said, "but I needed to write about those of us who are being forgotten. And I wrote about how the average American needs more respect. I used that exact phrase. Then, you called."

I did, to gather clues about where the Average American was living.

"I've always pictured the average American as someone standing in front of a farmhouse in the Midwest," Jim said. "Where is Larry Bird from?" French Lick, Indiana. "That's the backdrop," Jim said.

"No, it's much deeper than that," Judith said. "I see the average American as a state of mind. Belonging is on Maslow's hierarchy of needs. Think about it. If you're in the average American group, you've got one of your needs satisfied already."

"As you can see, she's the serious reader in the family," Jim said.

"I'm not like Jim," Judith said, shrugging off the compliment. "His mother is in Mensa; he comes from brains. Being above average, whether it's smarts or talent, that doesn't mean you'll be happier than those who are average. I remember seeing the Bob Fosse movie [*All That Jazz,* about the life of the Broadway show choreographer] where he's driving his dancers to be better, better, better, just absolutely driving them, when they are doing the best they can. But he continues to rant about how mediocrity is ruinous.

"That was once part of my struggle, feeling inferior because I am average," Judith continued. "But Fosse didn't get it. He was so obsessed about work and he died of a heart attack, didn't he? After a lot of self-therapy, I now understand that average doesn't mean mediocre. It can be uplifting. Spiritually fulfilling."

Ralph Waldo Emerson wrote that those who "complain of the flatness of American life have no perception of its destiny. They are not Americans." Although more focused on spirituality than Americanness, Abbot Francis Benedict, a modern-day California monk, believes that focusing on ordinary, everyday events is the antidote for boredom. "When you do the same tasks over and over, you can go beneath the surface, beyond the task itself, to the landscape of the soul," Benedict explained to the *Los Angeles Times* in 2003. "People fear there's nothing there, nothing inside themselves worth exploring. They give up too soon." And for centuries, Buddhists have believed that the average existence is the secret to reaching nirvana and to understanding the meaning of life. The Buddhist goal is to set out on a journey to what Buddha called the Middle Way, the midpoint between a life of hardship and one of overindulgence. Zen masters believe that to reach this Middle Way is to then—here's the twist—transcend all the mundane conditions of life.

Judith asked about my take on average existence. I confessed that I needed to learn to be less Fosse-like if I expected to be more educated about the average American. I needed to find a way to be more flexible about and comfortable around averageness.

"I don't know if this is what you're saying," Jim said, "but I don't think we can divide the country based on our perception of how smart or dumb the other side is. I see the portrayal of the dumb American, and it's always based on the same clichés. Either he's ignorant on a subject that the person doing the ridiculing is into, or he eats fast food and generally takes advantage of other conveniences. But I think he is more knowledgeable than his critics on other topics. And taking advantage of conveniences seems pretty smart to me."

The average Joe is smart, at least as smart as the average Jacques. The vast majority of IQ tests are established so that the mean standard is 100, and the most exhaustive and widely accepted study on national IQs—Richard Lynn and Tatu Vanhanen's 2002 book *IQ and the Wealth of Nations*—gives the United States and France each an average of 98 (the United Kingdom was set as the 100 standard). America landed within ten points of world leaders Hong Kong (107), South Korea (106), and Japan (105) and ahead of neighbors Canada (97) and Mexico (87) and many other countries such as Russia (96), Greece (92), and India (81).

H. L. Mencken, the most influential American journalist of the twentieth century's pretelevision era, often expressed his outrage that the nation had ceded control to the average American, a species he famously dismissed as the dimwitted *Boobus americanus*, or, collectively, *booboisie*. "If x is the population of the United States and y is the degree of imbecility of the average American, then democracy is the theory that x times y is less than y," he once wrote. He also opined, "No one in this world, as far as I know, has ever lost money by underestimating the intelligence of the great masses of the plain people."

However, the average IQ level in the United States has jumped roughly four points per decade on wide-spectrum intelligence tests since Mencken's day, even though Americans on the bottom half of the IQ scale have consistently had more children than the smarter half. Those who scored in the top 10 percent in intelligence among all Americans in 1920 would be in the bottom third today. And with Internet access skyrocketing in the new millennium (when it first reached the majority of U.S. homes), average Americans now view millions of websites and read a wide array of opinions on web pages, which surely must be raising their collective intelligence. Oft-derided media such as television and computers are arguably two big reasons why Americans are getting smarter. Despite depictions of the average American as being dulled by too much TV and other visually enhanced media, Cornell psychology professor Ulric Neisser, who studies the American IQ phenomenon and edited the 1998 book *The Rising Curve* observed, "There has been this new kind of visual literacy. Movies and television and video games, with their rapidly changing images, have had an effect on the way people think." Video games have significantly raised gamers' eye for detail. Because home computers routinely show 3-D images and other artistic renderings, experts have seen an explosion in the way most Americans are able to intellectually dissect visual puzzles and solve problems creatively. Even corporations' daily offerings to consumers are helping to strengthen this skill set. "You can hardly go to a McDonald's without having a puzzle on your food wrapper," Neisser offered as one example.

Moreover, as Steven Johnson covered in depth in his 2005 book *Everything Bad Is Good for You*, subtitled *How Today's Popular Culture Is Actually Making Us Smarter*, media and technology are the likely reasons for the rise in average intelligence, because it is these very aspects of our lives that have made the largest advancements over the past few decades. Johnson's most interesting theory: To make money in today's DVD culture, Hollywood operators know they must give consumers a reason to see a story more than once, and as a result the industry is smartening up its programming, with multiple plotlines that work the mind and take multiple viewings to sort through, the type of layered experience that gamers have come to expect. "All around us," wrote Johnson, "the world of mass entertainment grows more demanding and sophisticated, and our brains happily gravitate to that newfound complexity. And by gravitating, they make the effect more pronounced. Dumbing down is not the natural state of popular culture over time—quite the opposite."

Julianne Conry, an educational psychologist who studies ability testing at the University of British Columbia, pointed out that each time U.S. testing companies revise their tests, "you have to know more to be average." In his 2004 book *The Wisdom of Crowds,* James Surowiecki used solid evidence to refute the notion that the average American is some kind of half-wit. He gave several examples of how, when a large cross-section of individuals is asked a question, the most average answer is usually the most accurate. "And why do we ignore the fact that simply averaging a group's estimate will produce a very good result?" Surowiecki asked. After citing a study, he concludes, "We assume averaging means dumbing down or compromising."

"I think Americans' intelligence is, in large part, a product of our education," Judith said in her living room. She added that one of her earlier letters to the editor had been a plea for "more quality education."

"The more our education rises, the more we will be able to deeply engage each other on a wider variety of issues," she said. "That's a good thing, whatever your political bent." (She is a left-leaning Democrat, I would later learn.)

Today, 91 percent of Americans aged five to fifteen are attending school, an improvement from 83 percent in the supposedly idyllic year 1950. And there are exactly half the number of students per teacher today as in 1950. On average, high schools now require two years of both science and math, double the 1983 average. In 1954, there were three library books per public-school pupil. By 2002, there were seventeen books per public-school student, and 99 percent of students also had access to the Internet.

Americans rank first in the world in educational commitment, with the average stay in school now more than twelve years (Sweden and Japan follow at fewer than 11.5 years). Moreover, the Census Bureau has long tracked the median years of school completed by residents twenty-five years and older, and this statistic has risen each decade. In 1940, it was 8.1 years. In 2000, a record 80.4 percent of those in this age group had graduated from high school, a jump of more than 5 percent from the previous census. In 2005, this number is expected to top 85 percent. For the first time in history, more than half the entire population of the United States has successfully made it through high school. In 1904, only 6 percent of American citizens had made it that far.

*The Bakers,* both college grads, said that education should be a mark of the Average American, that it is vital to establishing our employment potential. So—per the numbers—I decided that my search pool should include only those with a high-school diploma.

Judith was born fifty-five years ago in the small town of Chittenango in northernmost New York and stayed there until after she earned her college degree nearby. "If you've heard of it, it's probably only because Frank Baum grew up there," she said. L. Frank Baum wrote *The Wonderful Wizard of Oz.* He was also, incidentally, a torchbearer for the Populist Party, which was built on the message that average Americans should lead the country.

"It's funny about the tourist attractions we have in the country," Jim said. "In a way, that's how we got the idea for our business. We were driving through the Midwest in—what was it Judith, 1999?— when we started wondering if we could do a better job."

"It was 1998," Judith said. "We were at the point of our life where we wanted to come up with a way to make money doing something together that we loved."

"We started brainstorming," Jim said.

"No, we started flipping out," Judith said. "At one point, the best idea we had was to open a business in Nebraska we were going to call Six Socks Over Sagebrush. We came up with the name first. Then, we said, 'Okay, what's the big attraction? Do we make the six largest socks in the world and fly them in an open field?'"

"I think we were going to have the world's biggest ball of twine there, too," Jim said. "We were not only thinking big, but gigantic. We thought we had latched on to quite the idea."

That is, until Judith took the wheel and her husband started reading a golf magazine. Jim has played the sport for years, and Judith first hit the links at age fifty.

"Jim came across an article that described someone as an 'average Joe golfer,'" Judith said. "It really struck him. It led to a discussion about how that term defines most golfers, and about how we never see them being celebrated. The focus is always on the elite golfers. We felt being average in golf is to be admired and sensed that it also resonated in other ways." This makes sense in golf more than in other sports: Par is the goal of the game; to be playing on par is, for most players, to be in heaven.

Only, it turned out that wearing the Average label on one's sleeve—literally—does not necessarily elicit a sunny reception. Judith said that Jim had recently played golf at a club in Myrtle Beach wearing an Average Joe Golfer shirt.

"Don't tell this story," Jim urged his wife.

"We had a wonderful time in Myrtle Beach," he explained, turning to me. "The people we met there were very hospitable. We started some friendships. The memories away from the course are all positive." Eventually, I got the story. Jim was in the ten to fifteen handicap group he believes defines the average golfer, but in Myrtle Beach he was having a particularly fine round and asked a club employee about the course record. "What are *you* asking for?" the man scoffed. "Anyone who would wear that shirt on the course would never come close."

Jim said, "I also have friends who are golfers and when I told them about the business, a few of them said, 'Who wants to be average?' They may be correct. It's still to be determined."

"It's been a tough three-plus years for us," Judith said, "but I truly believe people are getting more and more comfortable with embracing average—as golfers, athletes, with other lifestyles. For most, Average Joe and Jane is a more authentic brand name to wear than The Enforcer or something else they're not. Those are the type of labels people should be laughing at. I tell Jim that we're just ahead of our time. I hope we can both get to the point where the business is successful enough to become our full-time job."

I asked the Bakers what criteria should define the Average American.

"Dedicated to working for a living," Jim said. "I think that's your foundation."

Mr. Q noted that most Americans are either in school working toward a career, or in the full-time workforce. Being in this group would be another criterion, my seventh so far after U.S. citizenship, a minimum of five years in the same home, resident of native state, resident of the nation's most average community, the belief that family is extremely or very important, and having completed high school.

"I think marriage is a good indicator," Judith said. "Marriage and parenthood, do you have that?"

Once she said it, I did. Ninety percent of Americans marry at least once in their lifetime and between 51 and 52 percent of U.S. homes are headed by a married couple. The decline in the percentage of married-couple homes—from 80 percent in 1910 to 78 percent in 1950, 69 percent in the early 1970s, and 51.5 percent in 2003—is actually now slowing, in large part because of the increase in the percentage of married immigrants. J. Average would live in a home where at least one married couple resides. Moreover, as a couple of parents' groups had reported and as the Census Bureau would soon confirm, most Americans, like Jim and Judith, are parents. So J. Average would be a mom or a dad.

Automatically eliminated were the nearly 26 percent of Americans who live alone, including those in 40 percent of the homes in the Midwest strongholds St. Louis and Cincinnati. The ratio of single-person residences in the United States has risen nearly 18 percent since 1940. In 1900, these households represented a mere 1 percent of the nation.

I told Jim and Judith that I was looking for a type of geographical community, the one that best represents most Americans. Could a state qualify?

"From our perspective, I don't see our community as New Hampshire," Judith said.

There are other definitions for community, some even legal. In 2000, the South Dakota Supreme Court defined community as "within 60 road miles of a person's residence." In 1988, the Nebraska attorney general proposed "neighborhood" as the best legal definition of community. Judith opposed using the state as a defining factor for other reasons. She said it's too big, and that part of their own lives takes place in another state. Her letter to the editor was written for a local paper in Vermont, and her husband's daytime job is also in the Green Mountain State.

"I wouldn't even say the city is small enough to be our common area," Judith said. "Probably a neighborhood or the area between the central shopping location and home. Those are the people we see the most around here."


*"Midnight is past our bedtime,"* Judith said, politely letting me know that she and her husband needed to call it a night. Okay by me; she had just tossed me one more criterion. In what can't be great news for late-night talk-show hosts, the vast majority of Americans are regularly in bed before midnight, a criterion that fully eliminates the roughly 10 million night-shift workers in America.

Judith offered me golf-tee-shaped pretzels for the road and took me on a quick tour of company headquarters—a packed office across from the master bedroom. Nearby were standard cardboard boxes, one overflowing with golf towels emblazoned with the "Because Average Is Good Enough" trademark. On a shelf outside the door were a number of small plastic golfer figurines. One carried the inscription "I Hate This Sport," another, "World's Worst Golfer."

"We go through a lot of golf catalogs and there is so much clutter out there with all the greatest-this and the worst-that type items," Judith said. She fished a small commemorative plaque from the collection of plastic golfers.

"It's from the Myrtle Beach Chamber of Commerce," she said. "They sent it to Jim because he made a hole-in-one there," Judith continued. "They send it to everyone who hits one. I guess they want to remind us of what's special about the town."

# Four

# ORDINARY MAGIC

*Candidates remaining: fewer than 100 million*

$\mathcal{D}$*oes the Average American have to be white?*

It is the last question Judith Baker posed to me in Keene.

"The reason I bring it up," she said, "is that Jim and I were out shopping a couple weeks ago and we saw a mother walking with her child. The boy was obviously from a mixed-race marriage—a beautiful combination of races, a sort of dark coffee brown. And we thought, Wouldn't it be wonderful if race didn't matter?"

With New Hampshire, Maine, and Vermont the nation's three whitest states—each at 96 percent or more, well above the national percentage of 75—perhaps upper New England is not the best place to further investigate race.

I remembered my visit to the Census Bureau, located in Prince George's County, Maryland, where I had learned that between 97 and 98 percent of Americans consider themselves to be of one race, and that Prince George's County matched that Census 2000 statistic. I had also been told that of all the counties that are predominately black, it has the largest percentage of middle-class African Americans. The county has a much lower percentage of rich people and poor people than the nation as a whole.

I decided to return there. To prepare, I perused phone directories from the area and, lucky me, found a listing for a business named Myklar the Ordinary. I did some more research. It turned out that

Myklar the Ordinary was a sixty-year-old African American magician in Prince George's County.

I phoned Myklar (Hello, Mr. Ordinary?) and, after a few formalities and a brief overview of my travels, asked if I could attend his next gig with him. "It's no coincidence that you'll be joining me," he offered. "You're just following the signs being laid out for you." At his suggestion, I met him, a handsome man, not quite six feet, with an engaging smile and a full mustache, in Maryland in front of a Safeway (was that supposed to be a sign?), where he offered me a ride.

Stepping into his red Chevy van, I spotted a caged white dove in the cargo area and a black tuxedo draped over the back seat. Myklar was wearing brown shoes and pants and a yellow pullover. Nice, I realized during our drive, the five colors most used to define the races.

It was early on a Sunday in February. Myklar said we were en route to the Zion Baptist Church in a rural town named Hill Top and that he was scheduled to perform for the congregation after the morning service. Nice, again. I knew from Mr. Q that the largest religious classification in America is Protestant and the largest Protestant denomination is Baptist.

"The Bible tells us that Zion is the utopia we reach after we are welcomed into heaven," Myklar said. A tad uncomfortable with such intense religious talk, I lost myself in my map, and found that our destination was one town past Welcome.

"Do you know Joan of Arc?" Myklar asked, referring to the fifteenth-century French youngster who channeled messages from God, led a victorious French army, and was burned alive for being a witch, then dubbed a saint centuries later.

"For years, she was afraid to reveal what she knew," he went on. "You should feel comforted knowing you are not taking your journey alone." I knew he was not talking about Mr. Q. And I knew that this conversation would probably not be about the average American and race, as I had anticipated.

We were headed to an address outside of Prince George's County, in southern Maryland. Myklar neared a stop sign and took his eyes off the road. "You are on a divine journey and God's hand is on your shoulder, guiding you," he told me.

For a Sunday morning drive in the country, spiritual signs pointing to the Average American are a lovely notion, and they were clearly in Myklar's bag of tricks. He seemed to have already picked up on the fact that I was predisposed, particularly on this journey, to spotting "messages."

"God guides your thinking," Myklar was saying. "So even if you are overly aware of your surroundings, it is God who is making you see things the way you do. He's not showing anyone else what he's showing you, right?"

I had to admit that from Fitchburg through Keene to here, to chart my route to the most representative American, I had followed signs, clues, foreshadowings, call them what you will. What other guide did I have? If the phone calls David Letterman regularly used to place to the heartland and an ongoing CBS News feature titled *Everybody Has a Story* are any indication, the most popular alternative seemed to be blindly landing a finger in the phone book. Although the results would no doubt be less dangerous than in the Steve Martin film *The Jerk*—in which a gunman finds his ideal target, a "random son of a bitch, typical run-of-the-mill . . . average victim bastard," when he randomly plucks a name from the white pages—they would be no less haphazard, and not where I believe the truth lies.*

I asked Myklar if he had any problems with some churches disapproving of magic.

"When it comes to the actual acts, I always use the word 'illusion,'" Myklar said. "I look at myself as an illusionist, historian,

---

*Speaking of Martin, his 2003 novel, *The Pleasure of My Company*, features a Californian named Daniel who is named the Most Average American after winning a national essay contest sponsored by an apple-pie manufacturer, despite the fact that he suffers from obsessive-compulsive disorder and lives in a town where "average is not the norm." Daniel is also a runner-up in the same contest that he won, having submitted another essay under an assumed name. In the winning essay, Daniel compares his averageness to "the still power of an apple pie sitting in an open window to cool."

storyteller, and philosopher, not a magician. I enjoy that it's a venue where people pay close attention. I appreciate religious settings because the people there are usually deeper into observation."

If that's the case, then America is a veritable magnifying glass. Those aboard the *Mayflower*—the first colonists to settle with their families in America—were looking for religious freedom. John Winthrop, the founding governor of Massachusetts Bay—the first self-governing American locality—joined the Pilgrims with a wave of emigrants and a promise that the new territory "shall be as a city upon a hill" and that a Protestant faith, Puritanism, would lead the way. The Puritans' rejection of material wealth eventually gave way as a societal standard. As economist Max Weber, one of the founders of modern sociology, posited in a landmark 1905 thesis, the Protestants created a work ethic that gave rise to American capitalism.

Alexis de Tocqueville, the Frenchman whose 1835 *Democracy in America* remains the most quoted travelogue about the nation, said, "On my arrival in the United States the religious aspect of the country was the first thing that struck my attention." And even though the nation's founders established the world's first secular government, the Pledge of Allegiance was reworked in 1954 to include the phrase "one nation under God"—"reaffirming the transcendence of religious faith in America's heritage and future," explained President Dwight Eisenhower.

According to Gallup, more than 80 percent of American adults believe in God, and about 10 percent believe in a "universal spirit." The latter percentage is about the same ratio, according to an AP survey, of those who don't believe in "a personal God" but do believe in "a higher power." Today, membership in religious groups is more than double the membership in other types of organizations. J. Average, I decided, would believe in God.

Said Myklar, "I am Catholic, but I see myself as a Christian first."

About Christianity, Tocqueville observed, "There is no country in the world where the Christian religion retains a greater influence over the souls of men than in America. Christianity, therefore, reigns without obstacle, by universal consent." In both the nineteenth and twentieth centuries, the Supreme Court concluded, "We are a Christian people." Today, there may be a higher percentage of Christians in the United States than Jews in Israel, Hindus in India, or Muslims in Egypt. Ninety-nine percent of U.S. workplaces have only one type of official religious holiday: Christian. One hundred percent observe the A.D. calendar years. (A.D. is the abbreviation for *anno Domini,* Latin for "year of our Lord," a reference to Christ's birth.)

In 2004, Christians represented more than 80 percent of the nation. The Jewish population in America, at about 4 percent in the 1920s, is between 2 and 3 percent today, although a Gallup poll found that on average, Americans believe this number to be at 18 percent. The 2003 National Jewish Population Survey found, according to the *Jewish Week,* that "the average American Jew leads a more modern, less family-friendly lifestyle than the average American. Proportionally fewer Jews have ever been married, while Jewish women average fewer children than other American women." There are now more Muslims in America than Jews, and with the average Jewish couple having 1.8 children, below the minimum population replacement figure of 2.1, the percentage of Jews is expected to continue declining. And Americans without a religious affiliation constitute a larger populace than Jews and Muslims combined. Rabbi Aaron Schonbrun, who practices at Congregation Beth David in California's Bay Area, said in 2004 of those who share his faith: "We were not meant to be average Joes. There is nothing average about Jewish living."

Does Myklar the Ordinary see himself as an average Christian?

"C'mon, look at this van," he joked of his worn Astro. "Is this the vehicle of an average anybody?" He said it was a couple months past its eighth year. As had become my compulsion, I checked with Mr. Q, who placed the age of the average American vehicle at eight years old.

I spotted a car with a vanity license plate. Myklar didn't have one of those on his van, so it was another potential check in his average column.

"Funny you would see that," he said. "I'm thinking of going to Motor Vehicles next week to get a new plate. I want it to read, 'You and I Lord.'"

I didn't think it would fit.

"U-N-I LORD," Myklar clarified. "The letters."

Wouldn't someone read it Uni-Lord?

"Sounds like you just did," he said.

I played along: another omen. The most average American would be someone whose primary faith is Christian. However, J. Average would need to respect others' religions. Two out of three Americans oppose the creation of a constitutional amendment to officially proclaim America a Christian nation.

It wasn't always this easy. During the early years of the first American colonies, Protestants rejected association with other religions, even conspiring to keep Catholics away from the new nation and forbidding saints' names for children because, in 1545, the Catholic Church had made them mandatory from baptism forward. In 1789, the year before the first census was conducted, American citizens were close to 100 percent Protestant, with Catholics at about 1 percent. Many historians attribute the growth of Catholicism in America to the one place where its population found refuge and expanded in colonial times—southern Maryland. "The unsung heroes are the plain people," Timothy O'Rourke wrote of his subjects in his 2001 book *Catholic Families of Southern Maryland*.

Although the Average American would be a Christian, I could not pinpoint a specific denomination. Catholicism may be the nation's most common religion, as it is the largest single denomination, at about 25 percent of the population. However, Protestantism, although a large collection of many distinguishable denominations— from larger branches such as Methodist and Lutheran to smaller ones such as Quaker and Foursquare Gospel—is more prevalent. But I could not place Protestants in the clear majority of the U.S. population. In 2004, the University of Chicago's National Opinion Research Center reported that Protestants made up 63 percent of the population in 1993 and 52 percent in 2002, and that it was possible that Protestants had already lost their majority.

Perhaps certain practicing Christians had the best chance of being the most average. When compared to the full U.S. population, the average conservative Protestant has only about half the tangible wealth of the average American, but Catholics and mainline Protestants come in close to the national norm. According to the 2004 National Survey of Religion and Politics, Catholicism is the faith most evenly distributed between the two major parties, as Catholic Democrats outnumber Catholic Republicans by only 3 percentage points.

Myklar said he is a regular speaker at the Catholic church in his hometown. I added two criteria: J. Average, like around 60 percent of his or her fellow Americans, would need to be a regular church-goer—attend church services at least once a month—and believe that religion is a "very important" aspect of his or her life.

At the Zion Baptist Church, a deacon spotted us talking in the van and enthusiastically waved for us to join him.

*President Gerald Ford once remarked,* "It's the quality of the ordinary, the straight, the square, that accounts for the great stability and success of our nation. It's a quality to be proud of. But it's a quality that many people seem to have neglected." The adjective "ordinary"—meaning routine, usual; also, of common quality, rank, or ability—is from the Latin *ordo,* denoting order. In Britain, an ordinary is a kind of tavern or restaurant (a usage once popular in America, and the likely reason a tiny hamlet in Kentucky is named Ordinary). In America, three meanings of the word as a noun are religious in nature, but that's not what inspired Myklar the Ordinary to use it as part of his moniker.

"When I first started performing, I wanted to be truthful," Myklar said as we set up an audio system for his performance. "I was just an average magician. I would joke with the kids, 'If I was an ordinary magician, this is how I would perform.' I recognized that it was nothing to be ashamed of. Many of us strive to be the best in everything we do, but for those who do the same and come out looking ordinary, they need to realize they are still special. I tell kids it's not important to be Number 1, because only one person can be Number 1."

What one thing about his life did he wish was ordinary?

"I regret not knowing my daddy," he said. "Really the only time I saw him is when he showed up at my high-school graduation." Before entering high school, Myklar spent four years at Sisters of the Blessed Sacrament for Indians and Colored People, a school outside Philadelphia. He realized his life would have meaning around the time he laid eyes upon the school's aging founder, a nun named Katharine Drexel. Soon after, at age ninety-seven, Drexel passed away on campus.* Myklar remembered attending the funeral and thinking that one day he would preach about love.

"You need to ask yourself if you love all people," Myklar said. "No matter what their station in life, no matter how ordinary you believe they are."

The Hill Top church service let out, and an older gentleman dressed in blue overalls over a green and white checked shirt walked over to where we were standing. Myklar said we had been talking about the average American.

"Mason Proctor," the man said, extending his hand to me. "An average man. Course, most people in this church I say is average."

How so?

"If we hit the lottery tomorrow, I don't see us leaving the community or probably changing at all," he said. Proctor is a local bus contractor and a deacon at the church, where he had been a member for fifty of his sixty-seven years. "I'm happy with where I am," he said. "Like the pastor said today, 'We don't own anything.' So what if someone has more money or not than me? My friends are here."

The ability to acquire possessions is usually seen as a plus, but research shows that the advantage most likely lies with those in the middle of the material-worth scale, especially if they have religion in their life. In his 2004 book *The Paradox of Choice*, Swarthmore College sociology professor Barry Schwartz explained, "When people have no choice, life is almost unbearable. As the number of available choices increases, as it has in our consumer culture, the autonomy, control, and liberation this variety brings are powerful and positive.

---

*Drexel is the only person born a U.S. citizen to have been canonized as a saint. She is credited with performing miracles that involve getting deaf people to hear.

But as the number of choices grows further, the negatives escalate until we have become overloaded. At this point, choice no longer liberates, but debilitates." The fact that many choices are taken away from churchgoers—thou shalt not commit adultery, do drugs, etc.—or that their choices are simplified, means that along with some of the other benefits of religious faith, those with religion and of ordinary means are typically happier than others. There is no fork in the road to fret over if the road is straight.

That said, there have long been Christian clergy intensely critical of unexceptional Americanness. Baptist educator Frank Benjamin Fagerburg wrote a text in 1934 entitled *The Sin of Being Ordinary*. William Edelen, an elderly minister who holds services every Sunday morning at the Palm Springs Tennis Club in California, recently repeated much of the sermon against average Americans that he delivered thirty-four years earlier at Plymouth Congregational Church in Wichita, Kansas. "One of the most insulting cults that exists in our society today is the religion that has as its object of worship the common man," he said at the start of his homily. "What a pathetic distinction to be known as a person who can't compete with the best. . . . Here is the problem, may I suggest to you: too many want to be a bunch of average Americans, just a bunch of common people."

To the contrary, Mason Proctor believes there is a possibility that Americans are like sports referees, in that the most glorious can be those who are noticed the least; they are not so shallow and insecure that they seek or need public recognition. And for many Christians nationwide, there is a sense that ordinary is okay. Today, there is a Common People Baptist Church in both Cummings, Georgia, and Cleveland, Ohio. At the Crossroads Church in Cincinnati, a 2001 newsletter read, "Jesus was an average and normal guy in many respects." And Pat McEwen of Melbourne, Florida–based Life Coalition International said in an address to fellow Christian missionaries, "Jesus chose the ordinary working people. Peter was fishing. Matthew was collecting taxes, not a popular profession in any times. What made them special? They were special because they were ordinary."

—

In a 2003 sermon at First Congregational Church in Ridgefield, Connecticut, minister Dale Rosenberger said, "Jesus keeps our feet on the ground and points us back toward ordinary people. . . . Many of Jesus' followers . . . couldn't get beyond the incongruity of the miracles and the message located in this plain man. . . . Why did they leave? Because Jesus was so uncharismatic, so unexciting, so everyday." Kindergarteners at the Brainerd Baptist School in Chattanooga, Tennessee, have a relaxed but standardized dress code (such as sneakers "to be worn at all times") because, as a guide for parents explains, "Christ was an ordinary and modest man."

*Seated on folding chairs* in the community center of the Zion Baptist Church, a couple dozen children and about as many adults were surrounded by wall posters of Martin Luther King, Jesse Owens, Shirley Chisholm, and other black luminaries. But if the kids' open-mouthed stares were any indication, the star of the room was the gentleman sporting a tuxedo and a rainbow-colored scarf who had just pulled a dove out of nowhere.

"This is not magic; it's called an illusion," Myklar the Ordinary told the children, many now standing. "If there was such a thing as magic, what would it look like? We *can* find magic in other places. I'll tell you: You will find there is magic in what's considered ordinary in our lives—for example, the magic of love that we find in 1 Corinthians 13."

Myklar wove together some standard tricks and a talk about love and the importance of belief and self-confidence. And keeping a balance.

"Your aspirations are the things you hope to be," he said, holding a balloon and a sword. "This balloon represents your aspirations, your hopes, your dreams. Stay away from negative people. All they want to do is bring you down and burst your bubble. All you have to do is stay above their level. Then, no one will try to burst your hopes and dreams."

Myklar slid his sword through the air-filled balloon. The children applauded loudly.

"See?" he said, taking out the sword. The balloon remained inflated.

"But without that balance . . ." This time, the sword popped the balloon.

"It's Black History Month," Myklar said. "It's important to realize that blacks are responsible for so much in this country, even though at times in the course of our nation's history, they were under incredible and inhumane duress," he continued, then described the achievements of many African American inventors. "But there is no reason to be proud of being black, just as there's no reason to be proud of being white or any other color. It is not an accomplishment. What's more, we are all closer than you probably think.

"There's been some speculation that Jesus was not the lily-white person we've seen portrayed. Jesus Christ became really white mainly through painters like Michelangelo and Da Vinci." Myklar launched into a well-supported litany about why Jesus must have been dark-skinned. "Once you understand this," he concluded, "you'll begin to understand why our color does not limit us."

Before he was ousted as the CEO of mortgage giant Fannie Mae, Franklin Raines was quoted in the *New York Times* on September 26, 2004, about African Americans, "Look at what we could achieve if we got to be average! We don't need to take everybody from the ghetto and make them Harvard graduates. We just need to get folks to average, and we'd all look around and say, 'My God, what a fundamental change has happened in this country.'" In another forum, Raines explained, "If America had racial equality in education and jobs, African-Americans would have two million more high school degrees, two million more college degrees, nearly two million more professional and managerial jobs, and nearly $200 billion more income. If America had racial equality in housing, three million more Americans would own their own homes. And if America had racial equality in wealth, African-Americans would have $760 billion more in equity value, $200 billion more in the stock market, $120 billion more in their retirement funds and $80 billion more in the bank."

Myklar said that just as white Africans who become American citizens are African Americans, so, too, are all Americans. "I have a guest here," he continued, lifting his wand toward me, "and he'll enjoy hearing this. There's a well-known study called the Human Genome Project, and one of the things they wanted to do was trace humanity back to its origin. Well, they have, using DNA which is only found in women, and they said that all of humanity traced back to Africa. Other anthropological studies were more precise, showing how from a single woman—some people like to call her Eve—the DNA spread from Africa to the rest of the world. They show an amazing journey. Yes, we truly are all the family of man. So, I'd like you all to please welcome your cousin Kevin."

My first job out of grad school was at Louisiana's Southern University, the nation's largest predominately black university, where I listened to a number of professional presentations regarding race. But I was much more moved by Myklar's pronouncement, in large part because, unlike most of the other speakers, he was inclusive, not divisive. I had not yet told Myklar about the question I had brought to Maryland—does the Average American have to be white?—and here he was giving me more food for thought.

One of the weakest religious beliefs in this country—supported by less than half the population—is that God made humans in their present form (even the Vatican under Pope John Paul II, although this may be changing under Pope Benedict XVI, concluded that there is no conflict between Christian faith and evolution). But Myklar said it is "a blessed time" in that creationists and evolutionists at least can agree on a "coming-from-a-single-source theory." The Human Genome Project and a study by a group of European geneticists and DNA specialists both concluded in 2003 that Africa is our universal home. Oxford's Stephen Oppenheimer, a DNA expert on the key Eve study, confirmed, "The fact that we look different is because we live in different environments. We are really, truly the same under the skin." In December 2003, the cover headline of

*Scientific American* claimed, "Science Has the Answer: Does Race Exist?" The answer inside: "If races are defined as genetically discrete groups, no."

This all marks quite a change from 1790, not only the year of the first census but of the nation's inaugural naturalization statute, which determined that only "free white persons" could be citizens. At the time, about 20 percent of the population was black. Census 2000 was the first one to allow residents to choose "two or more races." The Census Bureau predicts that by the 2060 census, non-Hispanic whites will be in the national minority. (Hispanics and blacks are becoming a larger percentage of the population in large part because Hispanic women are having an average of three children and black women 2.3, compared to 1.9 among non-Hispanic whites.)

Many Americans already feel we are there. A recent Gallup poll found that on average, Americans believe that 32 percent of Americans are black and 21 percent of Americans are Hispanic, although the true percentages are each under 15 percent. In recent years, most Americans have not known with certainty what their own true racial heritage is. In 1989, Gallup asked Americans if they knew anything about their great-grandparents, their great-great-grandparents, or their great-great-great-grandparents. All three responses were in the minority, at 46, 19, and 13 percent, respectively. This got me thinking that race, as important as it is in people's lives and their sense of self should perhaps, surprisingly, not be considered as a criterion.

To conclude his performance, Myklar gestured toward the poster of Martin Luther King and alluded to his famous "I Have a Dream" speech. "We should all have many wonderful dreams and believe in them all," Myklar said.

After his audience departed, Myklar joined me at a long table for a makeshift lunch of potato salad and punch from the church kitchen. My first question: Should the Average American be white? "It's not so black and white, is it?" Myklar said, smiling. I kept in my research pool the 25 percent of the population that is not white.

However, Myklar and I agreed that J. Average, like most Americans, would express acceptance of all races. If the findings of a 1989 study were still accurate, this would disqualify 20 percent of white Southern Baptists, the proportion that objected to having black neighbors. Further out of the mainstream, Ku Klux Klan members believe that to be an American, one must be white and Protestant. In 1924, a year before the KKK membership peaked at around 5 million, KKK chief Hiram Evans, a Texas dentist, told *Time* magazine that he was "the most average man in America." In my search for the most average American, anyone with Evans's religious or racial views would be out. The average American's rising acceptance of other races is perhaps best illustrated by a string of Gallup studies about mixed-race marriage. In 1948, only 4 percent of Americans were in favor of marriages between blacks and whites. In 2002, 65 percent of the population approved; in 2003, 72 percent.

In 1943, President Franklin D. Roosevelt declared, "Americanism is not, and never was, a matter of race or ancestry." And the Average American would not need a specific, limited heritage. Today in America, no one ancestry meets the majority standard (although German and Irish—the blood of my grandfathers—are the most prevalent, claimed by 15 and 11 percent of the population, respectively).

Myklar told me about his wife and their three adult children and of his late mother Geraldine, a former Commerce Department assistant who had passed away thirty years ago. Myklar—"the first professional in my family," he said proudly—was born Michael Russell, graduated from Howard University in Washington, D.C., and went into sales, hawking everything from encyclopedias to campsites. Soon after Geraldine passed, he found solace in magic.

"I was walking through a mall and saw a magic kit for sale," he said. "It just drew me in. I know in my heart that it was a signal from God to bring joy to others."

After lunch, he told me to keep looking for signs. We packed up his belongings and carried them toward a side exit. After a few steps, he put down his birdcage and pointed to a placard on a distant wall. The sign read, "WHEREVER YOUR TREASURE IS, THERE YOUR HEART WILL BE ALSO."

When Myklar dropped me off at Safeway, he reminded me of my promise to follow signs to the doorstep of the Average American. As I thought further about this, it seemed most appropriate for my next destination to be the city of magic and signs: Las Vegas, here I come.

# *Five*

# YOUR NAME
# IN LIGHTS

*Candidates remaining: fewer than 80 million*

*U*nder *a brutal sun* on a rocky mountain pass high above Las Vegas, about forty locals talked in small groups. Off to the side, a large, bearded power-shop steward named Tom Bennett sat alone on a log and played catch with his black Lab. I joined him and told him what I was doing there.

"I don't relate to a lot of people," Bennett said, sidearming a stick. "And I can't stand some of the yuppie jerks. They join these races so they can be middle America, but they're not. But, I guess we do have a common bond. I mean, how many people drive these models and never leave the pavement?"

Ringing a makeshift picnic area were the types of SUVs most commonly used for nothing more treacherous than toting kids and groceries over speed bumps. Eleven of the vehicles had successfully completed the Shamrock Rally, a 61-mile race that snaked through streets and rough mountain trails in and around Las Vegas. Entrants—commonly more than one per vehicle—had not been given course maps but had to advance by following clues found at checkpoints (and, because the roads were not closed to other traffic, they also had to decide how much they wanted to bend the traffic laws). As was the custom, there would be only three race awards presented, and one happened to be Most Average, for the most average finishing time. I had joined a team as a wingman to help decipher the clues, figuring Myklar would approve.

Bennett was a course marshal for the fourth annual affair and an officeholder of the local Land Rover club that promoted it. The race founder, Vinny, a Vegas musician, is a lean, deep-tanned man with long gray hair. He quieted the groups to announce that he had tabulated the race results and would soon present the awards. As a clocked race with staggered starting times, the finish order was still a mystery to them.

"You say you are interested in the average American," Bennett said. "I am an average American. To me, that means people who are forgotten by their fellow Americans. . . . I know what it's like to be ignored. I've seen it ever since I came back from Vietnam."

A girl jogged over and taunted Bennett's dog with an oversized branch. Earlier, her parents had proudly talked about a Special Olympics award she had recently won. "You need to stop that," Bennett chided her. She put her head down and walked away. "I know she's special, or whatever the word is, but c'mon," Bennett said. The girl, the preteen daughter of one of the drivers, had Down Syndrome.

Vinny shouted that Team Braganza, named for the driver of a two-man squad, had earned the fourth annual Most Average Award.

"Yes! Average!" squealed Emil Braganza, a rail-thin Filipino American standing next to the dirt finish line in a polo shirt, plaid shorts, white socks, and sandals. He high-fived his larger teammate.

It was the only time I caught Bennett applauding. Only the citation is not exactly meant as an honor.

"I started it as a stab at ironic humor," Vinny would explain later. "I wanted to show that there was a fun element to the day. I'm certainly not saying being average should be celebrated. Hell, no. I'm what you might call a Land Rover snob."

This brought me back to one of the first reasons I had started the search: wondering how America thought of averageness. The language origins of the word are negative, as it comes from the medieval Arabic *awArIyah,* meaning damaged goods. But does being average in our culture mean losing, or winning?

"For an overachiever, it's a slap in the face," said Braganza—Captain Average—standing beside his teammate, an older-looking man named Jeff Lantz. "You may as well call me a loser."

"Looo-serrr," Lantz obliged.

Braganza explained that he did not want the average tag because he did not want his proud work ethic to be questioned. I asked about his background. He said he arrived in Las Vegas from the Philippines in 1970 at age three and that he had grown up with seven siblings, supported by his casino dealer dad and his nurse mom, that he had a wife and a six-year-old son, and that hard work had led him up the economic ladder to a manager post at the Environmental Protection Agency, where he had been employed for nearly fourteen years. Lantz also worked there.

After Braganza learned of my team's standing (third place, no hardware), he said he had just pretended to celebrate with Lantz.

"I'm not so sure," Lantz said. Braganza winced.

"C'mon," Lantz prodded, looking at his teammate. "It feels good to be Most Average. We were singled out for a finish we should be happy with."

Lantz's philosophy is carried out in other sporting endeavors around the country. Founded by a sculptor in northern California in 1969 and now contested annually in several locales, the Kinetic Sculpture Races showcase elaborately decorated vehicles that transverse streets and waterways. Its most coveted prize—given to the middle finisher—is called the Mediocre Award. One Baltimore race participant, whose entry was meant to resemble a Victorian teapot, told a local reporter in 2003 that the event creator's philosophy was that "we are all losers, so lighten up and spread peace and joy."

In Major League Baseball, "ordinary effort" is the level players must reach to have their defensive play praised in the history books. Official scorers apply that standard when deciding if a fielder should be credited with an error-free play. On offense, players are predominately defined by their "average." For more than sixty years, every major league hitter has finished the season with an average of under .400; they each failed as a batter more than six out of ten times. In the other two major American professional sports, football and basketball, coaches are notorious for saying that winning is everything, not acknowledging that by losing they secure the best college draft picks for the next season. The draft rules are in place because the premier competitive goal of the professional leagues is parity—a perfectly average win-loss record for each team—to increase the likelihood of competitive games and to show fans that each team has a fighting chance. If kids were in charge, there would still be a retreat from a win-only mentality. Some 64 percent of young athletes would rather play on a losing team for a coach they like than on a winning team for a coach they dislike, a November 2004 *Sports Illustrated for Kids* survey shows.*

Lantz, the Most Average wingman, offered the simple reason why he felt his finish was worthy. "Last year, we finished last," he said. "Last is worse than average, right?"

"But saying we were average just sounds so blah," said Braganza.

To another group—storytellers—average can be hell. In his 1997 book *Story,* the most popular screenwriting guide in Hollywood, author Robert McKee declared, "We stretch toward the 'bests' and 'worsts' because story—when it is art—is not about the middle ground of human experience."

But screenwriters aren't always right. Indeed, *Inquiry* magazine

---

*Acceptance of average performance is more common when animals are competing. At dog shows, the most average competitor wins—that is, the canine that judges believe has the fewest deviations from such standards as number of inches tall, chest and neck measurements and color, nose shape, and fur thickness. Champion horses have also benefited from average physical features. In 2004, Dr. Alan Wilson and his colleagues at the Royal Veterinary College, with funding from the Biotechnology and Biological Sciences Research Council, studied the remains of the great undefeated racehorse Eclipse, who was born in 1764 and is in the pedigree of about 80 percent of today's thoroughbred racehorses. As the *New York Times* reported, the scientists "found that the great racer and stud, was, in fact, average in every way by today's equine standards—and, Dr. Wilson said, in that very averageness lay the secret of his greatness. At a gallop, a horse's legs strike the ground and rebound with the springiness of a pogo stick. Because the horse's measurements were 'right in the middle of normal,' he said, the bones are neither too long nor too short, too flexible or too stiff." Wilson added, "When they all come out optimum, it looks like average."

reported in 2001 that Dr. Leslie MacAvoy, a professor of philosophy at Eastern Tennessee State University, has defined authenticity as "a deepening of the self-understanding expressed in everydayness." In the new millennium, we are even seeing an understanding of this from Hollywood. A full-page ad on the front cover of the January 22, 2003, *Daily Variety,* the entertainment industry's lead trade publication, touted Jack Nicholson's title role in *About Schmidt* without even mentioning or picturing Nicholson. It was headlined, "That Mythic American Hero: The Regular Guy," a marquee borrowed from A. O. Scott's 2002 *New York Times* essay on the film. *American Splendor,* the hit independent film about the everyday activities of real-life Cleveland file clerk Harvey Pekar, was regarded by many critics as cinema at its best. The 2003 picture was promoted with the tagline "Ordinary life is pretty complex stuff" and featured this observation from Pekar: "We've got interesting lives, too. Mundane, everyday life is as interesting as any other kind, and as funny."*

The more the Most Average teammates talked about their lives away from the office, the less apologetic Braganza became and the more he surrendered to Lantz's upbeat assessment of their race performance. And of the concept of an ordinary life.

"No one can be above average in everything," Braganza said at one point. "If you are only focusing on one thing and you are great at it, you are probably below average in total, right?" This is a theory familiar to classrooms full of American schoolkids. SpongeBob SquarePants, the most popular children's TV cartoon character of our era, says, "Remember, everybody's good at something, but nobody's good at everything."

---

*Many of the most successful films actually feature "ordinary" characters. After all, to get pulled into the characters' lives, we need to relate to them (thus one reason why Everyman actor Tom Hanks may be the most popular film star of his generation). However, audiences also want to see the average citizen react to extreme circumstances, so that he can prove he can be as heroic as anyone, maybe even more so, if only given the chance. See Hanks, *Cast Away.*

Regarding Paul Giamatti, who has starred in *American Splendor* and other films, the *Washington Post*'s William Booth wrote that "it is now time to celebrate the Median Man as Leading Man."

If the beliefs of young Americans are any indication, being ordinary may be becoming more popular. In 2004, Gallup asked teenagers what they thought their purpose was in life. The top responses were "make a difference or help people" and "be a good Christian," together more than twelve times those who said "be successful or famous." In 1998, students at the middle school and high school in Wareham, Massachusetts, started an Ordinary Heroes Hall of Fame, honoring everyday people in their area. The Hall of Fame celebrates such locals as retired custodian Dean Pina, for forgoing his top slot on a heart transplant list and unceremoniously giving it to the sixteen-year-old who was next in line; and Kevin Donahue, for reconciling with his ex-wife and becoming her caregiver after she was diagnosed with cancer.

Braganza said, "I work very hard, but I'd rather be a hero with my son than a hero at work. I guess actually, yeah, I am pretty average in that I got married, became a father, and bought a house. But, it's all good. At work, I'm trying to get my top-secret security clearance, and the guy told me he needed names of those I spend time with outside of my family. I said, 'Well, there's this guy Jeff who I go to the movies with every couple of weeks. Other than that, no one.' He said he needed more names. But my wife and I spend time with our son and my son's acquaintances, that's our circle. I just looked at the guy and thought, *That's okay. It just means I am a husband and a father.*"

In other words, he's no loser; he's an average American.

Even his moviegoing interest would qualify him. Mr. Q had mentioned a Gallup report from a month earlier, about the average American watching 4.9 movies a year in the theater. The report also noted that 69 percent of Americans go to the big screen at least once annually, as would J. Average. Although the Gallup numbers would decline a year later, to 4.7 films and 65 percent as a result of the hot DVD and home-theater market and a long line of other entertainment options for consumers, moviegoing is still the average American's dominant paid-for public entertainment experience; not even sporting events or concerts attract a majority of American ticketholders on an annual basis.

As Braganza surmised, his domestic achievements are average, and commendable, in several ways. First, most Americans live in one home, which is occupied by the owner. The home ownership rate is nearly 70 percent, an impressive climb from the 20 percent rate of only a century ago. Second, like Braganza and most Americans, J. Average lives in a traditional house—a permanent, freestanding dwelling with a common entrance for all occupants, a "one-unit, detached," in government-speak. I applied these two criteria for J. Average. More than 50 percent of the homes in Los Angeles County were fully wiped from my search map—the percentage there that are not owner-occupied. The freestanding house criterion alone eliminated millions more homes, including 99.5 percent of all residences in Manhattan plus more than 90 percent in Philadelphia and more than 85 percent in Washington, D.C. Gone, too, were all of the nation's more than 2 million homeless individuals and the more than 15 million Americans who were living in mobile homes.

For most Americans, a home is the largest investment they will make—on average, Americans create more wealth in their homes than in the stock market (incidentally, several reports note that most U.S. households do not own stock)—and the most expensive item they will own. The second most expensive item is a motor vehicle, Range Rover or not.

Mr. Q informed me that 70 percent of American households have direct access to one or two motor vehicles (the Census 2000 average was 1.72, up from 1.66 in 1990), that 60 percent of homes have a garage or carport, and that most Americans have a driver's license. I made each a J. Average criterion, eliminating those Americans without any motor vehicles or with more than two.

I considered Braganza's proudest achievement: his three-person family. In 2000, on average, U.S. households had 2.62 occupants, a rate that dropped to 2.57 in 2003 and is likely to drop to 2.4 by 2020. The nation's middle majority home size is between one and four occupants—another J. Average criterion. With a married-couple household already a qualification, I knew that the most average American would be living in a home of two, three, or four persons.

With five or more people occupying more than 30 percent of all Hispanic households, this significantly lowered the number of remaining Latino candidates. Those nearly 8 million individuals classified as living in "group quarters," such as dormitories, nursing homes, and prisons, were also gone.

American homes are the largest in the world. Although the average number of people in each home has shrunk, new homes in the United States have grown to an average of about 2,500 square feet, a full 1,000 square feet more than the 1970 home average. And the ten-person household of Braganza's childhood is more unusual now than at any other time in American history. In 1790, the average American woman gave birth to around eight children. In 2000, that number was down to 2.07. The average American household size was 5.8 persons in 1790, 4.8 in 1900, and 3.8 in 1950. The figure has continued to fall each decade since, as more Americans are living alone, more couples are waiting longer to have children, and fewer family homes include two parents. Just between the past two censuses, family homes with no husband present increased more than three times faster than married-couple homes.

Braganza's best friend understands the cultural changes. Lantz gained custody of his son many years ago, after he was divorced from the boy's mother.

"I think Jeff is a hero," Braganza said. "I respect him first and foremost because for about fifteen years, he's raised a child by himself, and he gave up a lot to do so. It required him to sacrifice personal relationships and accomplishments."

"I didn't sacrifice anything," Lantz said. "I can say that now. I learned the hard way that a stable home is what it's all about when you're a dad."

"Okay, let's not get all weepy," Braganza responded. "Let's get in this manly vehicle and rip through some twisted terrain. Arrrrrrgh."

In truth, Captain Average and his hero sidekick left because they were anxious to return safely home and spend some quality weekend time with their families. I noticed that they had strapped on their seat belts. Mr. Q had something about seat belts: that most Americans use them regularly. So would J. Average. With safety-belt use in America having jumped from 71 percent in 2000 to a record-high 80 percent in 2004, and with more than twenty states permitting police to pull over motorists who are not wearing the device, it has helped make the nation's roads safer. In 1975, there were 3.35 traffic deaths for every 100 million vehicle miles traveled. In 2004, the number more than halved, to 1.48 fatalities over the same distance.

Although Braganza said the simple act of his springing for an expensive Land Rover may show that he is not a typical parent, such a purchase actually keeps him in the ballpark. Today's average-income Americans are better off financially than over 99 percent of people who have ever lived. When Camille Sweeney interviewed families who earned around the median household income determined by Census 2000 for a story in the *New York Times Magazine,* she found that each had recently bought at least one of the following: a new car, a powerboat, a widescreen television, a three-bedroom vacation cottage, a swimming pool, or a pricey family vacation. In 2003, the average American family spent less than 50 percent of its budget on the four basic necessities of American life: housing, food, clothing, and health care. In 1999, *American Consumers*, an industry newsletter, reported that some 82 percent of American households had discretionary income (or "fun money," the amount remaining for spending or saving after taxes are paid and necessities are purchased). The only income group in the minority were households earning less than $15,000 a year. And even 49 percent of that group had fun money, as would the Average American. In 2002, the newsletter *Research Alert* reported some 74 percent of American households had discretionary income.

After Team Average departed Cottonwood Pass, I watched the child with Down Syndrome giggle with her sister; the only kids to finish the race, they had ridden in the back seat of their parents' car. Joseph and Ronae Fink were the previous year's Most Average Award winners. They said they moved from the New York City area eleven years ago in order to devote more time to their family. Ronae's retired parents had been living in Vegas, so she and Joseph had come to the city to be with them and to open a preschool. They had their two kids within three years of their move.

Joseph believes there is no shame in being common. "I am average and I love being average," he said, his voiced raised. "Let me tell you about before we moved out here. I had to report for jury duty in lower Manhattan. For two straight days, I passed a homeless man on the sidewalk near the front of the courthouse. On the third day, he was in the same position. I looked more closely and realized, *Oh my God, he's dead.* I found a police officer and told him. He just said, 'Not my problem. My shift is over.' Here you have someone who was unable to care for himself and someone who thought he was above it all. No thank you to both."

*I knew the spot of Joseph's revelation.* A month earlier, in a sixth-floor courtroom above the same Centre Street sidewalk, I had heard Judge Roger Hayes explain that government and religious leaders make many decisions for communities, and that the beauty of juries is that the average citizen is finally represented. On the street below, ten satellite trucks were parked and a long line of photographers were waiting to snap photos of Martha Stewart, the icon of American domesticity and privilege. She was in a nearby courtroom, in front of a jury of average citizens who would eventually convict her of a crime that would send her to prison.

It was the belief of Oliver Wendell Holmes, the legendary Supreme Court justice, that the law should be molded by what statistically average individuals in the community believed. "When men live in society, a certain average of conduct, a sacrifice of individual personalities going beyond a certain point, is necessary to the general welfare," Holmes proclaimed. He believed that the duties of the lawyer could one day be best served by "the man of statistics and the master of economics," who could determine which community characteristics are considered average and acceptable.

In front of Judge Hayes in New York, I was dismissed from a jury pool for being outside the average threshold. Hayes, presiding over a drug possession case, had asked if anyone had had any experiences that might influence his attitude toward police officers. This meant my revisiting something that I had not talked about for years. Some time ago in another big city, I had been roundly pummeled by a cop who had mistaken me for a suspect in the same vicinity. Outraged at my pleas of innocence, he had snapped. I had settled out of court after assurances that the officer would be seriously reprimanded by the city. The scarring in my groin area required multiple surgeries. And as doctors questioned whether I could ever have children, I seriously questioned whether I could ever fit into average society even if I wanted to.

For comfort, I ratcheted up my belief in objectivism, a philosophy founded by the late novelist, and atheist, Ayn Rand. Basically, objectivism rejects ordinary achievers and believes that only the most professionally ambitious, talented, and ruthless—from above-average capitalists to above-average celebrities—should be making decisions and receiving glory. In *The Fountainhead,* Rand's most well-known novel, her main character, Howard Roark, a New York City professional, appears in a courtroom and tells the judge that because juries present average decisions, the decisions are not as worthy as those made by an individual.

If I couldn't live like other businessmen, I would be significantly more independent and successful than them. I would shut off ordinary activities. I would bond with the well-known crowd. I would stop attending church. At the time, I was in my first committed relationship, with a hardworking and athletic woman. We had so much in common that we were even born on the same day of the same year. In her, I saw a woman I could settle down with, but I could not guarantee her a naturally conceived family. It quickly tore me, and the relationship, apart.

I devoted myself round-the-clock to an international post in professional tennis. And this dedication—myopia even—led to my working from the road more and more. Since convincing famous personalities in and out of tennis to promote the sport in off-court interviews and activities was among my initiatives, I was soon traveling in their circles. To complete the transition, I started a different job, in the entertainment industry in Los Angeles, in which I worked with celebrities. On the side, I started a celebrity Q&A column for a national magazine that had me interviewing a host of well-known entertainers. In Los Angeles, La-La Land, I had found a lifestyle where I could hide from reality. Indeed, in time I successfully eliminated any desire to find love, settle down, and start a family.

Or so I thought. I soon started spending time with a beautiful woman I had met at a business meeting. She was a successful sales executive at Tiffany & Co. in New York City and lived on Park Avenue. On our first date, she said that she was proud that her days growing up in Erie, Pennsylvania, were ordinary—a comment unsolicited by me. I learned that she was committed to maintaining the family values instilled in her during that time.

Maybe deep down, that's what made her so intriguing.

To spend more time with her, I left Los Angeles to take on a lengthy work project in New York. And I fell in love. We wed in the Catholic church where Kathy had regularly attended Mass during her childhood. I began to attend church services on an intermittent basis, but still searched for a reason to believe.

*On a Las Vegas mountainside,* Joseph Fink was making some big points. "Our children don't expect special treatment, although many people automatically assume that someone like our daughter does," he said, gesturing to his Down Syndrome child. "We teach her to be independent, but when she fits in, when she does things with the average crowd of 'abled' kids, it's a wonderful sense of belonging.

"To me, being average means you have a core," Joseph said. "It shows that you can stand on your own two feet and that you're a mature adult. Not one of those who drags down the country by feeling they are owed entitlements. Those who expect the American Dream are not American; those who think they are owed a hand-up by the government instead of a hand-down. That's not what our country was built on. They need to know we work for what we earn."

Joseph said he and his wife had recently retired, but they had grown restless and opened a business that custom-fits vehicles for handicapped drivers. He said the Average American should be someone who had worked hard for a living, even if currently retired. He meant the paid labor force and I applied that criterion. With retirees and late-shift workers already eliminated, I knew that J. Average would be a full-time, paid day worker. I pictured knocking on his door around dinnertime.

*Tom Bennett,* the road rally's grizzled course marshal, tapped me on the shoulder and said he and his wife, Christy, could drop me off at a hotel for the night. The Bennetts' dog barreled into my arms and then became my seatmate. Tom said his wife and his Lab were his best friends. We agreed that J. Average, like most Americans, would have at least one pet at home (neither dogs nor cats, the most common household pets, are in the majority).

The Bennetts started talking about guns. Tom, who has a concealed-weapons permit, discussed how I could earn a permit of my own, in case I was ever interested, while near the Las Vegas Strip we passed billboards that featured towering head shots of the implied average American. A brightly lit marquee for the Silverton resort with a photo of a middle-aged man read, "Tom won $15,500." "Not this Tom," Tom Bennett responded. We also saw that a matronly looking Linda had done much better at the Palace casino, taking in six figures, although her billboard was not as impressive.

The message to visitors of Vegas seemed to be that anyone could lose their average status overnight. However, although we live in a nation where seemingly ordinary Americans hold up signs outside of television studios in the hopes of being interviewed, where untalented singers line up in droves to be insulted by a Brit in a black T-shirt, and others try hard to live for a while in *The Real World,* the majority of Americans have never been identified on television and prefer to keep it that way. In 1998, Harris pollsters asked Americans if they wanted to be famous (fame was described as being "popular, well-known or widely recognized for your accomplishments, activities, abilities, expertise, or opinions"), and 69 percent said no. The media's notion that we live in a nation consumed with being well-known does not bear out. In a 2002 Gallup survey, teenagers were asked to name their heroes, and only 25 percent chose performers, personalities, or sports figures. Mirroring most Americans, J. Average would need to be someone who is not trying to be nationally known. To assure that finalists would be truthful on this point, I would look for a way to access their feelings, perhaps as a kind of "final test."

No doubt John Henry Kemp would never allow his face to be placed on a Vegas billboard. From Census 2000, the nation's median population center—the same population is north, south, east, and west of this spot—was determined to be next to a cornfield on Kemp's 119-acre farm in rural Daviess County, Indiana. At the time, Kemp was the father of ten and grandfather of thirty-two, and Old Order Amish. He told the local media that he did not have a television set and that he did not want any attention. Old Order Amish believe, among other things, that a life of worshipping fame is a waste.

Chances are, the Amish of Daviess County are happier than to-day's fame seekers. A national study headed by Dr. Tim Kasser, a professor of psychology at Knox College in Illinois, confirmed earlier research showing that those who most value image, status, and fame are noticeably less happy than others. Kasser found that this discontentment includes higher levels of depression and physical ailments, such as headaches and backaches, and a lower level of enthusiasm for life. "We found this in people age ten to eighty," Kasser noted.

For celebrity entertainers, their never-ending audition in front of average Americans is additionally isolating. Without the support of the ordinary, these performers could not be celebrities, and so everyday Americans hold the true power in this relationship, sitting on millions of thrones in front of our would-be court jesters. As Thomas de Zengotita, writing in *Harper's* in December 2004 about fame in America, noted of entertainers, "They are so needy, actually—dressing up, dieting, touring, posing, exposing privacies, cavorting desperately, endlessly, before us."

As the Amish have long understood, being well-known outside a tight-knit community brings attention, but it's mostly from complete strangers or from those with selfish agendas, not exactly cozy, un-conditional relationships. Of course, the reason many Americans are famous is because they have committed serious crimes or gotten themselves embroiled in unwanted controversies ripe for media cov-erage—hardly prime candidates for sunny dispositions. Like the writer character Trigorin in the Anton Chekhov drama *The Seagull,* we can also consider the likelihood that fame regularly does not make one happy because it only makes the seeker strive for more fame. This may be one reason, as Vanessa Grigoriadis reported in *New York* magazine in July 2005, that research shows "celebrities are four times as likely to commit suicide as noncelebrities and live, on average, thirteen years less."

Because Las Vegas has become the most popular tourist city in America, its visitors have often been portrayed as average Ameri-cans. However, on further inspection, this is unconvincing. At first glance it would appear that CBS constructed its 5,000-square-foot Television Research Center on the Las Vegas Strip because the city now draws some 36 million visitors a year who represent a nice cross-section of America. The center, a test-marketing attraction lo-cated in the MGM Grand casino, collects opinions from visitors on such topics as which new shows are apt to be successful, or asks them how they use certain household electronic products. However, CBS's lead researcher, David Poltrack, told *Business Week* in October 2004: "We get folks . . . who are generally more upscale and younger than the population at large. Those are our kind of people."

So, if Bennett believes he's average, what does he feel could most disqualify him? "I have killed," he answered softly, although with-out hesitation. A few minutes later, he opened up. "In Vietnam," he said, "the first person I killed was a boy. Grenade got him. Unfortu-nately, that's war. . . . Politicians need to face that."

A point that Tom had raised in anger earlier—"No one from 'the outside' ever really listens to average Americans, even though we *are* America"—had opened him up like a spigot. I sensed from Tom that no note-taking stranger had ever appeared in front of him to ask what mattered in his life and, as was the case with some others during my travels, he seemed to take his one opportunity to freely vent on both pedestrian and sensitive topics.

"You know, people listen to my politics and assume I'm pro-life," he said. "I'm not, and Christy and I undoubtedly hear, 'You're killing innocent children. You need to be pro-life.' I tell them they don't know a goddamn thing about killing innocent children.

"It drives me crazy that Christy and I still hear from people, 'What's the matter, you couldn't conceive?' They and their damn assumptions! Like not having children negates everything we have built together. We can have a fulfilling life that's full of love—hell, we do have it, God bless it—and we can have that with whatever our family unit is like."

Bennett is in the majority of Americans in that he is pro-choice and supports *Roe v. Wade,* the prevailing abortion standard, which gives women the right to abort in the first trimester and limits restrictions to abort in the second trimester. For many years, the majority of Americans have supported legalized abortion as the Supreme Court has defined it, while being opposed to the *act* of abortion, two more Average American criteria. In May 2005, Gallup asked Americans about whether they believed abortion was morally acceptable or wrong regardless of whether they thought it should be legal. Fifty-one percent thought it was morally wrong.

In 1992, when the American Viewpoint polling service asked Americans if they approved or disapproved of that year's Supreme Court decision on abortion, which upheld the right of a woman to abort until a fetus is viable, 58 percent of Democrats and 58 percent of Republicans were in support. In his dissent, Justice Antonin Scalia complained that the Court was merely advancing prevailing public opinion.

Although J. Average would be in support of legal abortion as it is currently allowed, he or she could be against abortion if he or she, and not another person, had the choice. Indeed, the majority of people who conceive choose to give birth. Christy Bennett said, "It's not an easy issue."

"But you've got to appreciate what you do have," her husband cut in. "Look, I'm not saying our marriage is all sex and sunshine, it's not. But I think that just makes us normal." Tom is right: A round-the-clock, chipper attitude is yet another myth of the average American. According to a Centers for Disease Control and Prevention study conducted between 1995 and 2000, the average American adult felt "sad, or blue, or depressed" three days a month.

Increased public acceptance of depression, including pharmaceutical companies' mainstream advertising of antidepressants, has helped fuel the myth that growing numbers of Americans—perhaps even a majority—will at some point suffer from the disease. Although it is the nation's most widespread mood disorder, in any given year less than 5 percent of Americans are clinically depressed, and the rate has remained steady for decades. In truth, America may have literally reached a happy medium. On a series of Gallup polls since 2000, the vast majority of Americans—93 percent on last count—have described themselves as very or fairly happy, another criterion. (Knowing that the Average American would be no sourpuss made at least one American—me—very happy.) Like most Americans, three out of four since Gallup started tracking this in 1992, J. Average would also be "generally satisfied" with the way things are going in his personal life. The highest mark, 82 percent, came in the last poll, in 2004.

One academic study on daily mood, headed by Princeton University psychology professor Dr. Daniel Kahneman and published in *Science* magazine in 2004, traced the "normal day" of more than 900 working women and found that unless women are poverty-stricken, their happiness level on a scale of one to ten is six or higher, with no real difference in daily moods seen between those residing in households earning below and above $60,000 a year (coincidentally, the median family income in the United States falls between $50,000 and $60,000). University of Illinois psychologist Edward Diener, known as Dr. Happiness, who has spent a quarter century analyzing happiness and who flies a smiley-face flag outside his front door, reported that American millionaires are no more happy than average-income Americans.

As Gregg Easterbrook wrote on Diener's conclusions in his 2003 book *The Progress Paradox,* "Once the middle-class level is reached, money decouples from happiness and the two cease having anything to do with each other." Easterbrook later wrote, in *Time* magazine: "Love, friendship, family, respect, a place in the community, the belief that your life has purpose—those are the essentials of human fulfillment, and they cannot be purchased with cash." In 2000, an AARP survey found that 61 percent of Americans believe money can't buy happiness, a view J. Average would need to hold. In a *Time* survey, which asked Americans to name their primary source of happiness, money ranked fourteenth. (Their relationships with their children and friends were the top two responses.)

Americans with average lives also achieve happiness and satisfaction more easily than pleasure-seekers. In his 2002 book *Authentic Happiness,* Martin Seligman, a University of Pennsylvania psychologist, breaks happiness into three parts: pleasure ("the smiley-face" part), engagement ("the depth of involvement with one's family, work, romance and hobbies"), and meaning ("using personal strengths to serve some larger end"). He said that pleasure has the smallest effect. "It turns out that engagement and meaning are much more important," Seligman wrote. He also noted, "As a professor I don't like this, but the cerebral virtues—curiosity, love of learning—are less strongly tied to happiness than interpersonal virtues like kindness, gratitude and capacity for love."

A few months after legendary Wall Street trader Jim Rogers, an old acquaintance of mine, completed a trip through 116 countries by car, I stopped by his Manhattan mansion. He was putting a few pricey belongings and a couple photos of himself with famous people into boxes for storage. The photos were replaced with those of everyday people along with one of himself running in a marathon. "Possessions and superficiality don't mean much to me anymore," he said. "It's about embracing the people who really are alive in this world." Rogers, in his sixties, soon after became a dad for the first time. He says his daughter is the highlight of his life. As he told *BusinessWeek* in October 2004, caring for a child "has given me feelings I didn't know I had."

People like technology guru Jim Clark are more prevalent among American multimillionaires. Before Clark founded Silicon Graphics, according to a *New York Times* report, he said that having $10 million would make him happy; later, before he founded Netscape, he said it would take $100 million; even later, before he founded Healtheon, he upped the figure to $1 billion. Finally, he conceded that even this was not enough: "Once I have more money than Larry Ellison, I'll be satisfied," he said. At the time, Ellison, who had founded Oracle, was worth $13 billion. If Clark's feelings are average for multimillionaires, then the average multimillionaire may never be as content as the average American.

For her 1997 book *The Golden Ghetto*, Jessie O'Neill, the granddaughter of former General Motors president and U.S. Secretary of Defense C. E. Wilson, interviewed a number of her fellow affluent Americans and found unhappiness common. "The myth which equates money with happiness is an outright lie," she wrote. "For the ambitious individuals who work long and hard for their wealth, the disillusionment they feel when and if they finally discover that their money has not purchased happiness and self-esteem can be doubly hard to bear."

A number of other studies also show that "materialistic attitudes" rarely lead to happiness, according to a December 2004 *New York Times* article, which pointed out that "wanting more and never being satisfied . . . increase the likelihood that a person will suffer depression, anxiety and low self-esteem." Average citizens who reap a major windfall, such as lottery and casino megawinners, regularly develop these problems. They often feel insecure about having all the cash, start chasing material luxuries, and end up broke and bummed out. Some 75 percent of Americans who win the big overnight money lose it all within five years.

As Tom turned down a road to the Vegas hotel where I would spend the night, we spotted a sign for a gun show in the city. Tom returned to an earlier subject. "You want to find a real average American, you need to hang out with some gun owners in Nevada," he said.

All right, pilgrim.

—

# Six

# GUNS, GAMBLING, AND GIVING IT AWAY

*Candidates remaining: fewer than 50 million*

*In Elko, Nevada,* some 525 miles north of Las Vegas, a windstorm whipped some sagebrush through the front entrance of Cimarron West, a rustic diner and country store. Over a lunch of omelets, toast, and coffee in a window booth, Danielle Kohler and John Carpenter explained to me that the establishment had long served as the social center of the neighborhood called Tree Streets. At Tom Bennett's suggestion, I had set out to find some gun owners in Nevada, and Danielle and John were the first I had befriended in Tree Streets.

I told them that Tree Streets was likely more statistically average than any other census neighborhood in Nevada.

"You kiddin' me?" Carpenter said, his voice deep.

"This is the Godfather, the Land Baron of the Tree Streets," Kohler whispered to me, leaning reverently toward Carpenter, Elko's Republican state assemblyman and the owner of Cimarron West, where he also manages a realty from a back office. A seventy-three-year-old former rancher, he had moved to a house in the Tree Streets several years back.

The Godfather said that although it's named for the Ash, Elm, Maple, and other "tree" streets that make it up, the neighborhood does not have any regimented boundaries, at least none of which he's aware. However, when I swung my laptop around to show him a computerized map for Census Tract 32-007-9509 (population: 2,250), he pushed aside his coffee, took a closer look, and said, "Well, I'll be damned. I'd say that's pretty much the heart of it."*

Compared to national averages as well as averages for Nevada tracts, Tree Streets is the most average on many fronts. One example: When I queried which census neighborhoods in Nevada fell within $2,500 of each of the three major census income factors—median household income, median family income, and per capita income—the computer kicked out only the Tree Streets.

After checking into Elko's Mid-Town Motel (across the street from the Centre Motel, naturally), I had found that Tree Streets was a full-service neighborhood, where residents can eat, shop, play ball, and attend school. Also present in Tree Streets are Second and Third streets, the nation's two most common road names (Main Street often replaces what would have otherwise been First Street). Elko is best known for an annual cowboy poetry competition. The town lies in the foreground of the white-capped Ruby Mountains, and on the hillside, thousands of rocks form a gigantic "E," constructed by Elko High School students in 1916 to honor a gym teacher who passed away while on a hike. When I was in Elko, the most visibility the outside world had to the area was a new television series that was shot locally. The Elkoans I met either laughed at the producers' attempts to make the backdrop look genuine or groaned at the show's premise. Animals were trucked in so that a property ap-

---

*More than ever, I believed that census tracts as a rule were the best examples of geographical community in the United States. The Census Bureau reports, "Census tracts, which are typically defined with local input, are designed to represent neighborhoods." The nation's leading primer on demography methodology notes that a census tract—I would also start to call it a census neighborhood—is based on "as much as practicable, uniform population characteristics, economic status, and housing conditions." In his book *Research in Community Sociology*, Dan Chekki noted that the community is "a society in miniature. It is the sociocultural milieu where people live most of their time and satisfy most of their needs." The neighborhood is the smallest census area that regularly meets that definition.

peared to be a working ranch. The goal of the "reality" show was for gay men to lie about their sexual preference in order to trick heterosexual women. Although a lot of the shooting took place in Elko, mercifully, it was done outside Tree Streets.

When I asked John Carpenter about values in the neighborhood, for a second he thought I was talking about real estate. "That's the first thing I thought of when you said average neighborhood, the homes we have here," he explained. "They're all about the same. People here try to keep things neat and tidy on their property, but we don't have anyone flaunting wealth, even those who have it."

I told Carpenter that in 2000, the nation's median home value, $119,600, was within $1,000 of the median for Tree Streets. The national average will stay under $300,000 for the foreseeable future.

"You're talking about the range of prices around here," Carpenter said. Indeed, only 1.1 percent of homes in the neighborhood were valued at more than $300,000 on the last census, the exact same ratio as all of Elko.

I decided that only those living in homes valued between $100,000 and $300,000 would be considered for the Average American. When Census 2000 was conducted, 50.2 percent of homes were valued in that price range. I erased some exclusive areas from my search—for instance, Rancho Santa Fe, California; Country Life Acres, Missouri; Barton Hills, Michigan; and Fisher Island, Florida—as each house there was valued above $300,000.

Kohler, who works in the trucking business, asked about life in Manhattan, where the average residence had recently topped a million dollars in value for the first time ever. In the diner were a few long-distance truckers—Elko is the biggest midway stop on the 500-mile run from Reno to Salt Lake City—so I mentioned that trucker hats were fashionable among many young, mostly male, New Yorkers. Some of the hottest American celebrities had been wearing them publicly. "Trucker's hat" had become part of the inner-city and fashionista lexicon.

"What's a trucker's hat?" Kohler said.

She was serious. I pointed out a couple of diners wearing adjustable caps with mesh backs. I said the hats often have foam fronts and sport farm-industry logos.

"Oh, those, we just call those baseball caps," Kohler said.

"They want people to think they're truckers?" Carpenter said, puzzled.

I muttered something about them wanting to look like authentic regular Joes, also the reason such items as wallets on chains and dish-sized silver belt buckles are considered in, for both men and women. The fashion industry is calling it "trucker chic."

"Maybe they're not comfortable being themselves," Kohler said. "They have to be someone they see as real. You know, rhinestone cowboys."

"You get a lot of people in the city—and I'm talking about Reno—who treat us like we're hicks here," Carpenter said. "But sure, we are the type of place where people are real. If that's being a hick, fine."

"People here tend to be individuals who care about the environment and conservation," Kohler said. I decided that J. Average would care, too, enough to support the nation's environmental protection laws. A 2003 Gallup poll determined that three out of four Americans believe there should be stricter enforcement of environmental regulations. Like the majority of Americans, J. Average also needed to be someone who recycles at least on occasion. According to a 2000 National Opinion Research Center survey, 56 percent of Americans "always" or "often" (the top two choices) "sort glass or cans or plastic or paper and so on for recycling."

"But we also respect that outsiders won't dictate what we do," said Kohler, the secretary of the local gun club. "And nothing says freedom in this country like the Second Amendment. With all due respect, more people use guns than you'd probably think."

According to 1999 Gallup findings, 67 percent of Americans have fired a gun. This would make the Average American someone who has shot one. According to a 2004 Gallup study, 40 percent of Americans had guns in the home or elsewhere on the property (this number is down from more than 50 percent in 1993). The study also concluded that the majority of Americans believe in the right to bear arms, as would the Average American.*

Of course, in many places in this country, toy firearms are also prevalent. In Elko's Round Table Pizza, a block outside the Tree Streets, I attended the monthly meeting of the Northeastern Nevada Pistol and Rifle Association and saw a boy no older than ten playing an arcade game named Legal Enforcers. It offers a choice of shooting any of six "special" guns—Magnum, automatic, assault rifle, shotgun, machine gun, and grenade gun. On average, some 22,000 Americans are injured every year by air rifles, paintball weapons, and BB guns alone. Kohler, thirty-nine, said many kids much younger should be allowed to fire the real thing.

"Some as young as five or six, we have developed enough sense of safety in them for them to shoot .22 rifles and pistols," she said. "Once people fighting against guns realize that we will always be a gun nation, it's best to work within that system and focus that same energy on [gun] safety. I think what you should really take away though is that the club is a wonderful place for people to meet, build friendships, and learn about discipline. Those are strong values. How is that bad? We're going to shoot anyway. We're teaching each other how to do it right. And you look at those who support us, and they cut through all social and other classes. So many people talk about equal opportunity, but we walk the walk."

Kohler said she understands that the majority of the country may be against citizens owning semiautomatic weapons and in favor of registration or waiting lists for gun owners. Indeed, these two views are in the majority, and I ascribed each of them to the Average American.

"The type of problems you hear about guns," Carpenter said, "you can attribute to Las Vegas and the big Nevada cities, but Elko is not Las Vegas." It turns out that Nevada is ranked the most

*Gallup also reported that on average, American households have 1.7 guns. This appears as if most American homes have at least one gun, but gun owners average 4.4 guns each, skewing the per-home average.

dangerous state in the nation, in part because of its high per-capita murder rate. Carpenter preferred to identify with the much smaller community profile. "There's a greater sense of fellowship in the Tree Streets than in a much bigger place," he said.

"Look, I've got slot machines in the lobby. It's a normal thing to gamble a little bit. It's very popular to visitors passing through here. But I am very aware that some people can get hooked on it. Sometimes I see people I know playing it, and I know they can't afford to gamble. I just say, 'I hate to take your money, so I don't want to see you playing. Please stop. The house always wins.'"

Although betting is often imagined to be a pastime primarily for those who can least afford it, most American gamblers are of above-average wealth. And gambling is an undeniable part of the nation's heritage. Lotteries supervised by the English monarchy were the major source of funding for explorations of the New World. American sports gambling started no later than 1665, when the first horse racetrack was erected on Long Island. The thirteen original colonies each ran lotteries, proceeds from which were responsible for building such universities as Harvard, Yale, and Columbia. Alexis de Tocqueville observed during his early nineteenth-century travels through America, "Those who live in the midst of democratic fluctuations have always before their eyes the image of chance, and they end by liking all undertakings in which chance plays a part." Public lotteries significantly helped finance the rebuilding of the South after the Civil War.

In 2001, more money was spent on legal gambling (more than half a trillion dollars, the equivalent of more than $1,750 per U.S. resident) than on movie tickets, DVD and video sales and rentals, and music purchases combined. In 2003, 75 percent of men and 57 percent of women bet—most often on public lotteries and bingo, casino gambling, and sports pools—and those numbers are increasing. Slot machines alone gross more annually than McDonald's, Wendy's, Burger King, and Starbucks combined. According to a 2003 study, more than 80 percent of Americans say gambling is "an acceptable entertainment option for themselves or others," as would J. Average. Of those Americans who said they go to church weekly,

52 percent had gambled within the past twelve months. No doubt, this acceptance can be attributed in large part to the church's generally open-door policy on betting, which is in turn due to the popularization of and reliance on weekly bingo fundraisers at many churches. Wayne Allyn Root, the CEO of the nation's only publicly traded sports handicapping company, even maintains in his 2004 book *The Zen of Gambling* that a commitment to God, including daily prayer, is a cornerstone of successful money wagering.

At the Elko diner, Carpenter agreed that the most average American, like most Americans, would be someone who had gambled with money in at least one organized game of chance over the past year.

"For better or worse, I have decided to keep the slot machines here," Carpenter said. "You want to talk values, you best go see Deacon Craig. He has done a lot to try and make the real problems go away."

I left the diner to walk deeper into Tree Streets and found Craig La Gier in his modest office at St. Joseph's Catholic Church. He immediately warmed to the idea of finding the Average American. La Gier was dressed in jeans and a plaid shirt. In one corner of the room was some fishing gear. The deacon said many Elko residents enjoy fishing in the nearby, picturesque Ruby Valley waters. Like most Americans, J. Average would need to live in a household where at least one person has a "craft or hobby."

"We may be in the middle of nowhere, but anybody says this is a hunky-dory community, they've got their head in the sand," he said early in our conversation. "Have you been in Angel Park?"

I had passed by it, but not checked it out. "You should go by there," he said. "It's normally a nice place. Unfortunately, you'll see some graffiti there. On the building where the restroom is, someone spray-painted 'Cimarron Dragons.' We need to put an end to this before they start trying to copy other gang behavior. I've talked with our sheriff about it. I want there to be punishment.

"We already have drugs here. Crystal meth is the drug of choice. Many meth labs in the area have been closed down. You want me to keep going? We had a young Hispanic man with a drinking problem. He drove under the influence and was killed behind the wheel.

He lived right down the street here. Worked for the railroad. Five kids and a wife. She doesn't speak English."

La Gier had more examples, but his point was, no matter how big or small the community, hardly anyone lives in an environment of Rockwellian perfection. "It's around us, whether we want to admit it or not," La Gier said.

According to one national crime rating, the Relocation Crime Lab Index, which sets 100 as the annual average, Elko scored a 40, an enviable number (by comparison, Las Vegas scored 509), but this still amounted to 30 rapes, 66 robberies, and 192 motor vehicle thefts, among other crimes, per 100,000 people. Nationwide, the FBI reports that there are around 5,200 arrests per 100,000 people each year for offenses ranging from murders to curfew violations. However, arrests are not a true reflection of how many crimes are being committed. In his 1989 textbook *Society: A Brief Introduction*, Ian Robertson reported that "a large number of self-report studies, in which people were asked to give anonymous details of any crimes they had committed, indicate that close to 100 percent of Americans have committed some kind of illegal offense . . . .The 'typical' criminal is not the typical criminal at all, but rather the one who typically gets arrested, prosecuted, and convicted."

On the upside, La Gier said that he had seen a rise in community outreach within Tree Streets since he arrived five years earlier. "We took up a collection for the woman who lost her husband," he said. "She was working at the dry cleaners, making six dollars an hour. We collected over a thousand dollars to help the family. We also got toys and a turkey to give to them on Christmas. It certainly helps that there's a spirit around here of people helping where they can financially or volunteering their time where it's needed. It's become a tenet in so many of their lives."

J. Average would need to annually donate money and time to charity. In 2003, according to Gallup, 82 percent of Americans gave money to "a religious organization or other charitable cause" and 59 percent gave time to such causes. Americans easily lead the world in charitable donations, with an average of $953 in 2002—$938 more than the average Japanese citizen. According to *Philanthropy* magazine, each year Americans donate to charities more than seven times the amount of "the average German." In the United States, according to another report, those households bringing in less than $75,000 a year give a larger percentage of their income to charity than those making more. And most charitable contributions come from individuals, nearly three times more than corporations, foundations, and other public donations combined.

La Gier said such behavior is important because it provides a truer sense of worth than our material possessions. "I know we are seen as a country of conspicuous consumption," La Gier said. "But, if you ask me, a lot of that is a sin, point blank. Let's say you buy a $425,000 Lamborghini. It's still a vehicle with four wheels that takes gas and gets you where you need to go. I'm not bad mouthing good cars; I've got a Jeep pick-up. But when is there going to be a greater sense of not keeping so much for ourselves? The other day, I went fishing with someone who certainly has the money and land to build a monster home. But all he's done is replace his mobile home with a double wide. What's not important is the house; it's being close to his family and his people. He's found meaning."

In a nation that has 6 percent of the world's population, but 59 percent of the world's wealth, La Gier prays that we all are able to find more meaning. In 1999, he and his wife were living close to their native California and making above-average money—he $142,000 as a lumberyard buyer; she around $50,000 as a high-school teacher. For La Gier, it was a long way from his early days of playing minor-league baseball and delivering milk door to door (yes, some people actually did hold such iconic 1950s jobs). But when the bishop asked La Gier if he wanted to quit his job and become the deacon at St. Joseph's, he was not especially worried about the change in lifestyle and the drop in pay. His wife would take a job as detention chaplain for the Reno Diocese, working to, as La Gier says, "abilitate" prisoners. They would live in the Tree Streets next door to the church. Their two children, both in northern Nevada, would be within driving distance.

"I think materialism may be losing some of its dominance," La Gier said, "but still, there's a long way to go." Experts agree that through at least 2005, the mean net worth (assets minus debts) of American households will stay below $300,000, and that the median net worth will remain over $30,000. I decided that the Average American's household would fall somewhere in this majority threshold.

"If only people with all their cars and possessions would realize that such behavior is not going to make them any happier in the long run," La Gier said.

I thought about the fear of being ordinary and, having shared time with La Gier and many Americans who were comfortable and relaxed about being considered average, I wondered whether I'd be better off if I followed their example. I already knew that my uptight, go-for-it attitude could have a debilitating effect. It is one reason why those of us who exhibit Type-A personalities, who like to think we are in control, are twice as likely as the average American to define ourselves as "very unhappy." I once suffered the shame of bankruptcy as a result of my staying stubbornly focused on an international legal case and running up exorbitant litigation fees in pursuit of a relatively moderate, albeit principled, cash judgment. Justice did prevail, but I had refused to ask for a loan along the way, lest someone think I was not in control, or worse, not above average. I subsequently hit an emotional low, not only from my inability to pay others, but for not having maintained an overachiever's spotless lifetime public record.

I was not alone. Others, scared of being ordinary, have also made mistakes that have caused unwelcome emotions or consequences. In *The Golden Cage,* a June 2004 study of anorexia, medical doctor Hilde Broch explained that people with eating disorders are commonly overachievers who "have a great fear of being ordinary, or average, or common." Dr. Douglas Powell of Harvard Medical School, in a study published in the *Journal of Clinical Psychology* in 2004 on debilitating performance anxiety ("their condition is so severe as to threaten to end their academic or professional career"), wrote this about extreme public-speaking anxiety, stage fright, test-taking anxiety, and writer's block: "For many, it is the fear of being ordinary that prevents them from performing."

Roy Williams, a noted advertising professional and the author of a 1998 book, *The Wizard of Ads,* maintained, "The fear of being average robs you of contentment." Lorraine Hering, a West Coast bereavement counselor, claimed that the fear of being common "causes teens to take such extreme risks with behavior and emotions. The adolescent wants to prove that she or he is not ordinary and that his or her life will somehow matter. . . . In an almost violent urge to matter, many unguided youths will turn to violence as a means of making their mark." In a church setting, this fear can be described as having the most ancient of origins. In 2003, Raymond Rooney, Jr., the pastor at the United Methodist Church in Verona, Mississippi, told his parishioners, "What is the mother of all fears and anxieties? Who was it that was responsible for the first recorded sin, before Adam and Eve? The fear of being average. The anointed cherub wanted to be more than he was."

"This journey you're taking, it's really about yourself, right?" Deacon La Gier asked me as we faced each other from matching chairs in front of his desk. Being in a Catholic church and all, I was ready to confess. This was one of the benefits I saw in a religion I had long rejected as too regimented, too conformist—sort of the way I long had regarded the average American. Near the end of my spiel, I said that although I had some lingering issues about the fear of being average, I now recognized that it was hurting me in many ways.

"Life may have been passing you by," La Gier said. "We all have something to give to strangers. Everyone has talents that they can share. Share that knowledge. Show them that you care. It will make you connect with them, and you will appreciate them. I always say, 'We all have something else to give if we only think about it.'"

I thanked the deacon for his advice and walked two blocks to sit for a while in Angel Park. A few minutes later, a teenaged runner nodded hello as he cut a route in front of the statue of an angel that overlooks the grounds. I thought about all the miles I had run in pursuit of athletic glory. I had succeeded in that pursuit, but had I ever shared with strangers the things that I had learned?

*Seven*

# SOMEWHERE
# OVER THE RAINBOW

*Candidates remaining: fewer than 30 million*

*Over the radio,* a grocer named Fibber was getting ready to explain how a pile of coal happened to show up on his rural Midwestern street. It was dark and foggy, just past five o'clock in the morning, and I was driving through the middle of Kansas. I passed a gas station with a hand-lettered "We Got Worms" sign, rolled over some rickety railroad tracks, and heard a deafening crack of thunder. As I scanned the nearby train depot for a parking space, I refused to let go of my mental image of a sunny and peaceful day from 1940. A local radio station was broadcasting *Fibber McGee and Molly,* a sitcom from that year, complete with all the original commercials. Ol' Fibber McGee was about to get himself into quite a pickle.

Once a week from 1935 to 1951, up to a quarter of all U.S. residents tuned in to hear what was happening on *Fibber McGee and Molly.* Despite the fact that many Americans lived outside the reach of the show, no other entertainment series in electronic media history has attracted such a large share of the population.

The 1930s and 1940s were the golden age of radio; in the thirties, the medium's saturation passed 50 percent of American households for the first time. Two decades would pass before the majority of homes had television. Fibber McGee and Molly, played by a real-life husband-and-wife team, Jim and Marian Jordan, from Peoria, were widely loved as the average American man and woman; the voice of the middle class. Their big-screen feature-length comedy, *Heavenly Days,* even has Fibber being named the most average citizen in America by the nation's most prominent pollster.

Because radio was the nation's first instantaneous mass medium and considered even more psychologically and imaginatively moving than magazines and motion pictures (witness the panic that resulted from the 1938 radio drama "War of the Worlds"), corporations and the federal government saw *Fibber McGee and Molly* as more than just a hit comedy. Who better to use to endorse their wares and agendas than the average American couple as imagined by millions of Americans?

At a communications exhibit I had perused at the Smithsonian's National Museum of American History, it was written that during radio's heyday, programmers capitulated to the belief among advertisers that "network radio should reflect a white, middle-class America (although ethnic shows were popular)." The parenthetical point too often remains below the radar: the fact that everyday Americans regularly embrace diversity, while far-reaching and questionable media decisions are driven by national and multinational organizations pushing products—and politics.

Government influence has been a major part of commercial radio since the medium's first broadcast in 1920, when Leo Rosenberg of KDKA in Pittsburgh opened with the announcement, "We shall now broadcast the election returns." Two decades later, the Franklin Delano Roosevelt administration was helping to red-pencil the *Fibber McGee and Molly* script, using the perceived average American couple as a propaganda tool.

The radio division of the Office of War Information, which was created in 1942, worked with the War Advertising Council, a consortium of American advertisers, and *Fibber McGee and Molly* staffers to doctor episodes so that they could move public opinion in directions favorable to administration policies. By late 1942, the government had not effectively sold Americans on gas and rubber rationing, major domestic campaigns at the time. It wanted each American to consume no more than four gallons of gas a week, which did not go over well with most of the public. In a December *Fibber McGee and Molly* episode, Harlow Wilcox, the show's narrator, told Fibber, "Mileage rationing is the only fair way to cut down nonessential driving. When the rubber this country has is gone, it's gone. That's all there is. There isn't any more." After Fibber and Molly gave the policy a nudge, millions of Americans jumped aboard the mileage-rationing bandwagon. In a 1950 episode, the McGees served as the census takers in their neighborhood, prompting Molly to say, "A true picture of the size and condition of our country depends on true answers from all of us. And a true picture is of vital importance." Added Fibber, "Remember that the information you give your census taker is completely confidential. By law, no other agency of the government can ever use it—for taxation, investigation, or anything else."

When the nation's second instantaneous mass medium—television—overtook radio in popularity, the government looked for new ways to cowrite primetime dialogue to be spoken by average American characters. The most-watched result was *Red Nightmare*, a government-funded movie hosted by Jack Webb of *Dragnet* fame and televised in the early 1960s under the Warner Bros. banner. The script, originally entitled *Freedom and You,* hammered home the message that the average American, a husband and father played by a square-jawed, middle-aged white actor sporting a snazzy sweater vest, would be overpowered by Communists if he failed to fight all signs of the Red Party. In an ominous voice, Jack Webb said of the man's hometown, "It looks like Kansas."

*Enter Randy Barten*, a.k.a. Weed Man of Dickinson County, Kansas.

"Remember, you're not a young stud anymore," Randy said, handing me a bottle of pills near the railroad tracks where I had parked. "You may want to down a few dozen Advils, my friend." We were near the starting line of the county's annual community marathon.

I was standing with Randy, a cattle farmer and the county's director of noxious weeds, on an avenue in Abilene that he knows well. His office was just down the street. He was born and raised nearby and still resides in the area. His wife and their two kids are also natives. He was a potential Average American candidate; I had already been able to apply a lot of my updated search criteria to him, and he had hit each criterion so far.

The race would start at seven o'clock. As the rain picked up and we walked to the runners' registration table inside a local church hall, Randy continued his good-natured ribbing, burning off some nervous energy in the process. We saw two runners standing under umbrellas. I was donning raingear. Randy, a tall, rangy man who bears a resemblance to Ray Bolger, the actor who played the scarecrow in *The Wizard of Oz,* was wearing an orange cap, a flimsy cotton sweatshirt, and running shorts. "Here's my theory," he said. "If you're scared of a little rain, then a marathon is no place for you."

I could tell this was going to be an interesting 26.2 miles.

The previous year, Randy Barten had taken to long-distance running with the knowledge that it was a sport in which everyday Americans could feel comfortable participating. Abilene had started an annual marathon that year, but Barten did not feel he was ready for such a long distance. Instead, he had run in the simultaneous half-marathon, a distance he told me he liked "because it was halfway between running the marathon and not running." He had finished the half marathon in the exact middle of the 111-person race—56th place. His finish had been the most average of the race, using both the regular and median standard. After reading about the marathon and examining the results, I had tracked Barten down. (He had been unaware of his precise middle-of-the-pack status.) He had accepted my offer to volunteer as his mentor during the marathon.

If you want to get your name in the paper or on the Internet and keep it alive in a public historical databank into perpetuity, all while staying within accepted legal and ethical boundaries, run yourself a marathon. Because ordinary participants can compete in the same event with elite runners, because there are so many more of them, because they are out on the course considerably longer than the top finishers, and because they don't exhibit the negative characteristics that seem to be common with today's millionaire athletes, these everyday people are the stars to the many sponsors that make the competitions possible.

In 2004, after the stock price of American running-shoe manufacturer Saucony had risen 369 percent in less than two years, CEO John Fisher credited the company's praise of the common runner. "The sport has matured to become a people sport," Fisher told *USA Today*. "The leading marathon runners are fabulous athletes but virtually nondescript. Running is no longer about who wins, but who finishes." At the same time, Saucony competitor New Balance, also a U.S. company, was celebrating increased sales. New Balance CEO Jim Davis pointed to the company's advertising campaign, featuring the slogan, "Endorsed by no one," the message being that the masses are as important as the elite runners. Advertising for the 2004 Chicago Marathon ran with the tagline, "Watch the average person do the extraordinary."*

Unusual for a sport with professional competitors, marathoning has been all but taken over by average athletes. When I ran the New York City Marathon a few years ago, I finished 216th overall and 23rd among New Yorkers. Although the event has boomed to include more than 36,500 runners, the largest marathon in the world, my same time would now place me inside the top 100 overall and among the top 10 runners in the state. Marathons pride themselves on being truly equal-opportunity events. Perhaps it's only right that Walt Disney—whose grand success, as Disney biographer Steven Watts avowed, came from an honest connection with "average Americans and their hopes, fears, and values"—is the spirit behind the Disney World Marathon in Orlando, which in 2002 had a field

---

*In 2004, after a thirteen-year study, Harvard and University of Utah scientists discovered what most physically separates humans from primates—long-distance running ability. They concluded that the reasons man looks like he does—big brain, small guts, large bodies, and small teeth, to name but four traits among many—can be traced back to our ability to run distances. Dr. Dennis Bramble, a biologist and one of the lead researchers, said, "Running made us human, at least in the anatomical sense."

that was the same gender distribution as America, down to the exact tenth of a percent.

A detailed 2003 study by the Road Running Information Center concluded that when put together, all American road race participants "mirror the overall population of the U.S." for many reasons. For one, the average age for each falls between thirty-six and thirty-seven years. Incidentally, a detailed nonpartisan analysis of the recreational interests of self-described Democrats and Republicans revealed that the two groups are different from the average American when it comes to sports participation. For example, Republicans are 40 percent more likely to play golf than the U.S. average, and Democrats are 20 percent less likely. However, running (or jogging, if you prefer) is the one activity that the two parties had most in common with the average American, each scoring within 4 percentage points of the norm.

When I first checked out the website of the Abilene marathon, there was only one photo, of an unnamed runner, on the home page—not of a defending champion, but a competitor who was randomly placed there. He was, also, none other than Barten, decked out in a Kansas State football sweatshirt and grimacing toward the finish line of the half marathon.

Despite the brotherhood of the ordinary in running, I never ran to chat or meet strangers during races. Like everything else I pursued while growing up, there was no time to slow down; I wanted to put all my energy into the sport. In high school in Connecticut, when I was not getting straight A's and realized I would not be the best student in my class, I was intensely determined to find some way of being No. 1. It's the reason that in my high-school yearbook, I have the longest list of after-school activities.* After many starts in other

*This was somewhat comical, I realized in retrospect, especially after seeing a similarly ambitious student played for laughs in the 1998 film *Rushmore*. The lead character, Max Fischer, played by Jason Schwartzman, is even active in his school's beekeeping and calligraphy clubs. A more sober look at rejecting ordinariness came in *American Beauty*, 1999's Oscar winner for Best Picture, in which a flirtatious high-school cheerleader purposely becomes known as a sexual floozy because it fields, I found that I could make a mark in journalism and long-distance running. With an upperclassman, I started a school news-paper that led to my winning a statewide high-school journalism award from the *Hartford Courant*. As a high-school senior, I went undefeated in cross country, culminating with the state championship. And in my first marathon, I ran the year's fastest time in my age group in New England.

In my drive to excel at something, I had discovered these two interests, media and sports, and they motivated me through an undergraduate degree in journalism and a graduate degree from the nation's leading sports administration program. I wanted to stand out, so, to the surprise of many fellow students in high school, I went to a college in Alabama, in part because my guidance counselor told me that no one else in my school's history had ever enrolled there. Likewise, after completing my degrees I always attempted to move only into positions that could be associated with the top. Within the world's largest public relations conglomerate, I supervised the sports accounts of Philip Morris USA, then the deepest-pocketed corporate sports program in the nation. But while generating exposure for Marlboro's auto-racing team, Virginia Slims Tennis, and other cigarette-sponsored programs, I would not admit to myself or to others that I was promoting a product that killed people. To feel that I was above everyone else was good enough.

This is why, as an adult, running was the only real social outlet I had, and why I only knew how to treat it like work, with the blinders on toward maximum performance. When I finished races and saw competitors coming to the finish line laughing with friends, I didn't get it. I was convinced that they were lazy, not gutting it out to their fullest potential. In 2002, I ran in a 4-mile fun run that had been arranged for sponsors and their guests for the morning after a big New York City event. I went all out and won, no stopping for

covers up her greatest fear, of being an average person. "There's nothing worse in life than being ordinary," she tells a less popular friend, who later recognizes that being ordinary is not so bad.

pleasant banter. A year later, the *Hartford Courant* ran a story about an old achievement of mine on the front page of the Thanksgiving Day sports section. That morning, the largest annual running race in Connecticut was taking place, and I still held the event's high-school record. I was nursing an injury, but I had promised the newspaper reporter that I would enter the race. And I felt like I always had, pushing it even as I hobbled along among some average runners. They weren't trying hard enough. They were laughing. I was not.

Why couldn't I slow down and enjoy the company of strangers? What was my deal?

Maybe Randy Barten could shine some light. The rain had stopped, and he was having a grand old time shouting hellos to people he knew both in and out of the race. By the time we hit mile one in just under ten minutes, I had said I was impressed that he had introduced me to or pointed out no fewer than twenty of his friends and family members.

One of the buddies, a young man in a tank top, was running a couple strides behind us. "It's Kansas, we all know each other," he deadpanned.

There may actually be a drop of truth in Tank Top's wit, so far as Kansas has historically ranked last among states in tourists and first in its population of mythical average Americans. In his legendary 1947 travelogue *Inside U.S.A.,* John Gunther noted, "The Kansan is, as has been well said, the most average of all Americans, a kind of common denominator for the entire continent." In his 2004 best-seller *What's the Matter with Kansas?* native Thomas Frank acknowledged that Kansas is still seen as both most average and a kind of symbolic Blandland. "It may not do too well in other measurements, but in the quest for symbols of down-home, stand-pat, plain-spoken, unvarnished bedrock American goodness Kansas has everyone beat," Frank wrote. "Like Peoria or Muncie, Kansas figures in literature and film as a stand-in for the nation as a whole, the distilled essence of who we are." Kansas's longtime motto is "Where East Meets West and Farm Meets Factory." And the state's physical shape—as Gunther pointed out, it's almost a perfect parallelogram—and nearly center-of-the-country location often lead to its being used as America in microcosm, the nation's middle ground.*

Similarly, the American mass media have propagated the myth that the Midwest has spawned a standard national English, the primer for national television anchors and automated telephone voices. Many linguists divide the nation into twelve distinct dialect groups. The North Midland and South Midland dialects, which cut a wide swath from mid-Jersey to western Kansas, are most often associated with averageness. But even together, the two Midlands are not in the majority (the two most populated dialects are those in the West and South), nor are they accent-free. Even natives of Missouri—a state with places as different as Kansas City and the Ozarks within its borders—are split on whether they are in Missour-ee or Missour-uh.

"Although linguists believe that every region has its own standard variety, there is widespread belief in the U.S. that some regional varieties are more standard than others and, indeed, that some regional varieties are far from the standard—particularly those of the South and New York City," Dr. Dennis Preston, a University of Wisconsin linguistics professor and the past president of the American Dialect Society, noted to PBS. Every area of the country has a dialect with its own peculiarities, and there is no one dominant standard. For instance, the dialects of the Midland regions include such relative oddities as pronouncing our nation's capital as "Warshington" and leaving "to be" out of certain constructions, such as "The cow wants fed."

To be or not to be, there are many reasons why Americans customarily believe their own region's dialect to be the standard. Randy said he speaks "normal English" and believes that I do, too. Only, on the starting line of the marathon, he had told a friend, "The toad-

*The geographical center of the contiguous United States (excluding Alaska and Hawaii) is marked by a stone monument adjacent to a cow pasture in the north central part of Kansas. The actual geographical center of the United States (including Alaska and Hawaii) is 20 miles north of Belle Fourche, South Dakota, on a rural spot so snake-infested that the historical marker needed to be placed more than a mile away.

stranglin' should light'n up," a reference to rain uncommon in New York City, or anywhere else I have lived. Preston, the Wisconsin linguistic expert, conducted a study among Michigan residents regarding which states' residents spoke "correct" or "average" English. Michigan, which is not in the Midland, came out as most average, and the Michiganders incorrectly believed that they had no dialect. They also ranked Missouri, a state classified as Midland, in the lower third of all states, giving much higher marks to such non-Midland places as Connecticut and Colorado. They gave one of their six most abnormal ratings to Alabama.

As I can attest, having attended Auburn University, where a similar study was done, there is a local prejudice at work that linguists call "linguistic security." In this other study, also chronicled by Preston, college students at Auburn rated their state the same as Michigan, Indiana, New York, and many other Midwestern and northern states in the average-English department. They believed that residents of each New England state had more "normal" American accents than those from these other states, but when asked to rate states by their level of "pleasant English," Alabama was No. 1, followed by four other southern states.

More than 200 years ago, Noah Webster saw a need for a dictionary of American English and predicted that one day, 300 million Americans would speak a standardized version of the language he started to document. (America's population will reach 300 million as early as 2006.) And although we are supposedly watching the same television shows, and people are reportedly starting to sound more alike, our dialects in America are actually growing farther apart and spinning off new ones, some within the same state.

Randy Barten has his own way of talking, call it Midland Segue, a smooth way of switching back and forth between the serious and humorous, even when he is huffing and puffing in a marathon. As we approached a stretch of field that was once part of the historic Chisholm Trail, Randy felt obliged to give me a quick history lesson—in the 1860s, more than 3 million head of cattle were led on a treacherous route from Texas to Abilene—but when he caught a glimpse of our first real hill, he began joking about the promise from a marathon official that there would be no hills in the race. I taught Randy an old racing trick, that when one looks straight down at an uphill road while ascending it, a kind of optical illusion makes the road appear level, giving the runner a psychological boost. Although Kansas has long been mythologized as our nation's flatland, this, too, is an illusion. Kansas is far from being the flattest state, ranking twenty-second if calculated from high point to low point, and thirty-second if measured by the elevation changes in 1-kilometer sections. That places it around average for the country.

Feeling what some like to call the buzz of a runner's high, I connected some of these facts in an odd way. I wondered if it is wrong to consider averageness and routine to both be synonymous with flatness. Maybe reasonable highs and lows, like the fluctuations on a heart-monitor screen, are the truest signs of a healthy American life, whereas flat lining and off-the-chart blips are seriously dangerous.

I related this to my growing search criteria and realized that as long as these numbers stayed within the majority, they were best served by having some fluctuations not perceived as perfectly average. The Average American would not be someone who flat lines and hits averages exactly—he would not be a *precise* age or live with 1.59 other people—but, as the realest common American I could find, he would march to a steady beat of averages. Like all Americans, he would also be an individual, undoubtedly with some characteristics and past experiences that would be in the minority. As Irwin Edman, a noted American philosopher from the early 1900s, once remarked, "The standardized American is largely a myth created not least by Americans themselves."

About the nation's most average community, I felt comfortable that it, too, did not have to be a perfect match, but the best representative I could find. The most average locale would be defined by a series of blips that would mark it as the most average.

A bolt of lightning pierced the solemn sky. Randy was nearing the point where runners are allowed to veer off the marathon course and onto the remainder of the half marathon. He took the long road. But he immediately questioned whether he should have. His left knee, wrapped in a band to nurse a twinge he had felt earlier in the week, was starting to stiffen. Maybe there was something about leaning toward the halfway that ran in the Barten family. Randy said the year before, his son Eric, a college freshman, and another youngster had led a cow to the marathon's 13.1-mile turnaround point, then hung a homemade sign around the animal's neck that read "HOLY COW, YOU MADE IT HALFWAY!"

"I'm glad he'll be there again this year," Randy said. I assumed he meant his son.

I was keeping Randy on a pace of ten minutes and ten seconds per mile, as he had told me before the race that he would like to run the marathon in four hours and thirty minutes. Unbeknownst to him, the average finish time for community marathons in the United States is four hours and thirty minutes.

We passed through miles of road with open fields on either side, a heavy crosswind keeping us slightly off balance. By mile twelve, Randy told me his knee felt like a rusted hinge. Up ahead, on a usually lonely road, was the turnaround point, a hairpin turn where his wife, son, mother, and father were waiting. The spot was full of other well-wishers who knew Randy by name. Someone radioed word to the finish line 13.1 miles away, where an announcer told the crowd, "Randy Barten has made it halfway. But he's gimping."

After sucking down some water, Randy was unable to resume running.

His son Eric, looking rather devilish in a goatee and shaved head, was sans cow, but just as encouraging as the year before. He is on his college's cross country team and knows a thing or two about the importance of psychological reinforcement in long-distance running. He walked with his father, reminding him that to prepare for the race, there was a twenty-mile training run. "You know you can hit twenty," Eric said. "Just focus on that for now." Randy's wife, Judy, as I would find out later, wondered if he should have just stopped and climbed into their car. He could do some more damage, she thought to herself.

We were two hours and fifteen minutes into the race, on exact pace for Randy's target finish. A cemetery lay ominously in the background. It started to rain again. In Randy, I saw a forty-six-year-old man who was trying to show that he could do more than be average, more than go "halfway between running the marathon and not running." But no matter how hard he tried, no matter how thoroughly he calibrated his optimist's demeanor, he could not run another step. Despite his best efforts, maybe he was still a halfway man.

Dante wrote that in the darkness of a man's middle years, the three monsters that surround him are pride, desire, and fear. As Randy grappled with these emotions, I tried to help. There is no glory in stopping, I said. Although I didn't mention this, I had run over a thousand races and had never quit. While encouraging Randy, my overriding, if selfish, thought was, no one I coached was going to break that record either. Funny thing, competitiveness. All I had learned over months of travel, about average being okay, was momentarily kicked aside because I was seeking perfection; the completeness of finishing, even if it meant we would finish dead last. Randy said he would continue because I was his running adviser and he had put his trust in me.

So Randy walked in the cold rain. He was not in a great mood. The finish line was some 26,000 steps away.

Hail fell. With a heavy headwind, Randy and I were being pelted in the face. I told Randy that they were the biggest hailstones I'd ever felt and that the suckers hurt.

Randy broke into his first smile since the turnaround point. In fact, he was all-out laughing—at me. "These aren't hailstones," Randy said. "They may as well be large raindrops. They're gonna have to be a lot larger if you wanna call them Kansas hailstones. Get tough, buddy."

He had a point. The heaviest hailstone ever seen in the United States, found in a Kansas town southeast of Abilene, was the size of a cantaloupe and is estimated to have hurled to earth at about 100 miles per hour. Randy once saw a hailstone take out a car's front windshield. Abilene residents experience annual average wind speeds of more than 11 miles per hour, putting them in the top 1 percent of the U.S. population for living with windy weather.

Randy got me laughing like never before. Through his pain, he was making me realize that there could be more to a marathon than solitary pursuits. At one point, he pointed out a windmill—"You see, weather's all around us, city boy," he said—and started to explain how the device works. His family, driving behind us and waiting for Randy to call it a day, fulfilled my request for a paper and pen. I wanted to write some of his words down.

"Weather is always the best conversation starter around here," Randy said. "And because so many of us are into farming and are in love with the land, we really do care when someone asks us about the weather. It's not just idle talk."

Well, sure. It wasn't even ten o'clock and we had already experienced fog, rain, thunder, lightning, heavy winds, hail, and what then felt like sleet.

As the county's noxious-weed cop—his jurisdiction does not include marijuana, he qualified, for what must be the millionth time in his career—Randy was hip to acts of God. "We need to spray the weeds with chemicals to control them, but we need them to be actively growing for the sprays to work," he said. "Weather affects that growth rate."

Lightning hit about 100 yards to our left, into an open field. I wished we had been better protected.

"We should be fine," Randy said, although some runners had already dropped out of the race because of the danger.

"Snow, there's the real menace," Randy said. He talked about the birth of his other child, a daughter who was attending college in the state. "This was 1983," Randy said. "On her due date, we were hit with a blizzard. I plowed our place, but the roads were closed. She was not born that day, but if she was, I would have needed to plow a road for hours to get Judy to the hospital.

"But I love snow," he said. "You know what you and I have in common? We have real seasons. Real winters with real snow, you know what I mean?"

Yes. Mr. Q was sitting snug and dry in my car, but I told Randy I would turn snow into a criterion, if I could, when I got to my computer, as I would with other particulars that resonated with him.

Later, I would discover that most of the nation's population gets at least a "trace" of snow over "a normal," climatologist-speak for an average of at least 0.1 inches of snow a year calculated over thirty years. Of course, those who don't see snow outside their front door could spot it someplace else. "No, we live where we live," Randy would tell me when I called him later. "Seasons are part of our upbringing, our family. Gotta have that experience of snow in your neighborhood. It's American." Susan McLeer, the chair of psychiatry at Drexel University, once broke it down for the *Philadelphia Inquirer*: "There's a child in all of us, and we all kind of wish for a snow day. . . . There's a romance to being snowed in at home with people you like."

Any place without a normal trace of snow would be wiped from my search map. This criterion would disqualify more than 95 percent of Florida residents—all except a few thousand residents on certain spots alongside or close to the Georgia and Alabama borders. All New Orleans residents would also disappear from my search. Although Nevada comes from the Spanish word meaning "snow-covered," some of the state's southern residents were dismissed. Thousands of Arizona and Texas residents would become ineligible, as would the vast majority of Southern Californians. All beachside residents from Santa Monica to Mexico were erased, and, ironically, a number of Los Angelenos who might classify places like Kansas as boringly predictable. The nation averages 105 days of sunshine a year, and Los Angeles can regularly count on more than three times that. The majority of the nation receives more than 20 inches of rain per year. Los Angeles strikes out on this count, too. "I can't see how people can live where there is only one season," Randy said near mile fifteen.

Further, on that point, Randy asked about the average American temperature. I would learn that the National Climate Data Center places it between 54 and 55 degrees Fahrenheit and classifies average temperatures in five-point ranges. The majority of the country's population lives where the annual average falls in the 45- to 65-degree range. This would dismiss the last remaining Las Vegas and Florida residents from my search map. The heart of NASCAR nation would continue to peel away. All residents in Gulf Coast communities would be eliminated. All those in San Antonio and

Houston, the southern half of Louisiana, every resident along the coast from the southern tip of South Carolina southward, and thousands of Alabama and Mississippi residents would be similarly affected. On the cold side, all of Alaska and North Dakota, the upper half of Wisconsin and Minnesota, and the southwest quadrant of Wyoming were among the areas fully swept off my search map.

Randy soldiered on past more lightning and mentioned that despite his limp, running was helping him feel younger. He said that although some men seem to start having serious health problems at age forty, he had never had surgery and wanted to keep it that way. "I think I'm good for another ten years or so," he said.

I promised Randy that when I was back at my computer, I would find an age threshold for my search by taking the average American age and working out in one year increments from both sides until I hit the majority of the population. Thirty-six is the average American age from 2000 through at least 2005. Starting in 2002, thirty-six also became the median age. After extrapolating, I found that this makes the majority of Americans aged eighteen through fifty-three. J. Average's age would need to fall somewhere along that span.

The typical American age is dramatically older than when this nation was founded. On average, American residents in 1776 were only sixteen years old, and the life expectancy was twenty-three. In 1900, twenty-three became the average age. This century, America's life expectancy is expected to reach 100 years. In a May 2002 article in *Science* magazine, two demographers proclaimed that the linear graph showing America's rise in life expectancy by four decades since 1840 "may be the most remarkable regularity of mass endeavor ever observed." Of course, the average age has more than doubled since the birth of the nation in no small part because the class of infectious diseases that took the lives of most Americans at that time—influenza, measles, smallpox, and typhoid fever among them—are now rare.

Perhaps the age-fifty-three cutoff was most appropriate in that today's "mature" Americans are identified as those fifty-four and older by, for example, *Modern Maturity* magazine and Turk & Company, a California marketing and advertising firm. A 2003 study found that despite the myth that, demographically speaking, the eighteen- to forty-nine-year-olds count most to television advertisers, it is, as *Daily Variety* wrote in a July 2003 front-page story on the report, "actually the 25–54 demo that occupies the most hallowed ground on Madison Avenue." Advertisers seconded the study as valid, "considering baby boomers are climbing up through their 40s and 50s and nearing their 60s." As the *Wall Street Journal* reported in April 2004, "After decades of obsessing over people in their 20's, some of the world's best-known companies are setting their sights on older consumers, an audience habitually written off as poor, excessively frugal or stuck in a rut of buying the same brand." Well into the twentieth century, with the average life-span significantly shorter than it is today, most workers never had a chance to retire. Today, another Baby Boomer turns fifty about every eight seconds. Many demographers predict that as soon as 2050, the median age of Americans will reach the early fifties, a clear sign that in the foreseeable future a heavy burden could be placed on the nation's retirement programs and services.

Let's see what other Americans Randy blew off my map. Or not. "You tell me about the average American," he said between miles fifteen and sixteen, noticeably favoring his left leg. "I'm sure by now, you're a walking encyclopedia of the average American, emphasis, of course, on *walking*!" Randy said he pictured my subject as a whole lot of mismatched body parts. "What crazy facts have you dug up on this nutjob?" he said.

Did he say nutjob? Well, the Average American can name all Three Stooges (59 percent can) but not all three branches of the government (83 percent can't). When he takes a shower—for an average of 10.4 minutes with a water temperature of 105 degrees—he sometimes pees (86 percent do) but never sings (67 percent don't). He eats the equivalent of 20 whole animals a year but, as Gallup phrased it, "supports passing strict laws concerning the treatment of farm animals" (62 percent). His household throws away more than 100 pounds of food each year, but he drinks the milk in his bowl after the cereal is gone (67 percent). He spends over $100 more each year on footwear than he does on fresh vegetables. He believes nature is sacred or spiritual (62 percent) but spends 95 percent of his time indoors.

"Ninety-five percent?" Randy said. "Really? There's a difference between here and other places in the country. My God, 95 percent!" There's an easy new criterion for my search: The Average American would spend most of his time indoors. Randy asked how much the average American exercises. According to a 2003 Gallup study, more than 80 percent of Americans get "moderate exercise" at least once a week, giving me another Average American criterion. I may have had a better chance of finding J. Average in Kansas than Kentucky, North Carolina, Louisiana, or Tennessee, despite Kansas being less populated. The four other states are the only ones where the level of physical activity recommended by the Centers for Disease Control is met by less than 40 percent of the population. Eighteen states come in at over 50 percent. Of course, there are other ways of burning off calories besides active recreation. On average, Americans have fifty stress-related adrenaline rushes a day.

Trying to get his mind off his discomfort, Randy asked about certain, shall we say, after-hours characteristics of the common American. I was there to help. Today, the average American's favorite time to make love is 11 P.M., and he generally falls asleep within seven minutes of heading to bed, which is rather dispiriting when we also consider that the average lovemaking time before a man reaches orgasm is six minutes. This may explain why most American adults rate their sex skills as "average."

Ninety-three percent of Americans believe that having some form of sex education in schools is "appropriate," although only 73 percent believe it should include discussion of homosexuality (a larger group is okay with students learning about masturbation). The average American's sex life starts at sixteen and the average American adult has sex 116 times per year and has 14.3 sexual partners in his lifetime. (If you're wondering, the average measurements for certain grown-up male and female private features: between 6 and 7 inches—yes, fully extended—and size 36C.)

Randy, having just celebrated his twenty-fifth wedding anniversary, is among the 80 percent of married men who would wed the same woman if they could do it all over again. The wives who would marry the same men: 50 percent. On average, married American males have about 100 dates with women before tying the knot.

Randy proceeded to tell me about the time he went to his friend's house during the lunch hour one day and walked in on the man and his wife naked, going at it.

"Getting themselves a nooner," Randy explained. "You'll get to meet her tonight at dinner. She'll be dressed. All right, feed me some more random average American knowledge. I know you're dying to."

I would learn during my travels that the average American has a bottomless rattlebag of measurements, everything from his discarding 8 batteries to buying 800 gallons of gas annually, to eating 4.2 meals a week outside the home, to his being able to do 17 straight sit-ups, to his having 115 synthetic chemicals in his body, including dioxin, PAH, and other toxins proven to cause mammary cancer in lab animals. In 2002, he consumed 255 eggs, 70.7 pounds of poultry, 30.5 pounds of cheese and around 2 pounds of lard and 25 pounds of candy, and spent more than 350 hours in the bathroom, but not necessarily in that order. He acquires 52 items of clothing annually. The average American man has 41- to 42-inch hips, and woman 42 to 46, according to the National Sizing Survey. He hopes to die at home and believes his soul will travel to a spiritual place after he passes.

True to his image, the average American can be in the plainness camp. He prefers plain whole milk, at 7.4 gallons a year, over all other kinds; and smooth over chunky peanut butter (83 percent). Sixty percent of Americans eat peanut butter at least once a week and the average American eats three pounds of the substance annually. In 2005, Harris pollsters reported that 53 percent of Americans eat PB&J sandwiches at least once a month. Considering its widespread (pardon the pun), everyday use, and the fact that it was invented in the United States, peanut butter is more American than apple pie. Not that the average American is as wholesome as some would have him. He doesn't floss regularly (90 to 95 percent) and by age fifty has lost twelve teeth; he believes it's inappropriate for the F-word to be used on broadcast television (83 percent) but swears in public (63 percent). He does not properly wash his hands after going to the bathroom (83 to 84 percent).

*It's worth noting* that the fifty-three-year age limit that became one of my search guidelines is also the ceiling that is used in establishing many professional control groups for health studies. For example, research led by a physician at the University of Maryland Medical Center and published in the *Journal of the American Medical Association* had Americans of that age span eat some fatty McDonald's breakfast items—think Egg McMuffins and hash browns—over multiple days and found that when subjects added vitamins C and E to the diet, the antioxidants noticeably decreased the risk of heart disease. The subjects' arteries reacted as if a low-fat bowl of corn flakes had been consumed. A separate study, out of Penn State University, examined 242 subjects up to those aged fifty-three and found that a life with urban conveniences can account for why many people are fat.

I mention these particular studies because they serve as examples of what Randy sees as an urban myth—that eating meat and other fatty foods is the major reason why people have health problems. "It really is about balance," Randy said around mile sixteen. "And exercise and staying healthy go a long way. See, I've learned something in my old age." On average, most Americans have health insurance, as would J. Average.

Randy is right in that so much of health is about staying average. An educational campaign by LifeScan, a manufacturer of blood glucose meters, was titled "Be Average," as a reminder that hitting the average blood glucose levels is a sign of optimal health. "Avoid the highs and lows," the campaign urged. Humira, an arthritis drug, runs its commercials with the tagline "More Normal Living."

Around mile twenty, Randy's son had joined us on our walk to the finish line in case his dad literally needed someone to lean on. Eric Barten said we were fortunate to be without any major ailments and that he had learned not to take running for granted. Commendably, mainstream races have been opened to all people, with wheelchair races increasing in popularity and many wonderful programs created in which disabled runners are helped along the course by the direct assistance of others. However, the Bartens believe that whether it's fair or not, when you lose your good health, you're not so average anymore. Most Americans can walk under their own power, an act that I made an Average American criterion.

"So what does the average American weigh, anyway?" Eric Barten asked.

I thought of Adolphe Quetelet, my muse. More than 150 years after his passing, an obesity index he created was bastardized by federal agencies, and it's still regularly used to characterize the average American as dangerously overweight. But here's the real rub: To be clinically overweight by the Quetelet Index, one must merely hit a measurement calculated solely by height and weight, with no distinction made between muscle and fat, and no thought given to gender or trouser size. Because these studies routinely leave out those under twenty years old, an analysis of 2000 findings showed that most Americans, contrary to various media accounts, were not "overweight" that year. And if body fat percentage, a more modern and fair measurement, were used as the standard, the clear majority of Americans, both children and adults, would be classified as neither overweight nor underweight.

Yet, certain government agencies, headed by officials who know full well that extreme statistics will get more dollars appropriated for their departments, and the brunt of the mainstream news media, which has never shied away from taking the agencies' ginned-up numbers and repackaging them as gospel, love the Quetelet Index. It allows them to blare their trumpets of doom with proclamations like these, made since the start of this millennium: "60 percent of Americans are fat" (CNN.com); "more than 60 percent of Americans are obese" (*Pittsburgh Tribune-Review*); and "80 percent of Americans are overweight" (*Better Nutrition* magazine).

When the Quetelet Index (also known as the body/mass index, or BMI) is changed, it is always to make more Americans fat. For example, until 1998, women who were 5 feet 5 inches and 164 pounds were not considered overweight; then, overnight, those who were 5 feet 5 inches and 150 pounds were. About 30 million Americans instantly became overweight. If anything, the Quetelet Index should be revised in the other direction. According to Dr. David Williamson, a statistician for the Centers for Disease Control, all Americans are getting heavier, despite their physical condition. "Competitive cyclists weigh more than they did 20, 30 years ago; HIV patients weigh more," he told the *New York Times*. And Dr. Timothy Lohman, the director of the body-composition lab at the physiology department at the University of Arizona College of Medicine, wrote, "We're overfocused on fatness."

Looking at the most reliable figures, less than 8 percent of American adults weigh more than 250 pounds, and less than 8 percent weigh less than 125 pounds. As we can learn from the animal kingdom, size can be misleading. Of all American land animals, the cougar has the most impressive speed and leaping ability, but it is a large animal: The vast majority of cougars weigh between 135 and 205 pounds—the same parameter as I would find applies to the average American.

From studies released by the *Journal of the American Medical Association* and the National Center for Health Statistics from 2000 forward, which found that American adults on average weigh somewhere between 145 and 195 pounds, and working out from that center to make sure I would capture the majority, I decided to set the range for the Average American at between 135 and 205 pounds. J. Average will therefore weigh between the first amount acceptable at some American blood drives (135) and the first five-pound increment unacceptable for those who want to experience the American tradition of riding a mule into the heart of the Grand Canyon (205). Leaving my search would be many heavyweight boxers, who weigh more than 200 pounds, and many department store Santas, who at last count averaged 218 pounds. Goodbye, too, to most fashion models, who continue to model product sizes their target customers will never buy (by one count, women models depicted in American advertising weigh 110 pounds on average, placing them on the 2 percent fringe).

Don't be surprised if the Saint Nicks live longer than the models. The Centers for Disease Control was recently forced to admit that it overestimated the number of deaths from obesity by the tens of thousands. The weight problem that truly exists in the United States can be attributed, in part, to the national smoking decline. In contrast, many fashion models still smoke like chimneys as a replacement for calorie cravings, putting them at a serious health risk. The national life expectancy has soared more than six years over the past three decades, and the national smoking rate declined 27 percent from 1980 to 2000 (and 38 percent among middle-aged Americans during that time span). "There is no question that smoking affects the epidemic" of overweight Americans, said Dr. Neil Grunberg, a neuroscientist at Maryland's Uniformed Services University. Grunberg noted that after smokers quit, they gain an average of ten to twelve pounds and their metabolism slows down. As for the nation's weight problem, Dr. Williamson of the CDC said, "Maybe the sky isn't falling quite as much as we think it is."

The nation's weight gain can also be attributed, oddly enough, to Americans' increased intelligence, or at least our increased job and education level. With the majority of Americans having earned at least a high-school degree, we have a record percentage of American adults with jobs that do not require physical activity. A 2003 study by the U.S. Department of Health and Human Services showed that more than 40 percent of those with some schooling beyond high school sit down at their usual daily activity, compared with 31 percent of those with less than a high-school degree. The percentage of adults in jobs that require heavy lifting has shrunk to less than 10 percent, which affects our weight index and shatters the recurring myth that the most common American must be a calloused hardhat or bale-tossing farmer.

Randy Barten and I talked about how government subsidies to farmers started in the 1920s as a response to severe weather conditions and the need to lower food prices. (There's a lot of time to talk when you walk a marathon; indeed, by the end of this one day in

Kansas, I would cover much more ground in my search than I had imagined.) In 1929, Americans spent, on average, around 25 percent of their money on food. Today, owing to increased farm subsidy programs—$457 million went to rural areas in 2002 alone—the share has dropped to about 10 percent. Farm subsidies have helped push Americans to their highest-ever weight level. Healthy fruits and vegetables are not supported by the government programs, but fat-happy crops such as wheat, soybeans, and corn are—and this includes high-fructose corn syrup, the sugar replacement that drives most weight gains, along with rice and cotton.

As a result, the subsidized foods are much cheaper than other foods. Consider that about 75 percent of Americans snack. This raises the demand for more snack ingredients. The farmers, paid by the government to produce corn for corn syrup, therefore focus on this ingredient. And, as Kansas newspaper reporter Alan Bjerga explained, "If farmers overproduce, prices fall, but government aid encourages production anyway. Oversupply means food companies can buy more, cheaper crops, driving down the cost of snacks. So Americans eat more snacks. And get heavier." This helps explain why poor Americans are often the fattest, a seeming contradiction. In 2003, Mississippi, the poorest state in the nation, was also the most overweight. In defense of farmers, Republican Senator Pat Roberts of Kansas, who has authored farm subsidy legislation, said Americans are lazy people who pig out, "followed by 10 to 12 hours of television" (he more than doubled the true daily TV intake). On average, American workers earn enough money in thirty-six days to pay for their food consumption for the entire year, eighty-one days fewer than it takes to earn our annual tax payment. "Which I guess proves that the government is hungrier than we are," quipped Republican state senator Bob Waldrep of South Carolina.

The majority of Americans, asked to define themselves as underweight, average, or overweight, chose average. However heavy Americans are, they may appreciate the physically imperfect more than the professional lookers. A 2004 survey of women from ten developed nations, including the United States, Great Britain, France, Italy, and Japan, conducted by researchers at Harvard University and the London School of Economics, gave several choices as to which attributes make a woman beautiful. The United States was the nation that chose "happiness" at the highest rate (89 percent) and the country that was most overwhelming in its belief that "the media sets an unrealistic standard of beauty" (81 percent). When asked how the media could do a better job of portraying beauty, the U.S. respondents again went against the norm, preferring "the use of everyday women as well as models." The research was commissioned by Dove soap, and the brand responded by rolling out the Campaign for Real Beauty, an advertising effort featuring everyday women—wrinkled, freckled, full-faced, or otherwise structurally normal. (However, some would complain that the campaign's featured models were under the average American woman's size 14.)

During the Civil War, Abraham Lincoln shared a dream he had about being surrounded by plain-looking people. "You are a very common-looking man," observed one of those in the dream. Lincoln retorted: "Friend, the Lord prefers common-looking people. That is the reason he makes so many of them." American faces that are not girded by cosmetic patchwork or otherwise blessed or besmirched with irregularities may miss the wow factor in the short term, but they are the ones most comforting for others to be around. After measuring how Americans respond to many types of faces, the biologist and anthropologist Donald Symons defined beauty as "averageness, the average values of the features of faces."

A few years ago, in a study funded by the National Science Foundation, the National Institute of Mental Health, the National Institute of Child Health and Human Development, and the University of Texas Research Institution, researchers photographed the faces of many undergraduates. Dr. Judith Langlois, a professor of developmental psychology at the University of Texas, reported that when sixteen and later thirty-two random faces were digitized into composite photographs and shown to 300 judges along with the individual faces, the averaged faces "were judged to be significantly more attractive. . . . By using advanced computer technology, we demonstrated that 'averaged' faces are perceived as attractive; we replicated this finding in two populations, male and female, and in three samples from each population. . . . We do believe that 'averageness' is a necessary and critical element of attractiveness. Without 'averageness' even the most youthful, smiling face will not be judged as attractive."

Langlois added that the findings of Symons and her own team are not exclusive: "Many studies show that after seeing several examples of a category—for instance, schematic animals or schematic faces—one responds to an averaged representation of those category members as if it were special or familiar to us even if we have never seen it before." In the 2002 book *Facial Attractiveness,* a group of U.S. researchers rejected the maxim that "beauty lies in the eye of the beholder" and wrote that averageness is "the only characteristic discovered to date that is both necessary and sufficient to ensure facial attractiveness." In 2002, researchers at the University of Western Australia took these discoveries a step further. Here's professorial fellow Leigh Simmons, one of the study's leaders: "We wanted to see whether for human faces people who were average had in fact been healthier." The result? "That's in fact exactly what we found in a large sample of people."

The natural attraction to average beauty is not simply a case of people preferring faces that are symmetrical. A team of researchers from the University of London conducted an experiment that purposely followed the one by the Texas group, only judges were shown a facial profile, which has no axes of symmetry. After looking at morphed images created from faces unfamiliar to the judges, the composite of average faces was rated the most attractive, at a rate of more than 75 percent.

Maybe it should come as no surprise that the obsessively surgically enhanced are often shunned as both freakish—outside the norm—and clones of each other. Referencing other research on average beings, Simmons reported, "We seem to actually like average members of lots of different categories, . . . like birds and fish and dogs as well as other people and so it seems to us that there's probably two things going on. We have a brain that tells us what's average and then somehow we like that."

*At mile twenty-four,* Randy Barten looked pretty good for a man who was hobbling from side to side. He said he thought he could make it to the finish line, inspired by the family members who were there to cheer him on. They'd been doing just that for four hours by this point. His son was back in the family car.

"I think if your family values are a guide, the average American could be from a rural area," Randy said. He mentioned that like those in the Presbyterian church where he and his wife have been rotating their term as deacon for many years, he likes it when people show they still care deeply about manners.

"But you know, I don't believe most Americans have the best manners," he said. "And I wonder if that's because they live in a community where that's not a given. As places get bigger and more diverse, that's not holding us all together. Maybe the rural setting is where we can be the most real and share the best values, but I don't know if we are in that society anymore. People are heading to the cities and the suburbs."

Randy had tapped into a major change in American society that Kansas residents know all too well: The average America with rural roots is becoming more of a fantasy every day. Disney World reports that millions of its tourists come simply because they enjoy roaming the park's rendition of an old rural Main Street. Multiuse buildings close to the sidewalk, a standard feature of this type of Main Street, are now illegal in most U.S. municipalities.

The vast majority of Kansas counties that have lost population since 1980 are rural. Between 2000 and 2010, the Census Bureau estimates that the nation's metropolitan population will rise by 12 percent and the rural population by a mere 2 percent. After analyzing Census 2000, demographers discovered that for the first time in our history, the majority of Americans are suburbanites. "As a statistic, this is up there with the Census Department's announcement 100 years ago that there was no longer a detectable frontier line," Nicholas Lemann proclaimed in *Washington Monthly.*

Suburbia is the part of a metropolitan area that lies outside a principal city of 50,000 or more residents (urban and suburban America overlap), and there are more than 250 metropolitan areas in the United States. The concept of suburbia was pretty much nonexistent until the mid-nineteenth-century writings of Catharine Beecher, a Connecticut-schooled author. Her books on everything from gardening to motherhood were all premised on the notion of living on the outskirts of the city. She promoted the suburban area as the best place to raise a family (she suggested ten children per marriage) and proclaimed that the suburban family and house constituted "the home church of Jesus Christ." By 1910, 12 percent of Americans lived in the suburbs. Over the next forty years, the percent nearly doubled, to 23 percent.

Today, suburban areas are growing much faster than central-city and rural areas. In fact, suburban population is growing at twice the rate of central cities. More than 72 percent of the overall metropolitan-area population is suburban, a ratio expected to increase at least four more percentage points by 2020. Since most Americans live in the suburbs, all central-city residents—from those in New York City to the fewer than 55,000 residents of Carson City, Nevada—would be excused from my search. All rural places would also be purged.* All those living in the 50-plus percent of the nation's counties that are exclusively rural would be fully dismissed, including the majority of Missouri's counties. Gone was the city of Washington, D.C., and all of Michigan's Upper Peninsula, which is rural. Alaska was already history, but this criterion would have ditched it anyway, as the state's one metropolitan area, Anchorage, is suburb-free. Any point 50 miles south of California's northern border was erased. Iowa and Vermont were seriously affected, as their populations are each more than 75 percent rural. Most of Wyoming's population was gone, as were the majority of residents in Arkansas, Idaho, Kentucky, Maine, Mississippi, Montana, South Dakota, and West Virginia. The western half of Kansas was removed from my map. Neighboring Ne-

*Despite much media talk—particularly as the results of the 2004 election were analyzed—about areas such as exurbs (just outside established suburbia) and micropolitan areas (essentially, cities outside of metropolitan areas), they and all of rural America contain less than 30 percent of the population.

braska had been reduced to two small blips, not surprising for a state in which the population at any University of Nebraska football home game is larger than all but two of the state's cities.

These decisions meant completely erasing more than 90 percent of the entire U.S. landmass—all the acreage outside of suburbia. My search map looked like an atlas of islands, with one large vertical streak of land in the northeast quadrant. As New Jersey is the only state that consists entirely of metropolitan area, this kept in play Salem, New Jersey, which NBC News singled out in 1964 as the most representative American small town in voter makeup and other selected variables tied to that year's election.*

Like the farmer, the suburbanite has also been frequently cast as the mythical average American. However, before we get the sense that the typical suburb is a lily-white comformist haven of bake sales, minivans, and soccer moms, let's consider the fact that since 2000, most suburban households have been non-family homes, and that about 40 percent of the nation's poor live in suburbs. There are now twenty poor suburbanites for every twenty-one poor urbanites. More than one out of every five homeless Americans lives in the suburbs.

Let's also consider that among the foreign-born population, which has historically been attracted to urban centers, and which has been regularly left out of sunny commercial portraits of suburbia, more actually reside in the suburbs than the city. James Cain chose the Los Angeles suburb of Glendale for the backdrop of his acclaimed 1941 novel *Mildred Pierce* because of its already famous homogeneity. Today, over 50 percent of Glendale's population is foreign-born. Here's Delores Hayden, a professor of architecture and urbanism at Yale: "As suburban couples have become more diverse and millions of housewives have found paid work, the male-breadwinner family with stay-at-home mom and two children, in a peaceful three-bedroom colonial with a leafy yard and sociable

---

*Host David Brinkley noted the criteria that 15 percent of the residents made over $15,000 a year and that Salem was "29 percent Negro—not average, but not unusual."

neighbors, predominates only in reruns of old sitcoms." The common American suburb as a bedroom outpost is part of that same myth. However, for the first time, there are now more jobs in suburbia than in both urban centers and rural America.

The suburban prerequisite for the Average American certainly changed my perspective, as my subject could not live in any of the Midwestern cities where so many people had predicted I would end up—among them Cincinnati, Columbus, Des Moines, Peoria, and Indianapolis. Of the many other cities, Muncie, Indiana, has probably been cast the most over the years as the average American place. This is a direct result of the 1929 book *Middletown,* from Indiana sociologist Robert Lynd and his wife Helen, that used then-rural Muncie as a stand-in for the typical American town (a sequel, *Middletown in Transition,* came in 1937). Today, the Muncie population's collective marital status, income, and Hispanic presence are but three indicators of why Muncie is not the best example of average America. (Although most Americans of marrying age are married, only 41 percent are married in Muncie; its median household income is more than $15,000 below the national norm; and its percentage of Hispanic residents is less than one-eighth of the national figure.)

Randy wanted to know how I avoided feeling suffocated as a resident of densely populated Manhattan, and I told him that he may have touched on the true divide between rural areas and the rest of America. The Census Bureau prefers to see Americans as living in one of two residential areas—urban or rural—and considers urban any census block that has at least 500 people per square mile. Many suburban towns are partially rural, but as noted, urban Americans are in the vast majority of the U.S. population. To ensure that the Average American lives amongst the same population density as most U.S. residents, he would not only live in suburbia, but in an "urbanized" suburbia. After Randy asked about the average home acreage of American residents, I learned that although the mean American lot size is growing, to nearly two acres, the median lot size has shrunk to 0.5 acres (a surge in construction of ranch homes on vast rural spreads accounts for much of the widening gap). The majority of Americans live on between zero and two acres of property, and most Americans have a private lawn, two more things I needed to look for in the life of the most average American.

There are about 30 million acres of lawns in the country and about 80 percent of U.S. homes have private lawns. According to a 2004 story by Mark Clayton in the *Christian Science Monitor*, each year the average U.S. homeowner spends forty hours mowing the lawn. "The EPA estimates that the amount of pollution emitted by a lawn mower operating for one hour equals the amount of pollution emitted by a car driven for about 20 miles," he added.

Randy, who raises less than a dozen head of cattle as his secondary profession, is a good example of the change in rural America since the era when the Populism movement was founded in Kansas more than a century ago. Populism championed farming as the ideal profession for average Americans and a rural upbringing as the national standard. Today, less than 2 percent of rural residents earn their primary living through farming. Moreover, only 5 percent of the foreign-born population lives in rural America.

Part of what suburbia has over both rural and urban America is more impressive educational, income, and health service results. The College Board, which oversees the SAT program, analyzed the 2003 SAT scores and found that suburban students averaged 1066—forty points over the national average—whereas the rural and urban groups failed to top 1000. The suburban average was fifteen points higher than only nine years previously. The median household income in suburbia is more than $12,000 over the average of each of the other two regions. In 2004, a study published in the *American Journal of Emergency Medicine* found that the response rate for those suffering cardiac arrest was quickest in the suburbs. And suicides and homicides are more common in urban and rural areas than in the suburbs. A recent analysis in the *New York Times* concluded, "Suicides occur at a higher rate in rural areas than in cities or suburbs, with the rate rising steadily the more rural the community. With homicides, the trend works in reverse."

Suburbia has become Car Nation. Office parks make many errands and commutes a piece of cake, with drive-through services, shopping centers, and fast-food outlets offering suburban residents retail conveniences. Because so many of today's suburban areas are built to accommodate vehicle traffic, they are increasingly devoid of long stretches of sidewalk or other pedestrian-friendly amenities. This goes a long way toward explaining why only 10 percent of American children walk to school (versus 50 percent in 1950), why the number of miles Americans travel via motorized transportation has doubled since 1963, and why the average suburbanite is heavier than the typical urbanite (ranging from about two extra pounds in San Francisco's suburbs to about six in the most sprawling suburban areas, such as Geauga County east of Cleveland and Walton County east of Atlanta, according to separate studies).

To understand how suburbanites formed a majority, we can start with the first president of all fifty states—Abilene native Dwight Eisenhower. Flush from Ike's successful stint as supreme allied commander in Europe during World War II, Americans had the money and security to buy new homes. As a result of the nation's newfound prosperity, middle-class couples started large families and needed the room to raise them while still being within driving distance of the booming big-city job market. Suburbs became the natural choice, and millions of tract homes were erected to fill the demand.

As a result of Eisenhower's 1954 initiatives allowing significant financial incentives for homeowners and a major tax break for commercial developers, houses, malls, office parks, and fast-food joints sprang up quickly throughout suburbia. In 1956, Eisenhower founded the nation's Interstate Highway system, allowing those in suburban areas quick access to the cities, and vice versa (to get the billions needed for the program, Ike presented it as a national defense project, even ordering one mile in every five to be straight and therefore usable as a military airstrip). Suburban shopping malls appeared everywhere, so much so that by 2000, the nation had almost twice the amount of retail space per capita of any other large country—almost twenty square feet per resident. American suburbs now have more "big box" stores, and more roads, sewers, and water and gas lines, per capita than any other region in the world. Of course, some social critics have a name for all this activity—sprawl. Today, fifty acres of farmland are lost to sprawl every day, but more than 90 percent of the nation is still open rural space.

On State Road 15, a Toyota forced Randy Barten and me to the curb. We were in the last mile of the marathon. Past our 25-mile point, the course had been opened to traffic, as we had hit the six-hour cut-off mark. Someone in a pick-up honked his horn and yelled Randy's name. Randy's family was at the finish line. "This is pretty bad, isn't it?" Randy said. "Let's just get to Eisenhower's." Huh? "The finish line is in front of Ike's house." The race is called the Eisenhower Marathon for short, but I had only made it to the Kansas border the night before and hadn't had time to brush up on the local landmarks, let alone Eisenhower's boyhood home. "The station where you parked your car, that's where he made his speech announcing he was running for president," Randy said. Ike gave the 1952 address in rolled-up pants on account of a rainstorm that he called "a gullywasher." The Union Pacific station is on one side of the marathon finish line, and Eisenhower's childhood home is on the other.

Eisenhower did not go to college immediately out of high school. After doing some jobs around town, he decided to leave Abilene, and a local physician helped him get into West Point. This was in 1910, the last year that rural Americans were in the nation's majority.

Eisenhower is considered the most average American to become president in the modern era. Unlike so-called average guy George W. Bush, Eisenhower did not come from an elite family, nor did he enroll in private schools. Neither of Ike's parents had held elective office. His father worked as a mechanic at an Abilene creamery. In his freshman year in high school, Ike did not receive any A's, and in his adulthood—although this assessment would be revisited and revised by some historians—he would be ridiculed by many pundits as intellectually mediocre (in 1952, he didn't even realize he could choose his own running mate).

At West Point, "Eisenhower was content to stay in the middle," Ike biographer Stephen Ambrose wrote. "He preferred enjoying his classmates to competing with them." Ike himself likely believed that when he did stand out, it was because of what he had learned in the middle. He felt he was no better than the average American, and if people thought West Point was about conformity, so be it. Eisenhower recognized that it was the men who represented this brand of conformity who defended the nation. The day after Ike died, the *New York Times* ran a front-page obituary that stated, "As President he governed effectively through the sheer force of his popularity among average Americans of both major parties, and it was the average American who was the real source of his power."

Randy and I made it through Eisenhower's boyhood neighborhood, where the roads, now paved, were dirt in Ike's youth. We closed in on the small home where Ike grew up. At the finish line, only a few spectators remained. Randy's dad, a tall, frail, bespectacled man of few words, draped a finishing medal around his son's neck as a couple dozen friends and family members looked on. "That's good there," senior Barten whispered to his son. Our time was six hours, fourteen minutes, and two seconds.

"My leg doesn't feel so good," said Randy. Although we were walking stride for stride, the marathon officials had scored me finishing ahead of Randy. We met a runner who said he'd been so scared of the lightning that he had stayed in a ditch for a while. A few minutes later, we learned that someone had finished behind us. "Probably some guy in a ditch fell asleep," Randy said and got me laughing again. "I'm not last. I'm still in the middle of the pack."

Four hours later, after I had been in my hotel room checking some numbers with Mr. Q, Randy and his wife picked me up for a night out at the local Elks lodge. Randy said a ton of his friends would be there. "Yeah, you can regale us with all with your shower-peeing flow charts," he said, laughing. I laughed again, too. We were soon making plans for a year ahead, for a weekend together with the wives in New York City.

As we spotted a remote Dairy Queen with a sign out front that read "Welcome Runners," I started to mention that my first summer job was at a Dairy Queen in a mid-sized town. But a scene up ahead stopped me. Transversing a field was the most impressive weather phenomenon of the day. It was my first-ever double rainbow sighting, I noted. "Whoever sees it first gets good luck," Randy said.

*I heard from Weed Man* after I left Kansas. I should have paid more attention to his bum knee. By putting undue stress on his left leg, he had broken his femur, the bone that runs from the knee to the hip. And this meant Randy had undergone his first surgery, to put a rod in his leg. His doctor said he never should have finished the marathon.

I told Randy I was sorry that I pushed him past the midway point, that I recognize full-bore competitiveness is not always the answer, that I had spent my whole life running away from being average, but that one of my best race experiences was with him, even if we just counted the first half of the race. I told him I didn't want to lose his or Judy's friendship.

"Wow, seems like you've learned a lot," he said warmly and reminded me that I had some luck to burn, having seen the double rainbow first. As Ike may have said, maybe being first is only best when you recognize the value of the middle.

*Eight*

# GOING COASTAL

*Candidates remaining: fewer than 15 million*

*It was the last Friday in April,* but in a small schoolyard in the up-country of Maui, Hawaii, it was all about the first of May. A number of young girls in brightly colored sundresses smiled broadly as they skipped around a maypole to the strains of piano music. Five young boys seated on a giant tree stump tapped their feet. Over by an expansive tree shedding purple flowers, the children's minders cheered and clapped in rhythm.

When it comes to celebrating the mathematically average, May Day has no equals. The holiday started in the British Isles before the birth of Christ because the first day of May was the exact midpoint on the Celtic calendar. The Celts and Saxons believed this midpoint symbolized nature's bounty and fertility, whereas New Year's Day was viewed as a sign of death. As a result, May Day became the preferred day to be married and for couples to attempt to conceive. The month-long period beginning on May 1 became known as "honeymonth," a word that eventually became "honeymoon." Presumably unbeknownst to many of the parents who were around me, the may-pole signifies the male phallus, and the colorful ribbons attached to its tip represent the womb.

I had come to the nation's most remote state to better focus my investigation of community—and to follow a symbol. The rainbow, which had graced the end of my time in Kansas, is most prevalent in the fiftieth state; the image even decorates license plates. After tooling around for a couple of days and speaking with various natives, I had finally spotted a rainbow in Maui, arching over a small hill in the lush inland town of Kula.

On the hill, I came across a quaint, peculiar-looking Catholic church named Holy Ghost Mission. It had eight sides, the same number of colors as there are in a rainbow. The first person I spotted on the church grounds was a weather-beaten man toiling in a small cemetery. That evening, I attended Mass at Holy Ghost, and the same man, and his wife, sat across from me—Gerry and Barbara Tavares.

Gerry's Portuguese grandfather, Manuel, had helped build the small church more than a century ago and is now buried outside it. After the service, when I learned that Gerry was a retired Maui County fire chief, I asked him how he defined community. He brought me to the grave of his older brother Albert, who had died at the age of ten months. Gerry reached down and plucked a blade of grass that had barely touched the headstone. We walked to a second, larger cemetery. The grounds, well manicured, overlook a hillside tree called an angel's trumpet and, much farther below, the Pacific Ocean. Several more of Gerry's relatives are buried there.

"This has become a real community to me," Gerry said.

Thanks to the 282nd chapter of the Korean War Veterans Association, Tavares, a former military engineering officer, proudly serves as the church's volunteer graveyard custodian. For years, on the third Wednesday of each month, he has attended the association's meetings. When the group initiated a program to restore neglected gravesites, Gerry was assigned to repair and maintain the two cemeteries at Holy Ghost. He then arranged for his brother's tomb to be transferred from an abandoned graveyard many miles away to this cemetery so that he could offer daily care and prayers to the sibling he never knew. At the grave, a sign reads, "Budded on earth to blossom in heaven."

Gerry's membership in both secular and religious organizations represents a growing rarity in the United States. Although religious commitment may be on the rise (the number of Americans who attend church weekly moved up three points, to 27.5 percent, from

2002 through 2004) America is arguably the most individualistic—one could say atomized—nation in the world. Outside of religious congregations, there is no other type of organization in which most Americans have membership. In his 2000 book *Bowling Alone,* Harvard political scientist Robert Putnam presented an avalanche of evidence to show that America's membership in social organizations had reached an all-time low. Wrote Putnam, "The dominant theme is simple: For the first two-thirds of the twentieth century a powerful tide bore Americans into even deeper engagement in the life of their communities, but a few decades ago—silently, without warning—that tide reversed and we were overtaken by a treacherous rip current."

No doubt Tocqueville would have been amazed. When he toured the country some 170 years ago, he observed, "Americans of all ages, all stations in life, and all types of disposition are forever forming associations." For social organizations such as the Elks and the Knights of Columbus, membership peaked in the early 1960s. At that time, the Parent-Teachers Association was the largest secular organization in America; nearly 50 percent of families with school-aged kids had a PTA member. Today, this figure is well below 20 percent. By 1995, only 3 percent of Americans on a typical day spent time in any community organization. In 2003, the government's American Housing Survey determined that more than 75 percent of American homes exist in an area with no community center or clubhouse.

During the nationwide decline in secular organizations, veterans groups have continued to grow—likely more than any other kind of traditional group. Since 1980, the number of independent veterans organizations has nearly tripled. The members of these groups are still serving, at gravesites and in many other community outreach programs.

"I'm thinking about going back to Korea," Gerry said, "if only to see if the medical hospital we built in Taegu is still standing." I told Gerry my dad had been a medical aide in the Korean War.

"God bless him," Gerry said. "Did he go back?" I shook my head.

"Yeah, maybe that's for the best."

The current nationwide support of American servicemen and women is, by far, one of the population's largest commonalities. I decided that, like more than 90 percent of Americans, J. Average would "support the troops." However, he or she would not necessarily support the government's decision to go to war—in Iraq or elsewhere. Reminiscent of Vietnam—by 1972, 60 percent of Americans saw the Vietnam War as a mistake—the nation's majority support of the war in Iraq disappeared in 2004, and, by the summer of 2005, over 60 percent of Americans opposed the U.S. decision to go to war there.

Gerry and I headed to the church hall, where some women were pounding dough. "The Bread Ladies," he said by way of introduction. When Holy Ghost had been in need of an expensive facelift a few years ago, a handful of Portuguese women in the parish started making secret-recipe sweetbread to sell to the public. Through enthusiastic word of mouth, Hawaiians of all stripes began arriving at the small church to purchase loaves. The product went on sale in some island stores, and the Bread Ladies raised more than half a million dollars.

Gerry said it was appropriate that the church benefited from sweetbread because it had originally benefited from the local sugar industry. The Portuguese who built Holy Ghost immigrated from the Azores and the Madeira Islands in the late 1800s to take jobs as contract workers at sugar plantations. One-third of the cane sugar, and one-tenth of all sugar consumed in the United States, comes from Hawaii. Gerry also noted that being an islander, he enjoys "the best coffee in America"; by default, maybe, as Hawaii is the only state that produces it.

On average, sugar accounts for 15 percent of the population's daily caloric intake, and, on average, each day Americans consume twenty teaspoons of "added" sugar (that is, beyond the sugar found naturally in foods and beverages such as fruit or milk), twice the maximum recommended intake. More than any other product, those calories come from sweetened soft drinks. Indeed, an average twelve-ounce serving of soda contains nearly ten teaspoons of sugar, or 150 calories, and in 2005, a study in the *Journal of Pediatrics* reported that soft drinks are the leading cause of childhood obesity. Mr. Q noted that each year, the average American consumes fifty-five gallons of soft drinks. I found a statistic I could apply. More than three out of four Americans drink soda. All other Americans were no longer J. Average candidates. As for coffee, 80 percent of American adults drink it regularly or occasionally, and 61 percent of U.S. homes have electric coffeemakers: two more search criteria.

Before I said goodbye to the Bread Ladies, I tossed in the need for the Average American to eat bread, maybe even our daily bread. According to the Grain Foods Foundation, 50 percent of Americans consume bread daily. I decided that J. Average must routinely eat it on a weekly basis.

Probably not realizing how much he had helped me, Gerry apologized for not being of more assistance. "You should go speak with Jimmy Aarona," he said. "If anyone can tell you about community, he can." Aarona, the Kula postmaster, was active in several area organizations, Gerry noted.

When I reached the front entrance of Kula's yellow, flat-level post office, I saw a number of people going to the May Day celebration, which was being held in a woodsy area across the street. I joined them and watched the group of girls dancing around the maypole for awhile.

"So you went to the May Day program," Jimmy Aarona said when I finally made it to a seat in his office. "I may go there later. I try not to turn down the opportunity to hear the local sounds." It turned out that Aarona is a singer for a choir that performs locally. A descendant of many generations of Hawaiians, he spoke in a soft native lilt. I told him about my journey and asked him if there was anything that made him average.

"You tell me," Jimmy said. Because he was musically inclined, I had enough to start.

Two thousand years ago, Plato said, "Music is a moral law. It gives a soul to the universe, wings to the mind, flight to the imagination, a charm to sadness, gaiety and life to everything." Mr. Q noted that most Americans feel the same, in so much as about nine out of ten

Americans, according to a 2000 Gallup survey, believe that music is a way to bring families closer together, a view I decided the Average American must hold. Although most Americans do not play a musical instrument, J. Average needed to have a stereo in the home, as do the majority of his or her fellow citizens. In part because there are more entertainment options today than in years past, and because more schools are phasing out music programs due to budget cuts, our number of music-listening experiences are in decline. In 2005, the average American aged twelve and older is expected to spend only 166 hours listening to recorded music, down from 258 hours in 2000 and 201 in 2002, according to a Census Bureau publication.

On Jimmy's desk, in a jar next to a large stack of clipboards, were many jumbo-sized jelly beans. Nearby, a wooden Easter bunny was displayed. Jimmy's large face was framed by silver hair, silver-rimmed eyeglasses, a thick gold necklace, and an open-collared shirt with large blue and brown flowers. Mr. Q had a 2000 statistic from Gallup about glasses and contacts—that 71 percent of Americans wear them. Four months after I left Hawaii, AP more clearly noted that the majority of Americans use glasses or contacts "to correct their vision," better articulating the J. Average qualification. I would add that as a criterion for my search. Eyesight is the only one of our five senses for which most of us require medical assistance. With the vast majority of Americans still retaining vision along with the other four senses—hearing, smell, taste, and touch—use of all five became one combined search criterion. The Average American had to be able to see, hear, smell, taste, and touch the world around him.

Jimmy believed that the list of reasons stating why he could not be an ordinary American was "probably longer than any list of averages." He explained that he was in the process of moving to the Hawaiian Homeland—an area where the land is given for free to native Hawaiians—with his wife of thirty-eight years. They wanted to strengthen their Hawaiian roots.

"I'm a federal agent, so this may sound weird, but the truth is, I see myself as a Hawaiian first and an American second. But I have pride in both. America has done things that aren't right—with blacks, for instance. Things happened in the Hawaiian kingdom that shouldn't have happened. And some of the answers aren't so easy. The monarchy owned the land here, but on the other hand, they let people live and farm there. The white missionaries brought God, but took the land."

I decided, reluctantly, to ask Jimmy more about perceived differences between those in his community and most other Americans. Since the beginning of the search, I had consciously advanced candidates not for what made them a minority but for what made them common.* Near the beginning of my search, I had even taken a side journey in order to better understand the history of Americans' commonalities.

*I* had decided to begin at the beginning—with our roots. However, because the Western Hemisphere was the last to be peopled, one thing that everyone in America has in common is that our roots come from someplace else. A landmark 2003 study by Harvard and Oxford scholars placed the first-ever native birth in Alaska some 18,000 years ago, when America's future nuclei—places such as Boston and Philadelphia—were frozen under about a mile of ice. By most accounts, the first natives of the future America were born to spear-wielding Siberian nomads who traveled in big-game hunting groups of fifteen to fifty. They emigrated from northeastern Asia by foot after the polar ice caps sucked up enough ocean water to turn the Bering Strait into a land bridge between the two continents.

Expert dental, genetic, and linguistic analyses indicate that the Siberian emigrants were the ancestors of most of today's American Indians. The other present-day Native Americans descended from

*Throughout the search, I only applied statistics that were both affirmative and in the majority; candidates needed to "earn" their average status. For example, I could advance candidates for having flown on an airplane (an affirmative statistic that captures the majority of Americans). Conversely, I could not apply statistics that expressed inaction. For example, I could not advance candidates for never having flown to Wichita (although this group is in the majority), because the would-be qualification refers to inactivity.

Asia's Athabascans, Eskimos, and Aleuts, who mastered boat building and used the Alaskan gateway after it became ocean. Getting to Hawaii, which is more than 2,000 miles away from the continents, was likely a tougher journey. Between 250 and 450 A.D., daring inhabitants of the Marquesas Islands in the South Pacific probably became the first Hawaiians after reaching the islands in voyager canoes.

Of course, the formation of the United States is specifically traceable to those who arrived via the Atlantic, and not just to the Brits of the Jamestown colony and the *Mayflower* voyage. "Europe and not England is the parent colony of America," Thomas Paine remarked in 1776, when America had many citizens from France, Germany, Holland, Portugal, Spain, Sweden, and other European countries.

The first New World native of European descent was one Virginia Dare, born on North Carolina's Outer Banks on August 18, 1587. To better understand our common characteristics from her birth forward, I had set out to learn more about her, and this meant a visit to London's St. Bride's Church. It was an unseasonably hot afternoon when I met with James Irving, an administrator at the church, in the stuffy southwest corner of the Catholic stronghold, in front of a marble effigy of a young Virginia Dare. Her parents were married at St. Bride's, itself an emblem of pedigree: Its multitiered steeple is the original model for what has become today's prototypical American wedding cake.

Although St. Bride's has been rebuilt several times, the land it sits on has been a base of Christian worship for more than a thousand years. In a church storage room that houses generations of history, located a floor above some ancient crypts, Irving handed me a dusty book. Inside, it reported that Virginia's mother, Elenora, was the daughter of John White, a watercolorist; Virginia's father, Ananias, was White's assistant. Irving reminded me of some of the character traits that distinguished Virginia's parents and their traveling companions.

"They were commoners," he said. They were looking for a better life. The Dares, along with the other fifty-seven men, sixteen women, and nine children who anchored twenty-seven days before

Virginia's birth in what is now Dare County, North Carolina, left behind a London rife with plague, poverty, and crime. In rural Great Britain, a vast number of laborers had been devastated by a program called "enclosure," in which aristocratic landlords fenced off for their own estates land previously inhabited and worked for profit by the peasants. Many of the peasants were left unemployed and homeless and came to the city to beg. "Day labourers have no voice nor authority in our commonwealth, and no account is made of them but only to be ruled," statesman Sir Thomas Smith wrote in 1565, when real wages were half of what they had been in 1500.

"We often have this image that the first English settlers were all wealthy," Irving lamented. "Not so." But they shared goals. And, declared Irving, "they did share a common language." Even more than wealth, it was the colonists' ability to understand each other that led to their creation of an enduring nation.

Virginia Dare was the first person from an English-speaking household and the first person from a family familiar with the printed word to be born on what is now American land. The St. Bride's churchyard was home to the first movable-type printing press, placed there in 1501. Generations of English writers, from Shakespeare to Dickens and beyond, have known St. Bride's as the heart of the publishing industry. Today, the area is at the heart of the famous Fleet Street, home to a large assortment of newspapers, news agencies, and publishers.

"When the English came to America, language and recorded history were enormous contributions," Irving continued. And it was this cohesive discourse, historians believe, that initially distinguished the European settlers from the Native Americans, on whom they intruded. In 1492, the year Christopher Columbus mislabeled Indians because he was convinced his newly discovered land was in the East Indies, Native Americans spoke at least 375 distinct languages. When tribes crossed paths, they found communication difficult, often fought, and remained provincial.

*At the Kula Post Office,* Jimmy Aarona noted that his pending move to the Hawaiian Homeland was not the only thing that set him apart from most Americans: He was also planning to speak more native Hawaiian in the future. "It only has twelve letters, but it's a melodic language," he said. The language was first written down in the 1820s by Christian missionaries who had settled from New England. The first Hawaiian printing press soon followed.

I submitted to Jimmy that even today, language—and the extensive communication that it allows—is our most obvious heritage, as it has been for most cultures, and perhaps our most core commonality. The government has a general rule that naturalization is bestowed only upon those immigrants who understand words and phrases "in ordinary usage in the English language." I added two J. Average criteria: the ability to read English, and the ability to speak it fluently. When Census 2000 was conducted, there were more than 21 million U.S. residents of speaking age who spoke English "less than very well." A majority of them spoke Spanish.

One of the goals of the government's National Assessment of Educational Progress, often called "the nation's report card," is to discover the literacy proficiency of young American adults by focusing on how well they can read prose (books, newspaper articles, and the like) and other documents (paychecks, for example) and how well they can perform quantitative, everyday tasks (such as "deciding between two brands" in the supermarket). For one test question, respondents are asked to examine unit-price stickers from two jars of creamy peanut butter and then to name "the more economical" price. This is just one example of how literacy questions have gotten tougher over the years, as standard unit-pricing, for peanut butter and other consumer products, was not even in place when the government started the nation's report card, with earlier versions of the test, in the 1960s. As Harvard social-behavior specialist Rima Rudd concluded in a 2003 interview, the nation's "average reader" is being challenged because "the demand for more sophisticated reading skills has increased over time. The bar has gone up."

Native Hawaiians in Hawaii, who represent more than 20 percent of the state's population, have an extraordinarily high illiteracy rate—about 30 percent among adults, which is about 23 percent above the national rate. Jimmy said the racial and cultural diversity in Hawaii sets it apart from the mainland. Indeed, no one racial group in Hawaii is in the majority. The interracial marriage percentage in Hawaii is approaching 50 percent, and the largest percentage of Asians in any state is in Hawaii.

"So the average American has some Hawaiian blood?" Jimmy asked. He meant that because the country has a percentage of native Hawaiians, its human microcosm, the most average American, should as well. Although he was half joking, his question led me back to another serious issue—the one that I had tabled at the Baptist church in Maryland: Does the Average American need to be white? As discussed previously, most of us don't know definitively what our true racial background is. But perception—how frequently Americans see certain races in their communities—does have an effect on how one views the nation. Harvard political scientist Samuel Huntington concluded in *Who Are We?* his 2004 book on American identity, that Americans are becoming more colorblind, but he admitted, "Major differences in socioeconomic status and political power among races have always existed and continue to exist in America. They include differences in wealth, income, education, power, residence, employment, health, crime (both as perpetrators and victims), and other markers of class and status." Now that non-Hispanic whites are in the minority in Hawaii, California, Texas, and New Mexico, many of them are even feeling different about their communities. In 2000, the *Economist* noted that whites in California, "who were once so generous to newcomers, are beginning to behave like a minority under pressure."

My answer seemed simple: Although I could not measure the racial and ethnic makeup of the Average American, I could make sure that his *community* accurately reflected the profile of the nation. The census informs us that, as far as is reported by Americans, the nation is made up of—in this specific order—white, Hispanic or Latino, black or African American, Asian, American Indian or Alaskan Native, and native Hawaiian groups. The Average American's community would also have these groups, and in the same order. Because most of the community's residents would be classified as white (as a minority of Hispanics identify themselves), there would be a greater likelihood, but not necessarily a certainty, that the Average American would be, too.

What other differences did Jimmy see in Hawaiians?

"I see what's happening to so many of our youngsters with all the ice"—the smokable form of crystal meth, so named because the odorless drug resembles ice shavings, which is used more per capita in Hawaii than any other state—"and I hope they will allow others to help turn them around and find meaning.

"Every family in Maui is affected in some way," Jimmy said about the drug. "It's still everywhere." Indeed, I would spend the next afternoon in the heart of Lahaina, Maui's shopping capital, where I would be asked by a young white man in khaki slacks and a golf shirt if I needed some ice. When I started to jot this down in my notebook, the guy scrambled from the street corner through a parking area.

A study that was released a couple of weeks later by Peter D. Hart Research Associates showed that the lives of 63 percent of Americans were "impacted" by drugs or alcohol, and in 72 percent of these cases, the impact was due to a family member's use of the substance. Sadly, I had another search criterion.

"It's sad," said Jimmy, "especially because many of those doing the drugs are becoming parents and are not a safeguard to their kids getting into the same cycle. This is not normal."

By many accounts, most Americans have never used any illegal drug. (So much for one of my personal reasons for abstaining. I assumed it was a common occurrence.) The findings on marijuana, the nation's most popular drug, help tell the story. According to the government's Substance Abuse and Mental Health Services Administration (SAMHSA), "Based on SAMHSA's 2002 and 2003 National Surveys on Drug Use & Health, an estimated 90.8 million adults (42.9 percent) aged 18 or older had used marijuana at least once in their lifetime." The Department of Justice's National Drug Intelligence Center reports that "data reported in the National Household Survey on Drug Abuse indicate that 37 percent of U.S. residents aged 12 and older used marijuana at least once in their lifetime." However, Mr. Q would have some numbers I could apply. Like two-thirds of Americans, J. Average would be opposed to the legalization of pot for recreational use, but, like three out of four Americans, approve of it for medical use.

The first percentage may be high in part because of many Americans' own past actions. Indeed, in another sign that my search would not lead me to someone who could have qualified as one of Norman Rockwell's Boy Scouts his whole life, I learned that most Americans have a major regret over weaknesses they've had in the past with drugs, alcohol, or sex—the three areas most often cited when major past indiscretions are recalled. In 1987, a survey by Peter D. Hart Research Associates asked Americans what they most regretted having done earlier in life. Forty-two percent said nothing, refused to answer, or were not sure. Over 50 percent of the respondents chose a specific alcohol-, drug-, or sex-related regret—they either took illegal drugs, used alcohol heavily, drove while drunk, got someone pregnant or got pregnant before marriage, or had premarital sex. In their lifetimes most Americans will seek professional help for at least one of the behavior-related health problems that—though real enough—are always in the minority when taken individually. For some, it's drugs, smoking, or alcoholism; for others, it's eating disorders, sexually transmitted diseases, or severe anxieties and certain types of depression and psychological afflictions.

*After Jimmy had a quick discussion* about delivery routes with a female postal worker who had quietly showed up at his desk, I took advantage of his mailman's knowledge of regions. I mentioned that through my search, I had been trying to determine what type of geographic area best reflected a sense of true community among its inhabitants. Jimmy and I examined some maps and he concluded that the census tract—or, again, the census neighborhood—was the best representative of community. Using census neighborhoods served two purposes: They're small enough to mean something in the lives of all of the residents who live in them, and they're large enough to enable researchers to track trends. I told him that when I had left an average census neighborhood in Nevada, I was nearly convinced of the same.

I wasn't surprised by Jimmy's assessment. The census neighborhood was first championed to me two months earlier in Virginia by Warren Glimpse, a former Census Bureau official and one of the nation's most respected demographers. Glimpse is the founder of Proximity, which specializes in "geodemographics," a field that analyzes patterns to determine where like people live. For instance, his clients may include consumer-product companies in need of a national map that highlights where the highest concentrations of middle-income families reside, or school districts in search of which bus routes have the lowest graduation rates. "It's your journey, but if you want to be respected, go with census tract," Glimpse told me over lunch in what I had discovered was his usual no-nonsense style.

In Hawaii, I held off on making a final decision on the community type until I fully explored my options—from region to state and on down—in person. However, down the road I would choose the census neighborhood, with it having to be the standard census size of between 1,500 and 8,000 residents and it having to hit the same majorities on my J. Average profile. Glimpse, who had promised he could direct me to a computer database with the most-updated and complete census statistics from all the nation's tracts (and who had helped point me to the average tract in Nevada), would ultimately prove quite handy.

*In Hawaii,* Jimmy told me, "I've learned a lot from the outside world, the continent, through television. But I know now that it was an Eastern mentality. I remember watching Archie Bunker on *All in the Family* and hearing words like 'dago.' I had to ask my parents what he was talking about. And it became pretty obvious that we had to watch big [sports and news] events live so early because they were playing to you guys 5,000 or so miles away." With Hawaii five or more hours behind New York and Chicago for much of the year, some Super Bowls have started when many Hawaiians were still in their Sunday morning church services.

But the time difference is about much more than football games. Those living in places like Los Angeles and Las Vegas are also "second-class viewers" compared to the lucky folks in the Eastern and Central block, where the Times Square ball drop on New Year's Eve always starts another year of Eastern influence. Television is the primary news source for most Americans, but only the Eastern-most population can consistently count on seeing live programming— such as the network morning news shows—at or close to their airing. There's good reason: like my search, TV executives recognize majority populations when they see them; the Eastern time zone alone covers about 50 percent of the U.S. population and the Central time zone is the second most populated. Major news announcements are scheduled with this more than 75 percent of the country in mind. Incidentally, Indiana has long been in both time zones.

Jimmy volunteered another Hawaiian difference: how mainlanders usually think of Hawaiians as living their lives out in one large beach party. "I think we all enjoy being close enough to the ocean to enjoy it on short notice, but most of us are working and raising families, and not living down by the water."

Already a bit stressed wondering if I would ever make it to the end of my search—and in need of something that would help me make significant progress—I wondered if I had been handed a major gift by Postmaster Jimmy. And sure enough, on my computer in a hotel room in Maui, I confirmed that not only have most Americans visited the ocean, but, as Jimmy noted of Hawaiians, most Americans lived close enough to enjoy it on relatively short notice. And then the kicker—with most Americans living in the Eastern-Central time block, my search would be seriously altered. The West Coast and the Rockies had been zapped. As for how far most of the population lives from the ocean, there was some conflicting expert analysis—some reports put the threshold at within 50 miles and some within 100 miles. I put both distances down, but down the road, one distance over the other would prove moot. Those living more than 100 miles from the Atlantic and Gulf of Mexico waters—those near the Pacific were already gone—had disappeared. After I began to apply the ocean and time criteria, the remaining Texas residents dropped from the search. One commonality of fourteen of the remaining states: Interstate 95—that mainstay of Northeast-to-Florida snowbirds—cuts through each. Perhaps most interestingly, and appropriately, the fourteen states were on the land of the nation's thirteen original states (Maine and Massachusetts were combined until 1820)—the former British colonies that fought for America's independence.

And I knew when my next stop would be, now that I could afford to exhale a little.

"I guess you'll be going to a Fourth of July barbecue," Jimmy had said near the end of our conversation. "There's a day that celebrates the average American, right?" Well, clearly more so than the first of May. I set my sights on Independence Day.

*Nine*

# FANFARE FOR
# THE COMMON MAN

*Candidates remaining: fewer than 10 million*

*Common men beware:* In today's generation, you have some well-known competition. In 1993, when Barry Bonds was cementing his image as baseball's most dominant slugger, he told *Sports Illustrated,* "The other day, I mowed the lawn with my cousin. I eat at McDonald's. I eat at Denny's. I don't do anything different from anybody else. Off the field, I'm an average guy." At the time, Bonds was living in ritzy Los Altos Hills, California, in a multimillion-dollar mansion equipped with nineteen television sets. Mike Ditka, before rejecting overtures in 2004 that he should run for a Senate seat in Illinois, said, "Hey, I'm an ordinary, average guy." At the time, the former Super Bowl champion coach was starring in a national advertising campaign aimed at a minority population—men suffering from erectile dysfunction. And in a recent interview, the rapper Method Man described himself as "an average dude"; as an example of his average activities, he said he buys deodorant at the supermarket. But does an average dude stop using his real name? Does an average person's bank balance allow him to buy a $100,000 diamond pendant shaped like an ice pick?

No matter; with celebrities, ordinariness is in. Today, showing famous Americans engaged in such routine activities as grabbing take-out meals and opening car doors is a handsome business. *Us* magazine even has a weekly feature on this theme: "Stars—They're Just Like Us!" shows celebrities handling common American tasks. And with reality television growing in popularity, many entertainers have a better shot at steady work by promising to perform everyday activities for the cameras.

Of course, in time-honored tradition, politicians also jockey for a chance to be deemed ordinary. It was Herbert Hoover who said, "It is only when we get into politics that we are satisfied with the common man." With the explosion of media coverage, the strategy of emphasizing one's average roots has escalated, even among those from elite backgrounds. "And to the C students, I say, you too can be president of the United States," President George W. Bush reminded a Yale audience. According to backer Peggy Noonan, a former speechwriter for Ronald Reagan, Bush's presidency represents "the triumph of the average man." Bush's plainspoken, even butchered, language, and his sometimes rural wardrobe have played into this image.

During the 2004 campaign, Democratic challenger John Kerry could not shed his aloof and too-scholarly image, in part because of his own decisions (for example, he refused to release his grades from Yale, even though he was also a C student there), but also because when he did try to appeal to everyday Joes, many national pundits seemed to remain fixated on maintaining the established characterization of him—or maybe they just bought into it so completely that they couldn't see him any other way. Eight months before the election, *New York Times* columnist Maureen Dowd wrote of Kerry, "Even when he puts on that barn jacket over his expensive suit to look less lockjaw—and says things like, 'Who among us doesn't like Nascar?'—he can come across like Mr. Collins, Elizabeth Bennet's pretentious cousin in 'Pride and Prejudice.'" Only the NASCAR quote—later tarted up by several other media outlets to sound even more ridiculous and erudite: "Whom among us is not a fan of NASCAR?"—was not what Kerry said at the rally.* After the mis-

---

*Dowd got the quote secondhand, during a conversation with *Times* reporter Sheryl Gay Stolberg, who later admitted she may have made a mistake. She had—

reported quotes had made the rounds, Kerry—guided, no doubt, by handlers wanting their man to sound more Everyman—stood in front of reporters at a grocery store in rural Ohio and asked, "Can I get me a hunting license here?"

It's not clear whether such political posturing on the part of the leading candidates was good news—or irrelevant—for Joe Schriner, a balding handyman who ran for president in 2000 and 2004 on the promise that he was an average Joe.

On a hazy Fourth of July during his second campaign, four months before he would receive a total of 142 votes across the nation, I drove with Joe through the western Pennsylvania working-class town of Warren. His large van sported an Ohio license plate that read "AV JOE." 'Average Joe' SCHRINER U.S. President 2004 was written in large red, white, and blue lettering on a side panel. Trailing in a second vehicle were Joe's wife, named Liz, and the couple's three young kids. Their eldest, the only girl, was eight. The Schriners were able to afford their travel expenses by requesting "campaign contributions" in person and via a website. They had regularly slept in the van.

Within a minute after we met, Joe began reviewing a couple of recent newspaper stories about his candidacy. "But that's only a small part of the media coverage," he said. "We've had over a hundred TV stories. Liz handles the publicity." Joe's wife had been a public relations professional in her native New Zealand, and she is still a Kiwi. "I have some issues with America," she would later say, explaining her lack of U.S. citizenship. "But I don't want to get into that."

The Schriners were headed to a backyard barbecue. They had been invited by a man they had met only two days earlier. "Jack started a home for recovering addicts," Schriner said of the host.

How did they meet?

"I used to be involved in . . ." Joe paused. "Look, I don't want to talk about that. If it got out, it would be bad for the campaign."

Jack Wills's house was set on an old city block with cracked

the actual Kerry quote was plainspoken, kind of: "There isn't one of us here who doesn't like NASCAR and who isn't a fan."

sidewalks and houses close together. Next door was Phoenix House, the halfway home. In Jack's backyard, the scent of a roasted pig filled the air. Adults, many of whom he was trying to keep on the right track, talked, played volleyball, and prepared food. Children splashed in an aboveground pool attached to a large deck.

A month earlier, in a Quinnipiac College poll, 50 percent of Americans had said they would prefer to attend a barbecue with Bush—to Kerry's 39 percent. Maybe Joe was on a mission to pick up the remainder. In the food line, a middle-aged blonde woman with a heavily creased face asked us how we knew the host.

"I don't know if Jack told you," Joe said, "but I'm Joe Schriner. I'm running for president."

"Of what?" she asked.

"The United States," Joe said.

"Okay, good luck with that," she said. She turned to me.

I was looking for the most average person in America.

"So much for sobriety," she said.

*I knew there was something missing.* Because so many present had sworn off booze, this was a Fourth of July bash where no one was drinking beer.

In his old title track "Ordinary Average Guy," rocker Joe Walsh sang, of course, about drinking beer: The average American is often called Joe Six-Pack. But it turns out that beer consumption, incredibly, does not distinguish average Americans. Although more than $800 million is spent in the United States each year on beer advertising, more than on any other type of beverage, most Americans, and most American adults, do not drink beer. As a 2004 *Beverage World* study reported, "On a per-capita basis, beer consumption in the U.S. has been steadily declining." In a 2004 study of several nations, the United States was, in per capita beer consumption, behind Germany, Austria, the United Kingdom, and Denmark.

I needed to stay true to my search guideline that I would not make the *absence* of anything a criterion. Therefore, the most average

American may or may not be a beer drinker, or, for that matter, an alcohol consumer. Less than 50 percent of American adults are regular drinkers, according to a 2004 Centers for Disease Control report. Or a smoker: Three out of every ten Americans aged twelve and up use tobacco.

However, most Americans have consumed alcohol: About 25 percent of those eighteen or older are lifetime abstainers. J. Average, if not a regular drinker, has imbibed on a regular or occasional basis at some point. This knocked out certain people of faith. Jesus may have turned water into wine, and Saint Bridget may have written a poem 1,400 years ago describing heaven as a lake of beer, but orthodox Mormons, Seventh-day Adventists, Southern Baptists, and Pentecostals are among those churchgoers who eschew drinking alcohol, and those who have always been faithful could not be J. Average.

Over by a maple tree, I sensed from Average Joe Schriner that his political campaign was more a religious mission. An old-school Catholic, he told me that abortion and homosexuality are sinful. "When we oppose God's plan for heterosexual relationships geared toward building and strengthening the nuclear family, we are no longer spiritual, but nuts," he said.

However, most Americans—and J. Average would need to be among them—are tolerant of gay and lesbian relationships. Gallup reports that every year since at least 2001, most Americans have deemed that "homosexuality should be considered an acceptable alternative lifestyle." And a 2000 survey by Henry J. Kaiser Family Foundation found that 60 percent of parents with children aged eight to eighteen have talked with the youngsters about "sexual orientation, including being gay, lesbian, or bisexual as a normal part of some people's sexuality."

Americans' views on gays and lesbians have changed significantly since 1982, when Gallup determined that only 34 percent of the population found the homosexual lifestyle acceptable. In 2003, Gallup found that 61 percent of Americans believed that homosexuals should be hired as elementary school teachers, an increase of 20 percentage points from 1992. The percentage regarding high school teachers during the same span increased from 47 to 67 percent.

As another sign of the rising tolerance, in a 2001 Zogby poll of
high-school seniors, 85 percent said gay and lesbian relations were
acceptable. "The stigma of being gay is disappearing," according to
Gary Gates, a demographer at the Urban Institute. "This is a huge
change. Gay people in general are feeling more comfortable in society—and society is feeling more comfortable with gay people."
About 70 percent of Americans believe that same-sex marriage is
inevitable.

Considering Average Joe's preaching, is his campaign platform really average?

"We are not too blatant about it," he said. He told me that television was responding positively to his campaign because he and his
wife and children were "an average American family." As proof, he
cited a Fox News story on his run for the presidency that he claimed
a lot of people had seen.

But can someone actively seeking media attention really be an average American?

"We see Bush clearing brush on a Texas ranch to try to convince
people he is average," Joe countered. "TV shows us that he's average, so we believe the image."

Ironically, television, consistently a punching bag for so many
American fundamentalist groups—one of their primary symbols of
what ails the nation—seemed to be Joe's hope for success. Today,
most Americans have cable service and a color TV hooked up with a
VCR and/or a DVD player, three more criteria for my search. In
2002, the percentage of homes with cable television hit 69 percent,
and those with video or DVD components had climbed to more than
90 percent.

A collection of studies showed me that the Average American also
needed to—on a typical day—watch television. However, our devo-
tion to the possibly unfairly maligned "idiot box" may actually be
waning, if ever so slightly. Buried in a data report issued by the government's Economics and Statistics Administration is a professional
analysis concluding that between 2005 and 2006, the number of
hours Americans spend watching TV will decrease from 4.85 to 4.83
hours per person per day. From ten types of media—books, daily

newspapers, home video and DVDs, Internet, magazines, movies in theaters, radio, recorded music, television, and video games—the average American daily intake from 2005 to 2006 is expected to show an increase of fewer than ten seconds per day, to just under ten-and-a-half hours.

Maybe we're nearly filled up. After all, this leaves a little over thirteen hours a day—if one isn't multitasking—to eat, sleep, work, walk the dog, and what have you. The slowdown continues amidst growing media options. Today, the average number of television channels in U.S. homes is more than 100—up from 27 in 1994—and more than 15 of those channels are viewed regularly. The last time a particular television program of any kind was seen in a majority of television-equipped households, President Reagan was in his first term (the last episode of classic sitcom *M*A*S*H*).* Even the annual viewership for the country's perennial ratings champ, the Super Bowl, now falls below one-third of the national population. Today, no one favorite TV show—or song or movie, or any other entertainment product—can be a criterion for the Average American. There is no proof that the majority of Americans share an enthusiasm for any one of them.

*J*oe Schriner was not picking up a lot of votes at the picnic and had headed with Jack Wills to Phoenix House. After becoming sober in 1981, Wills overcame many complaints—several neighbors shared the concern that having recovering addicts on the street would raise crime in the neighborhood—before garnering the necessary support for the halfway home a few years ago.

Wills introduced us to John, a wiry man with a ruddy complexion who was wearing tight jeans and a muscle shirt and twirling a pair of sunglasses between his thumb and forefinger. John said that on the Fourth of July one year earlier, he had been living at an

---

*It was 1983, the year the Internet was launched in the United States as a military project.

Allegheny Mountains campsite a few miles away, zoned out on drugs and without hope. "Before I came here, I also did a little time in jail," he said.

Joe expressed his sympathy, almost certainly unaware of a study that reported that 52 percent of Americans would rather spend a week in jail than become president.

John said he was a former long-distance truck driver from southern Texas who had turned to uppers to stay awake longer and maximize his mileage. "I used to be rich," John said. "I was making $40,000 a year. I know money's important, but I never want it to control my life again. I don't make anywhere near what I used to, not even half. I work as a dishwasher at a restaurant. The Pepper Mill. I'm trying to keep it together."

*When he was rich,* John had been earning a below-average household income, an incongruity that stems from Americans having long been the world leader in financial privilege. In 1750, the American colonies already had a higher per capita income than any other society on the planet. In 1900, if a family did not have a servant, many considered it lower middle class.

The Census Bureau does not define "class," but the most-cited barometers have a middle-income household earning between $25,000 and $100,000 a year and a middle-class wage for one person at between $15,000 and $75,000 a year. Many demographers define the middle class as those in households that earn in the middle three quintiles—the middle 60 percent—among all households. In 2003, this middle range stretched from $17,964 to $86,867. Census 2000 reported the average 1999 household income at $56,644 ($14,650 more than the median figure). Many Americans who make more than $100,000 a year do not consider themselves rich, in many cases because they are financially supporting children and have other expensive responsibilities. This may help explain why 64 percent of those earning $150,000 or more per year believe that those who are "rich" in America "have too much power." They may not be talking about themselves.

Americans have become richer, but not more financially equal. The Gini Index (named for an Italian statistician) is the benchmark for how evenly money is distributed within a society. If the richest person in a country owned everything, the nation would score 1000, whereas a totally egalitarian society would score zero. The U.S. Gini score was 374 in 1947. It fell to an all-time low of 348 in 1967. Between 2001 and 2003, it was between 425 and 450, the highest level of inequality since the Roaring Twenties.

I knew that income and the earlier criterion of total assets value were likely the most sensitive facts I would be seeking from candidates in my search. As a result, I decided that the dollar figures for assets and income should be the final points covered on my checklist. I would have to find some way to gauge from finalists—as a tiebreaker, if needed—how close they were to the dollar averages. As a starting threshold, I decided to go with the lowest and highest household figures in my income research, between $15,000 and $75,000 per capita. If there was a home clearly outside this threshold, I would toss it from my search.

*At Phoenix House,* John said he had put in more than a million miles as a trucker. Returning to Jack Wills's barbecue, Joe Schriner took a seat by the pool and talked about driving more than 30,000 miles on the road for his two campaigns. I thought about someone who, like Schriner, had both attended college in Ohio and worked as a newspaper reporter: Danedri Thompson, an America West flight attendant based in Indianapolis, the only real-life person I would find during my travels who had previously been selected as a most average individual. At a Rotary Club camp she had attended after her sophomore year in high school, attendees were asked to list such personal information as weight, birthdate, and eye color. Later, Thompson was proclaimed the most average of the group. I had originally learned this from an old newspaper column that I had found online. Later, I tracked Danedri down and she informed me of the reasons she did not consider herself average, with her high mileage among the reasons at the top of the list.

I had begun to realize that miles traveled could help me address American work life. Most workers in America have a maximum commute of 5 miles. Even if this number seems short—indeed, the one-way average commute time for those who did not work at home was 24.3 minutes in 2003—factoring in those who are still in school and those who stay at home, it was safe to extrapolate that the majority of Americans report to a primary weekday destination within 5 miles of home. So would the Average American. He would also need to be someone whose primary mode of transportation is the privately owned motor vehicle, as it is with most Americans. According to the Census Bureau, only 5 percent of U.S. workers used public transportation in 2004.

On average, in large part because of the increase in commercial conveniences closer to home, the rate of increase in America's traveling mileage is slowing down. Including airline travel, it is now at 40 miles per day, an increase of 14 miles a day since 1977, but up only 1 mile a day since 1995. However, most of our travel is for purposes other than working. Commuting accounts for only 15 percent of daily travel in the United States.

*A nice breeze was blowing* through the back of Jack Wills's home. Next to the giant pig, hot dogs were being grilled. Joe and Liz Schriner were relaxing with their kids in the pool. As I sat down for a two–hot dog meal on the back porch—a sign, I realized, that I was becoming more typically American, as I would not have touched red meat at the start of my travels—I recognized that I was missing a lot simply by not having the luxury of a deck or anything to kick back on at home whenever I wanted, a wonderful stress reducer, as many people know. Like many residents of Manhattan, I did not even have a place to fire up an outdoor grill—and, honestly, had not seen a need for one.

Mr. Q got me back to my search. According to the Census Bureau, more than four in five Americans live in homes with an external extension—a deck, porch, patio, or balcony. So, too, would J. Average. There would also be an outdoor grill on his or her premises, as is the case for about three in four U.S. homes. And to complete the scene, I decided that the Average American must be a meat eater, of both red and white meat. Those who do not eat red meat represent less than 5 percent of the population.

While Liz Schriner and her husband toweled off, she helped lead me to another criterion. She said it was not inconceivable that Joe could become president, because "the majority of adults in this country do not vote, and if Joe can convince everyone who didn't vote to vote for him, he could win."

Sticking with the Census Bureau, I explained that most Americans of voting age, some 55 percent, actually did vote for president in 2000. "I guess we need to update our message," Liz said.

I would later learn that the voting turnout for adults in the 2004 election was even higher: 58.3 percent of those of voting age. Because most Americans were not registered voters—I had to take into account the full U.S. population, and registered voters were in the minority—I turned to household figures. On average in the U.S., American households have between one and two registered voters, and the majority have between one and three. Only those homes with one to three registered voters would remain in my sights. Maybe this would help weed out a lot of convicted felons—thankfully, in the minority—who are not allowed to register.*

"We need to make values count in this country," Joe Schriner said later, deep in campaign mode. "What our legislatures are doing along party lines affects all of us. That's why we make sense."

---

*Incidentally, the felons may be hard to differentiate on first sight from the average American. A recent report noted that the average fugitive on the FBI's "Most Wanted" list is thirty-six, the exact same average age as Americans in general.

A nationwide *New York Times* survey reported in 2002 that 77 percent of Americans saw "important differences in what the Republican and Democratic parties stand for," a 27-point increase from 1992. Also in 2002, a Gallup poll found that 69 percent of the nation held the belief that Americans were "united and in agreement on the most important issues," a whopping 37-point increase from nine years earlier. This seeming incongruity is likely a sign of our discomfort with our national politicians, not with each other's views. Indeed, through their redistricting efforts, Senate and House members have been working hard to carve out areas that best match their political leanings (which helps explain why some districts are freakishly shaped). The result is a political atmosphere in which members of Congress have less incentive to appeal across party lines, which in turn has led to a more polarized, and gridlocked, environment in the capital.

And, it would seem, a political divide that has convinced more and more Americans that they are not in such close agreement with each other. In 2004, Gallup found that those who believed that Americans are together on the major issues had dramatically decreased, to 34 percent of the population. But despite continuing party efforts to dig ever deeper trenches around opposing camps, there is always ostensibly the one person the elected officials are looking out for: the average American, who they purport to know well and to care about. On the Senate floor recently, New York Democrat Chuck Schumer declared during a critique of Bush administration oil policy, "The average American is not looking at the newspaper and saying, 'Gee, the economy is great.'. . . The president should be standing up for the average American, not standing up for the oil companies, and not patting the Saudis on the back." In a House address, leader Tom DeLay, a Texas Republican, ripped Democrats by declaring, "They do not trust the strength and dedication of the average American."*

---

*These are just two examples from diametrically opposed politicians who are often in today's headlines. A full catalog of such appeals would grow in size to a book bigger than this one, from Jeffersonian and Jacksonian Democracy through William Jennings Bryan's invocations of the "common man" to Huey Long's "Every Man a

"I will come in as an average, independent American to help un-clog Washington," Joe Schriner said.

By talking of the political leadership in Washington, Joe would at least help me with my search: The Average American could be differentiated by the political party of those who represent him to the nation. I would have to wait until the fall elections to know what defined the majority of Americans in this regard, but the results would show that most Americans—as they had been when I was with Joe—were represented by at least one Democratic senator. (Most Americans are not represented by at least one Republican senator.) Among the states failing to hit this Democratic criterion: so-called blue states Pennsylvania and Maine. There are more registered Democrats in America than either registered Republicans or unaffiliated voters, but J. Average's House representative would need to be from the Republican Party. The congressional districts are based on equality of population, and Republicans have been in control of the House since the 1994 elections.

*S*truck *from J. Average consideration* would be residents of Massachusetts and neighboring Rhode Island. Massachusetts has not had a single Republican senator or congressperson in this millennium. Rhode Island has not had a Republican House representative since 1995.

"There are two big differences between our campaign and the big guys'," Joe Schriner said. "First, money. But we also do not look at any demographic match-ups to see which people we should be focusing on."

Indeed, in major-league politics and business, micromarketing, narrowcasting, and segmentation are now the buzzwords and driving forces. We can dismiss the quaint notion that the American

---

King" campaign, FDR's New Deal public works projects, Richard Nixon's "silent majority" utterings, the populist rhetoric of Democratic presidential hopeful John Edwards, and beyond.

majority is the primary target of presidential and national consumer-product marketers, even though the professionals may still dream in their off-work hours of capturing such an audience with a single message. Getting more than half the population interested in any one thing is nearly impossible in today's media culture, so to today's campaign puppeteers and marketing teams, American voters and consumers, respectively, are reduced to the simplest terms possible—for what narrow message they are most apt to "buy into" emotionally, from stem-cell research to kid-proof safety caps. The advertising messages—Americans are bombarded with an average of at least 500 a day—are then tailor-made for each of these "clusters" of consumers. To understand the future, think of the much-loved but increasingly rare general summer camps, which are slowly being replaced by more specialized and instructive experiences for the kiddies, from cooking to computers to rock 'n' roll.

If a presidential candidate speaks about the need to help the average American, chances are that a focus group or other market research finding has shown that those who see themselves as average are likely to want to hear whatever the candidate is saying at the time. Which helps explain why Karl Rove, George W. Bush's chief political strategist, came onto the scene from a career in direct-mail campaigning, where the seminal strategy has long been to mine databases of individuals' personal information, then narrowcast to clusters of these folks. It also helps explains why we have gone from a mass-marketing culture—in which Wrigley's sent four sticks of its chewing gum to every person listed in a U.S. phone book in 1915—to a new kind of advertising climate, one clearly reflected by a comment from Lawrence Light, the chief marketing officer at McDonald's, who was quoted in *Business Week* in 2004 saying, "We are not a mass marketer."

"We have a strategy to take the back routes through America, to the small towns that happen to be there," Joe Schriner said. "We were on a long Route 66 tour. Right now, we're on a Route 6 tour. When we get to the small towns, we always make sure we get off the main roads to talk with the people. Because they don't live on the thruways, they are not natural stopping points. I realize they generally see fewer outsiders."

Sounds like a demographic strategy to me. And an easy criterion. With all due respect to "Little Pink Houses," John Mellencamp's classic tune about the underappreciated joys of everyday America, the Average American will not have an interstate running through his front yard. Like most Americans, he would live on a local road. Those living on government numbered roads, such as I-16 or Route 6, were no longer candidates.

"For the most part, average Americans just want to be heard," Schriner said. "We strike a chord there. Let me give you an example: You hear a lot about taxes, so I asked myself, 'What's a fair way of paying taxes where we all feel we're being heard?' I now have a plan that we should look at how much we owe and then we each personally decide where the money goes. How much goes to the space program, how much to the military, how much to social programs, and so on. If there's a logjam preventing this, we encourage states to start it. It could work. There are already deviations as to how they collect their taxes."

From 1870 to 1912, there were no federal income taxes in the United States. Today, most Americans live in a household that files both federal and state income taxes, two more criteria for J. Average, I decided. As most Americans pay a sales tax in their home state, another criterion, I realized I would need to eliminate those remaining in one more state: Delaware is without this routine tax.

Joe Schriner told me that Sunday is "family day," and that one of the ground rules is that he and Liz make a promise to spend downtime with their children on that day of the week. Today, they had also promised their children ice cream. We left the barbecue and I headed with the family to a Warren supermarket, where the two oldest kids scrambled for an open bin of individual candies. They each wolfed some down. "Now, now," Joe said soothingly, when he caught up with them. "Let's save some for the shoppers." Joe bought ice cream for the kids, and afterward, we drove in separate vehicles through Warren. We crossed Pennsylvania Avenue, Warren's main drag, where many American flags were still fastened to telephone poles from the Fourth of July parade the day before. It started to pour. The Schriners found a park and dashed under a roof that was keeping a picnic table dry. It was probably time for me to depart and let them have their family day.

"My idea," young Sarah Schriner said of eating the ice cream at a picnic table. "They like the parks," Joe said. "They can run around here."

As was my habit, I would check to see if such tangibles were in the majority. I would add three criteria—J. Average would need to consume ice cream at least once a month, and live within 2 miles of a public park, as do about two out of three Americans for each, and use some recreational area annually. More important, I decided that the future of America—children, whom I had observed but not interviewed during my search—was well worth looking to for more direction.

As we got closer to that fall's elections, I drove several hours from Manhattan into upstate New York. There, on the eve of Election Day, I met another child named Sarah, who had a hand in her dad running as the first person ever to represent the Average American Party. And his odds were better than Joe's.

# Ten

# AVERAGE AMERICAN VOTER

*Candidates remaining: fewer than 8 million*

*Over the past ten years,* the city of Olean in western New York has been turning more Republican. On November 2, 2004, election morning, a heavyset Democratic official paced nervously around his party's Olean headquarters, still hopeful of spreading some dirt about the opposition.

"You didn't use my message?" he asked, as soon as Rich Bean came through the front door of the cavernous office, located in a converted store on Olean's main strip. Bean bit his lip and shook his head. A bespectacled man with an owlish face and a graying beard, Bean was running for one of the seven alderman seats on the city's Common Council. The party official had left word alleging that Rich's Republican opponent had failed to pay an out-of-town news-paper bill on time.

"I do not want anyone saying anything bad about her to anyone," Bean said. "I'm serious; that's not how I play ball."

On our subsequent drive to the polls, Bean said, "That's one of the reasons I hate politics. You get involved in a big political party, I guess I shouldn't be surprised. But I'm not interested in putting a wedge between people; I'm interested in bringing them together."

And that, he said, was one powerful reason why he was also

running to become the first politician ever to represent the Average American Party.

Rich is a mental health specialist at a government day program in Olean, a former oil, lumber, and steel city of about 15,000, located about an hour southeast of Buffalo. He resides in the same ward (in Olean, an area roughly the same as a census neighborhood) where he grew up, which he now would like to represent at the salary of about $3,500 a year.

"She's a neighbor," he said of his opponent. "Why would I want to say anything bad about her? Win or lose tomorrow, we're still neighbors. One of their kids is in Naomi's class. I'm not going to be slamming their mom."

*Then at fifteen,* Naomi Bean was the oldest of Rich's four children. There was also Rachel, fourteen; Ben, twelve; and Sarah, ten. It was the youngest who came up with the name of the Average American Party. Over dinner a few weeks earlier, her dad had mentioned that he was allowed to add to his Democratic affiliation another party line on his November 2 ballot. He had said that he was an average Joe. Sarah suggested Average American.

Rich and his wife, Becky, both in their early forties, are used to listening carefully to kids. They met while working as caseworkers at a government children's services agency in the area. In high school, Rich was in a foster home with five other children (his foster dad was the city's director of engineering); Becky had three siblings growing up. Their modest colonial-style house on an Olean city block doubles as Jellybean Daycare, which Becky runs.

Ten days earlier, during an online search, I had found mention of Rich's new party in an Olean newspaper story, and called the Beans. Rich told me about his daughter having christened the party, and I realized I needed to pay them a visit. Graciously, the Beans invited me to crash at their home for two days starting election eve. At the dinner table on the day I arrived, Rich talked about how averageness and normalcy had been themes in both his professional and personal life.

"Growing up, I knew I was different," he said. "There's a lot to be said for being average. . . . At the rehab center, our number one goal is to normalize our clients' lives. If we can get them to a day-to-day existence where they are just another face in their surroundings, then we have greatly succeeded."

"There's a certain level of self-esteem that comes from reaching normalization," Rich noted at one point. "With the mentally ill, they may not be able to have the concentration skills to do repetitive work, but we go places where they can work. We go to the Salvation Army thrift store and we straighten up the racks. The Salvation Army likes having us, because it's one less thing they have to worry about. Or we go to a home for homeless families and help them do household chores. So they are giving back to the community and building their self-esteem. You know what I find interesting? Our clients also help us reach normalization. If there were not mentally retarded adults out there, many of us may not have a job."

The concept of averageness as a goal for mental-health patients is perhaps best articulated through a self-help program called Recovery, founded by Dr. Abraham Low, a neuropsychiatrist, in 1937. The nonprofit Recovery, Inc., conducts weekly group sessions throughout the country, with the emphasis on repeating Dr. Low's writings out loud. "What Recovery teaches you, through its philosophy of averageness, is to endorse your successes and to refrain from condemning your failures," Low noted. "An attitude of this kind permits you to accumulate a vast fund of self-endorsement."

Before my trip to Olean, I had spoken with Tony Ferrigno, a Recovery counselor in New York City. In the 1980s, Tony, an iron-worker for more than twenty years, had developed mental-stress problems as a result of his job and his parents' declining health. Soon after his parents passed away, he retired, but his problems escalated into a debilitating nervousness that made simple tasks, such as boarding a bus and attending church services, seem impossible. Married with children, Tony thought about ending his life. In 1990, a cousin who once suffered from panic attacks recommended Recovery.

In 2002, Tony wrote these words about what he had learned there: "By understanding that our symptoms are distressing, but not dangerous, and that the things we fear and hate to do are the everyday things that the average person does, many of us turned what was once a vicious cycle of helplessness and hopelessness into a vitalizing cycle of self-confidence." During our conversation two years later, Ferrigno said that thinking like this had improved his mental health and helped many others. "The philosophy of averageness is a very powerful statement in the sessions," Ferrigno said. "If you can see things in term of average, you can cope. It works because averageness is not only a reachable place, but where many people find the most inner comfort."

"People feel more comfortable being average," Rich echoed in Olean. "Isn't that a good thing?" He talked about his travels to parts of Pennsylvania with his son, a budding hockey star who had made his age group's top-tier traveling squad. "We don't make a lot of money—let's just say $30,000 is a big salary to us—and one of the families sent around a notice about a nice inn to stay in on our next trip. Well, we can't afford $100 a night. We sent around a notice of our own, about a Motel 6 we learned about. We had a couple parents call us to thank us for basically giving them the okay to stay at a $50 place. Once we realize that being average is okay, maybe we won't feel the need to try to impress others."

Naomi, a studious girl with dark hair and glasses, entered the house and joined the conversation. I asked her if there was an acceptance of all students at her high school. She said there wasn't, especially from some students interested in standing out by their looks and style. "I think they spend too much time on that," she said.

Like generations of successful Penn State football players—powerhouse athletes and simultaneously the very model of plainness with their block-lettered, generic jerseys and helmets and their disdain for showboating—more students are starting to understand that being outside the beautiful crowd is not shameful. In a 2000 Gallup survey of students aged thirteen to seventeen, students overwhelmingly said they would rather be the top student in their class than the most physically attractive one. In addition, more said they would rather be captain of a "major sports team" than the best-looking student.*

Rich said that his Average American Party was against flashiness and for inclusiveness. "The way I see it, it stands for thinking about the citizens first, before any political loyalties," he said.

Although I already had a couple of national-level criteria—parties of senators and congresspersons—to help define the political tenor of the Average American's community, I realized that I would need to think about the local level when Rich, who had majored in urban studies and minored in sociology at Canisius College in Buffalo, said that it is the lowest level of organized politics that most impacts a person's lifestyle. "I have no desire to be politically involved in any more than city government," he said. "I want to know the people I represent. This ward is important to those around here because what goes on here is what directly affects all of our kids. We used to have a drug house on the street. Becky saw a cocaine deal go down at five o'clock in the afternoon with her daycare kids on the front porch. I hope to have a bigger hand in preventing those things and making this neighborhood a place that shows kids the right way." About 90 percent of the homes in his ward hold only a five-figure value.

Referring to how issues on the neighborhood level influence the

---

*As for how students define their level of popularity, a 2003 Gallup poll found that more than 80 percent of the thirteen-to-seventeen-year-old crowd believed that others in their school perceived them to be average or above average in popularity. When we look back on our high-school years, the popularity numbers are even higher. Gallup found in 2005 that 74 percent of those aged eighteen and older believed they were "very" or "somewhat" popular in high school. Incidentally, more than 60 percent said that those who were popular in high school ended up being "less successful" or just as successful in life than the unpopular kids, mostly the former. A 2005 University of Virginia study showed that the teenage "in" crowd is more likely to use drugs or commit "starter" crimes, such as vandalizing property and shoplifting, than other kids. Said Joseph Allen, a psychologist and the chief researcher for the Virginia study, "Popular adolescents look like leaders. But in reality they are tracking peer opinion. They do the same thing politicians do in tracking opinion polls. They are very much like politicians."

voting in Congress, former Speaker of the House Tip O'Neill once famously said, "All politics is local." O'Neill, a colorful Boston Democrat proud of his Irish heritage, had gone on to explain, "We don't talk about our constituency, we try to find Mary Byrne a job, smooth the palm of a cop who made a wrongful arrest, take old Mrs. McCarthy and her sister to the polls, get young Paddy off the bottle and into a job." As the *Economist* reported in 2003, the majority of local politicians are Democrats. The Average American's chief local elected official would be Democratic, and the local governing council—for example, city council, for which Rich is running—would be more Democratic than Republican.

According to the Economics and Statistics Administration, the largest types of local governments in the United States are municipalities (there are 19,429 in total), towns (16,504), and school districts (13,506). The local governments tend to swing Democratic, in large part because Democrats are more apt to support specific government programs—which are typically more successful in getting out voters on a local level than they are on a national level—and because there are over 15 million more registered Democrats in the country than registered Republicans. (For those keeping a red-blue scorecard, yes, there was a greater likelihood that the Average American would be classified as "blue.")

Rich and I moved to the living room, where he flipped the television channels between two news networks with pundits yakking about Bush versus Kerry. After a couple minutes, Rich, echoing Average Joe Schriner in Pennsylvania, talked about television's influence on successful presidential campaigning. "Everything is sound bites," Rich said. "There is no nuance. That's why Kerry's campaign is not running away with this thing. His messages are meant for newspapers."

Rich, who reads the Olean newspaper every day and the Buffalo paper on Sunday, correctly speculated that Americans are less interested in reading about national politics than they are in reading about local and other news. A 2004 Gallup study found that 58 percent of American adults read a local newspaper daily—high enough to be another search criterion—and that 62 percent never get their news from national newspapers. At last check, the ratio of American adults who get their news from the Internet at least occasionally was at 51 percent and rising. A 2004 study by the National Endowment for the Arts found that the percentage of American adults who read literature (novels, short stories, poetry, or plays) had fallen below 50 percent for the first time in our history, but noted that more than 60 percent of the population read books (which includes nonfiction). Gallup has been charting for many years the percentage of Americans who have read or have started to read at least one book within the previous year. In 2005, the number reached 83 percent, higher than the 81 percent figure posted in both 2002 and 1990. The Average American would need to fall into this majority.

Rich's best buddy, Mike, a landlord, stopped by the house. Mike had offered up his home as a campaign headquarters that evening so that he and Rich could call every last registered voter in the ward with a reminder to vote the next day. At Mike's home in a more up-scale neighborhood on the outskirts of town, they worked two phones to make the best use of their time. Today, about two-thirds of the people in the world have never made a phone call, but more than half of all Americans use mobile phones (about 10 percent use cell phones exclusively). The vast majority use landlines. I decided that the Average American must use both types of phones and must live within range of mobile service. This gave me three more search criteria.

"Mike's the only person who volunteered to help," Rich said on the ride back to his home. "He also took care of some expenses. He's a true friend." Mr. Q—I had long thought of him as an active participant in these conversations—cited a 2003 Gallup poll that reported that 79 percent of Americans believe friends are "extremely" or "very" important, another criterion. One national survey concluded that on average, Americans have nine friends and another that the average American is within five years of his best friend's age. (Most people I mention this fact to start counting, so you're not alone.) Incidentally, for those who attend church at least once a week, 72 percent say their best friend (not including family members) is also in the congregation, compared to only 39 percent of all church members.

"If there's one thing I've learned from social work, you see these houses and you can't always tell what the people are like inside," Rich said as he neared his home. He talked about how people pass judgment about others from what they see from outside features, such as garages (already a criterion), paved driveways (a new prerequisite; those homes with paved parking to their garage or carport are in the majority), and tidy lawns.

As staying in Rich's house was making for my deepest immersion into everyday family living on my journey, I was taking as many notes as I could about what resonated with the Bean family, which is how, by the next evening, I would have many more criteria for J. Average, based on topics discussed in and around the home.

In 2002, Gallup reported that among Americans, the "favorite way to spend the evening" was in the home, as the top responses were watching television, videos, or DVDs (26 percent); staying home with family (25 percent); reading (9 percent); and relaxing (9 percent: Are these activities not calming enough that we also need a "relaxing" category?). While he waited for his Election Day results, Rich gave me a casual tour of his house, during which he noted that the building had recently turned 100 years old, and that it now includes more rooms than when it was built. "I can't see living here without [the extension]," he said.

The average American home is thirty years old. Working out in ten-year increments to capture the majority, J. Average's home would be between ten and fifty years old. The Census Bureau reports that, based on the median, American homes have 5.3 rooms, a measurement that counts only areas used for "living purposes" and so excludes bathrooms, foyers, hallways, open porches, Pullman kitchens, unfinished attics and basements, and similar areas. Fifty-five percent of homes have between four and six living-purpose rooms, as would the home of the Average American. Two more majority criteria: The home would also have a kitchen and at least one full bathroom.

Rich and I talked about how New York may be a commonality, but that our neighborhoods are hardly alike, starting with their hours-long separation. Rich said he is fine with living on his old block. Most Americans live within fifty miles of where they spent the most time growing up, another criterion.

During the time I stayed in their household, the Beans talked about the miscellany of American life: laundry, dishwashing, showering, brushing teeth, dental appointments, a Christmas tree, and credit and ATM cards. More than 200 million Americans have ATM cards and more than 185 million have at least one credit card (and most households carry credit-card debt). All staples in most Americans' lives, each of these items became a qualification for J. Average. The Christmas tree and dental appointment would each need to happen annually; the showering and teeth brushing, daily. Like most Americans, J. Average would need to have a clothes washer, dryer, and automatic dishwasher.

On November 1, Becky launched into a discussion of the Internet and said that she had even been bonding with her children by playing computer games with them. In 2001, the percentage of the population using the Internet passed 50 percent for the first time. Today, over 90 percent of those aged five to seventeen use computers. J. Average would have this access, and would be someone who has played computer or video games over the past year, as have most Americans.

Rich and his son talked sports. But I would be able to apply only two spectator sports—football, which Rich played in high school, and baseball—as favored by the Average American. Since 2001, according to Gallup, they have been the only two sports attracting a majority of Americans as fans. Professional football is in the lead, with 64 percent of Americans as fans, including 51 percent of females. According to the National Sports Goods Association, exercise walking is the nation's top participatory sports activity—yes, it counts—but less than 50 percent of the population say it's a "sport" they do.

*On Election Day,* across from the boys and girls bathrooms at an Olean elementary school, in a converted room normally used for storage, Rich voted for himself by pulling the Average American

Party lever. "I didn't just vote for Democrats," he told me after he emerged from behind the curtain. He would later elaborate: "In college, one of my professors told me, 'Your butt must be really sore.' He said that's what must happen when someone sits on the fence a lot. I've always been a moderate. That doesn't mean my views are any weaker than anybody else's. I think the more informed you are, the more the chance that you'll end up in the middle. It should be a badge of honor."

Those Americans with more extreme views are more apt to vote, but voters and citizens alike are overwhelmingly centrist in their ideology. Since 1972, National Election Studies has asked Americans to place their ideological views on a scale from one to seven, from "extremely liberal" to "extremely conservative." In 2000 and 2004, the majority of respondents chose either three, four, or five, with four receiving the most votes. This was true of respondents from both "blue" and "red" states and of both voters and nonvoters. In 2000's "Bowling Alone," Robert Putnam wrote, "Ironically, more and more Americans describe their political views as middle of the road or moderate, but the more polarized extremes on the ideological spectrum account for a bigger and bigger share of those who attend meetings, write letters, serve on committees and so on." The Average American would generally consider himself or herself a moderate, regardless of any political party membership. When I learned about the seven-point scale, a three, four, or five became my guide.

Wrote Morris Fiorina, the author of the 2005 book *Culture War? The Myth of a Polarized Nation,* "The simple truth is that there is no culture war in the United States—no battle for the soul of America rages, at least none that most Americans are aware of. . . . A polarized political class makes the citizenry appear polarized, but it is only that—an appearance. . . . The most plausible explanation is that culture wars, two nations, and similar exaggeration make an excellent story line for the media." Indeed, *USA Today* noted in 2000 that the presidential election results that year would leave half of the nation "seething" and the other half "cheering."

What's often unreported is that in political surveys, there is often a large percentage of respondents who do not pick a side. For example, in a 2005 Pew Research survey that asked Americans to rate the Democratic Party on a scale of one to six, from very conservative to very liberal, 10 percent wouldn't choose (and 20 percent chose six, although only 4 percent classified themselves as sixes). The survey was especially interesting because, without a middle number, respondents had to go right or left when describing the party (most went left, and the most popular response was middle-hugging four). In a 2005 Democracy Corps poll, 27 percent of Americans would not say which of the two major parties they more closely associated with (for those who did answer, the Democratic Party led by 10 percentage points over the Republican Party). Also, according to polling, in most elections the candidates are more left or right of center than the public prefers, which helps explain why, in a 2001 Democratic Leadership Council survey, 63 percent of Americans said they would be more inclined to support centrist candidates.

Today, the image of a divided country—although triggered by both Democrats and Republicans in Washington—has been shored up by the president and many administration backers as a result of many of their staunch right-of-center activities. In 2004, 67 percent of Americans described President Bush as conservative or very conservative, but only 39 percent described themselves as the same (and only 7 percent described themselves as very conservative). The same year, a *Los Angeles Times* poll found that 58 percent of Americans believed that President Bush's life experiences had not prepared him to "understand the day-to-day problems of the average American." The same percentage felt that Bush had divided the country. In a June 2005 Opinion Dynamics poll, 54 percent of Americans said they believed that Congress was not in touch with the country.

Around that time, the president and his conservative congressional brethren were, according to Gallup numbers, arguably out of touch with the average American on such issues as abortion (65 percent of Americans preferred to keep in place the legal right of women to choose), the war in Iraq (58 percent disapproved of the president's handling of the war), terrorism (54 percent said that the war in Iraq had made the United States less safe or no more safe from terrorism), social security reform (54 percent disapproved of the president's proposal), euthanasia (75 percent, including the majority of evangelical Christians, favored the right to die), economic policies (73 percent claimed Bush's policies were hurting or not having much effect), and science (60 percent approved of using stem cells from human embryos for medical research).

Rich's alderman race was in the last column of the ballot. And with the Average American Party listed as the last of eleven parties, he was concerned. "If you look at the ward race, the Average American line is pretty much out of eyesight," he said. "I wonder if most people even saw that lever."

Sixty-eight percent of the registered voters in Rich's ward would come out to the polls. Walking out of the elementary school, Rich ran into a spry older citizen who had unsuccessfully run for alderman as a Democrat a few years back.

"You're dressed the part," the woman said, looking Rich up and down. Rich was wearing dark shoes, white socks, worn blue corduroy pants, a faded shirt with a college insignia, and a leather jacket. His "I Voted" sticker was crooked, and his thinning hair was heading in many different directions.

"Ann, what are you talking about?" Rich asked.

"When I ran, I was going door to door," the lady replied. "One woman said, 'I can't vote for you. Look at your clothes. You're too affluent.' I said, 'I just came from work.' She said, 'Sorry, can't vote for you.' Jeans versus suits, Rich, these are the choices that shape our democratic process." Mr. Q spoke up again to point out that Americans own seven pairs of jeans. At least one pair needed to be in the Average American's wardrobe.

Rich returned home to wait until all the votes were in. His friend Mike volunteered to pick up the results as soon as they were ready and to hand-deliver them back to the house.

Becky was hammering away on the computer when Mike returned. Rich was on the sofa eating Doritos. The girls were playing the game of Life on the family-room floor. Their eyes all turned to Mike.

"You did a hell of a job, buddy," Mike said to his best friend. "But it doesn't look like the votes are there. Let's not forget there are still some absentees."

Of the 764 votes cast that day, 352 went to Rich, almost all under his Democratic affiliation.

Rich headed to the Republican Party headquarters, where a short-haired woman with a bright red sweater—the winner—looked surprised to see him, and to hear his concession.

"I'm glad we know each other a little bit better now," he told her.

At Democratic headquarters, a couple of officials told Rich he was wrong for conceding. One announced in front of a group of about twenty that the Republicans down the street were in party mode. A woman in a "No Bush—No Dick" T-shirt started to boo. "I need to go home," Rich said.

At the Bean household, Rich found his youngest daughter and smiled. "Sarah, the Average American Party got eleven votes," he said.

"That's cool," she squeaked, jumping to her feet and galloping toward her dad.

Each of five established minor parties on the ballot of nine races—the Green, Libertarian, Socialist Workers, Builders, and Peace and Justice parties—failed to garner as many votes as the Average American Party did, so they may be on to something.

From a shopping bag, I pulled a little treat for the Bean kids—a gallon of chocolate milk and a gallon of strawberry, representing the two gallons of flavored milk that the average American downs in a year. "It'll last a day," Rich said.

"I've got some headphones for my TV upstairs," Ben said. He had graciously given up his upstairs room to me for two nights. "You know, in case you want to watch the vote for president."

I fell asleep at about five in the morning, when the national race was still being decided, and was awakened by Becky's knock on the door. Near Ben's bed, over a photo of him in hockey gear, was a Cub Scout award called Arrow of Light, St. Mary's of the Angels Roman Catholic Church. By now, I had realized that my very consciously catholic journey had once again taken on a Catholic flavor.

"Ben likes going to church," Becky explained downstairs, with an eye on her daycare kids. "But he prefers another church that's an hour away from here. It's in Maypole, where I grew up. I told him, 'Ben, we can't drive that far every weekend when there's a church close by.' He said, 'What, an hour is too far to drive for God?'"

Is religion important?

"I think it's more than important; I think it's necessary," she said. "There is a certain divinity at play in our lives. I don't think we can deny that. You know, Rich was real disappointed he didn't win yesterday. But I told him, 'You're still a voice. God has a reason for the path you take. Maybe they need someone at council meetings in the audience who is going to push and question and play that role.' Rich has done that and he can continue to. We have to have faith that we are on a purposeful path even when we don't recognize that's the case.

"You know, I can tell you this now: I have a friend who works at the newspaper and I told him we had a guest. He said, 'What do you know about this guy?' He said you could be some crazed maniac. I told him, 'You know, I prayed about it and got a certain sense it was just something we should offer.' But I don't know if we're any different than most people. . . . Growing up, my family never turned people away."

Most Americans say they would "do a favor for a stranger." If a finalist in my search would not answer at least a couple of questions about his or her life for me, a stranger, then maybe that person should not be the Average American.

When Sarah Bean waltzed by, I congratulated her on the first eleven votes received by the party she named. I asked her for her version of how she came to name it Average American.

"My dad said average Joe, and I thought that was just about guys," she said. "There can also be a Mrs. Average, so that makes more sense."

You need to look long and hard to find a female portrayal of a literal most average person. One exception comes courtesy of comedian Lily Tomlin and her Illinois suburban mom character, "Average American Mrs. Judith Beasley." For a 1990 television special, a tribute to Oprah Winfrey on ABC, Beasley, wearing a conservative blue suit and blouse and a high hairdo, said that although she is "quite a mover and shaker on my own block in Calumet City [Illinois], I am not, as they say, in the loop."

The same could be said for Rich Bean and his earliest campaign plans. On a promotional flyer, Rich had included the line "The Best Man for the Job!"—forgetting that his chief opponent was a woman.

From colonial times through the 1940 census, there were more males than females in the country. Females have been in the majority ever since, in part because of the combat deaths of military men. In 2002, there were about 6 million more female than male U.S. residents, bringing the female percentage to 51 percent. The Census Bureau projects that females will remain in the majority until at least 2050.

Most teachers are female. Most voters are female. For many years, Gallup pollsters have asked men and women what job they would suggest if a child came to them seeking career advice. In 1950, only 2 percent would encourage girls to seek a career as a medical doctor. In 2005, at 20 percent, medicine was the top suggestion for girls. Nearly twice as many women as men chose medicine as the best career advice for girls. Should the Average American be a woman too?

"That's a tough one," Becky said.

In 1998, when women were asked in a *Time*/CNN poll about the "main problem" facing them today, inequity—in the workplace and with men in general—was the category with the highest response. My search seemed an appropriate opportunity for some equity. On account of the nation's female majority, if more than one person matched my profile, I decided I would go with Jane and not Joe Average.

Speaking of her own daughters, Becky said, "I know this sounds cliché, but I just want them to be happy and to rise above where we are." Most Americans are at least as well off financially as their parents were, another search criterion. In 2002, *American Demographics* reported that 80 percent of adults today say that they "have done as well as or better than their own parents financially," although only 65 percent "are as certain that the next generation of adults will be as well-off." According to a fascinating 2005 *New York Times* series on class in America, most of the population believes that compared to their parents they are experiencing a "standard of living" that is either "much better" (39 percent) or "somewhat better" (27 percent). Compared to their social class when they were growing up, most also believe that their class is now either higher (45 percent) or the same (38 percent). A 2005 Pew Research poll found that 59 percent of Americans do not believe the country is divided into a society of "haves" and "have nots," although a separate 1999 survey found that most Americans believe it is "very common" to find parents who "sacrifice and work hard so their kids can have a better life."

Although the phrase "the American Dream" can have many meanings to Americans, a 2004 study commissioned by the National League of Cities reported that 63 percent of Americans believe they are living it and 62 percent believe it is achievable for most Americans. Of those who do not believe they are living the American Dream, 42 percent said they believe they will one day. Wrote the *National Review*'s Bruce Bartlett of the study, "For most, [the American Dream] means a good job and financial security. But somewhat surprisingly, living in freedom came in second. And when people were given a chance to mention what they felt are the two important factors in the American Dream, living in freedom was the most frequently mentioned."

Becky noted—as do most people when asked what makes them happy—that family is paramount to her. "We will always have each other for unconditional support," she said. Most Americans have at least one living parent, and the majority also has at least one living sibling, two more search criteria. This first statistic has risen dramatically among all age groups. In 1900, only 7 percent of sixty-year-olds had a living parent. The average U.S. life span has increased by more than thirty years since 1900, and today, nearly 45 percent of American sixty-year-olds have a living parent, and that number also continues to rise. For those Americans up to age forty-five, more than 90 percent have a living parent.

Before I departed for the long drive to New York City, Sarah sat down next to her mother and said she wanted to tell me about the difference between boys and girls in her class.

"At lunch, one class is supposed to sit at one table and the other fifth-grade class at another table," she said, twirling her long frizzled locks with her index finger. "Instead, all the boys sit at the boys' table and the girls sit at the rest of the tables. And one time, they decided to take over the girls' table. They're not as nice as the girls."

I promised to put her theory to a test. I would try to track down a real Mrs. Average and ask her some questions.

*Carmella Average?*

"Yes, speaking."

Back in my home office, after scouring nationwide public records online, I had found confirmation of one Mrs. Average, in Brooklyn, New York, a borough just out of view of my window. I phoned, told her what I was up to, and asked if I could swing by the most Average home I could find.

"You need to talk to my husband," Carmella said. "It's his name. I just got stuck with it. Can you call back later?"

On the redial, eighty-eight-year-old Harry Average answered. "Nothing we can't handle over the phone, I say," he said. I thought to myself, I would need to prepare a better approach if I wanted to find the Average American, such as only contacting the finalists in person.

I learned that Harry is one of only three Averages that he knows exists: himself, his wife, and a son in California who was unmarried and childless. His two daughters were married with different names.

Could I speak with Mrs. Average?

"I think she gave you her answer," Harry said.

Harry, born in Fall River, Massachusetts, moved to Brooklyn when he was still a kid. He said he only had a year or two of schooling, never making it through elementary school, and, as far as he recalled, never wrote his surname until he was in his teens.

"It was 1932 and I heard about the CCC," he said, referring to the Civilian Conservation Corps. "You probably don't know much about that." Wasn't it started by President Roosevelt?

"Don't talk to me about FDR," Harry said. "He's the reason Pearl Harbor happened. He threw the Japanese ambassadors out of his office. Next thing you know, they were bombing us. Ever since then, I have voted Republican."

The CCC, an organization created by FDR in which young men helped revitalize the nation's forests by planting 3 million trees, among other conservation tasks, required identification for new hires. "My mother found my birth certificate," Harry said. "I went to work with it. It said Harry Average. Then, I knew."

He never knew before then that his name was Average?

"Times were different then," he said. "All I knew is that I was Irish, English, and Jewish. But when I started working, I had to start using my name.

"My kids have asked me why I never changed the name. I said, 'That's what my mom gave me.' I am not going to disrespect my mom. Plus, I asked them, 'What am I going to change it to? Ginsburg? Galupi?' Say, how did you get this phone number?"

I said it was in a directory.

"So if we were unlisted, you wouldn't be needing us?"

Well noted. As do roughly 65 percent of Americans, the Average American needed to have a listed phone number for his residence.

So, about the one woman of the Average household . . .

"Why do you keep talking about my wife?" Harry said.

Fine. So what was it that Harry liked about Republican viewpoints?

"I didn't say I like Republicans," he said. "I said I hate Democrats. These Democrats, they are still talking about doing all they can to help the working man. That's always been nonsense. At least the Republicans don't say, 'No one else cares about workers but us.' I think they're at least more honest.

"And I do give the Republicans more credit for speaking out about how to keep children on the right path. I've got seven grandchildren, three great grandchildren. And I think with all this hoopla—you know, with these Britney Spears people, and Madonna and all that garbage—they aren't being given the best role models. And I felt the same thing forty years ago about Elvis."

Did Frank Sinatra pass the test?

"Sinatra, the man, was a disgrace."

So who are today's role models?

"People you've never heard of. The family member who took me and my wife on vacation five years ago just out of the goodness of her heart." Harry was helping me out a lot, despite his reluctance. On average, Americans take thirteen vacation days a year, and 70 percent of Americans plan a summer vacation. The Average American would need to take annual vacation time.

"But I have no respect for these people like what's their name, Alex [sic] Baldwin, and Sarandon, and this guy Springsteen. So you can act and sing? So *what*? Why does that make them an expert about what voters need? How about putting someone on my TV who can actually relate to voters? It's disgusting. That Alex Baldwin said if the election didn't go his way, he'd move to France. I hope he's packing. I don't want to see his face anymore."

A 2005 Opinion Dynamics poll would find that 72 percent of Americans believe that Hollywood is out of touch with "the life of the average American." So why does Harry Average still watch What's-his-face Baldwin and others he doesn't like?

"I can't help it. They come on my TV. I'm retired twenty years now, so I put the TV on a lot. Today, people know more about what celebrities think than they know about what their own family members think. What do you think that tells us?"

A lot. So being an ordinary American is okay?

"Of course it's okay! But the media, they only listen to those who have an ax to grind. That's all we see. I don't trust 5 percent of what I see in the media." On his not trusting the media, he is with the majority of American adults, according to a recent Pew Research poll. However, much as the public's anger at political parties stems from actions of politicians and not necessarily party-affiliated voters, the survey may be a sign that people are frustrated with the news media in general, but not with actual reporters.

By applying the traditional Kohlberg morality scale, which determines the respondent's degree of moral development (the test poses many questions about what to do when facing certain moral dilemmas), a 2004 study by Louisiana State University and University of Missouri educators found that journalists are more ethical than the average American adult. The reporters' scores increased with their autonomy from higher-ups. The same year, a Gallup survey found that more than seven out of ten Americans believe that journalists' honesty and ethical standards are average or above average (although television and newspaper reporters tied for eleventh among twenty-one professions in "very high" honesty and ethics in the public's assessment, well behind nurses and grade-school teachers, who ranked first and second). In the university study, the news journalists placed fourth among twenty-one groups, behind only seminarians, practicing physicians, and medical students. At the bottom of the scale were prisoners and junior-high students.

Harry met his wife in Brooklyn when he was a teenager. She's a couple of years younger than him. "She's Italian," Harry said. "My wife loves to cook and she still cooks for me. Lasagna, cannoli, you name it.

"Don't get me wrong. I'm not what you would call a connoisseur. I'm not impressed with a guy who says you need to have chicken a certain way. I'm interested in chicken to eat it, period. Food was meant for survival, not fancy dishes. You don't have to go far for a decent meal."

Like where?

"If I need to, McDonald's is close by."

In his 2001 book *Fast Food Nation*, Eric Schlosser notes that each month more than 90 percent of Americans between the ages of three and nine go to a McDonald's. Most Americans eat at McDonald's. I would also find that most Americans live within 3 miles of a McDonald's. The Average American would need to be in both majorities.

"I was in the food business, forty-two years," Harry said. He worked for Sucrest, a sugar refinery in Brooklyn. "Packing department, hands-on labor."

So, he's a sugar connoisseur?

"Oh no. I remember I was at the supermarket about thirty years ago. This woman in front of me bought sugar, but it wasn't our brand. It was thirty cents more expensive. She said her mother had always bought it because it was the best. I told the lady, 'Let me let you in on a secret. Sugar is sugar. It's all the same. The sugar from my place just costs less.' It made her think.

"That's like people who complain about big stores like Wal-Mart and Costco coming to where they are. The way I look at it, we need the big places. I like the Costco here. We also have some nice small stores in our neighborhood. I still go to the drugstore here. But there shouldn't be any hoopla about the big stores if the argument is just about prices. The big places are saving us money."

As they are, it would seem, for most Americans. There are now more Wal-Marts in the United States than colleges. More than one of every five retail dollars in the United States is spent at Wal-Mart, where more than 80 percent of Americans shop each year. In 2002, Wal-Mart saved Americans a total of about $20 billion, and nearly $8 billion more from discounts that other stores had to offer in order to compete with the retail giant, according to an analysis by New England Consulting. The same year, Gallup asked Americans, "If there were a Wal-Mart, K-Mart or Target store located about the same distance from your home, where would you prefer to shop?" Fifty-two percent chose Wal-Mart. The Average American would need to live within a twenty-minute drive of a Wal-Mart, and shop there annually, as do most Americans.

McDonald's and Wal-Mart just happen to be the two leading businesses where most Americans make purchases each year, and they can now be found under the same roof in some locations.* Wal-Mart's influence on other everyday-item stores is significant. According to ACNielsen, those U.S. households purchasing items at traditional convenience stores or gas-station stores is falling, from

---

*Wal-Mart and McDonald's are also the nation's two largest employers. With 1.4 million U.S. employees in 2004, Wal-Mart had more employees than the third, fourth, and fifth largest U.S. employers—UPS, Ford, and GM—combined, and

50 percent to 46 percent between 1999 and 2002 alone, and the drugstore percentage, although in the majority, also dropped during the same span. Today, about eight out of ten retail shoppers are female and, starting in 2003, women have made up the majority of online shoppers, too.

Incidentally, we can forget the notion that there is a cartful of specific product brands to which most Americans are loyal. Toothpaste is used by more than 99 percent of the U.S. population, but at last count, neither Colgate nor Crest products, the market leaders, were being used by more than 40 percent of the population. Coke or Pepsi? Each controls less than 45 percent of the U.S. soda market. Jif, the leading peanut-butter brand in the United States, accounts for less than 35 percent of U.S. peanut-butter sales. Even Tide, that iconic brand for the mythical average American family, has less than 40 percent of the nation's laundry detergent market. For a rare example of brand dominance today, we can always look to Microsoft Windows, the operating system that is in more than 75 percent of the nation's personal computers.

So, what is average about the Average household?

"People don't think I'm average," Harry said. "I'm only five-foot-two. When I tried to get in the Navy, I was told I was too short. When I tried to work for the telephone company, I was too short. You talk about prejudice. That's the way it was in the thirties. When the war came along, they didn't hesitate to draft me. I wasn't too short then, was I? They made me a cook."

The average American female grows to about 5 feet 4 inches, the average American male to about 5 feet 9-1/2 inches. To safely capture both averages, I determined that the Americans in the middle majority are between 5 feet 3 inches and 5 feet 10-1/2 inches, another search criterion. (Interestingly, as Malcolm Gladwell reported in his 2005 bestseller *Blink,* although only about 14.5 percent of

more employees than there are people in the U.S. military. Twenty-five years earlier, the nation's five largest employers were, in order of rank, GM, Ford, GE, IT&T, and IBM.

men are 6 feet or taller, 58 percent of Fortune 500 CEOs are, and in the business world, each additional inch translates to an extra $789 a year in salary.)

Harry would find another issue with large sizes. He asked about my project and I mentioned that the New York City metropolitan area was still on my search map. "The Average American can't be from around here," Harry said. "That's stupid. It's too big," he chuckled. "The average American from a big metropolis." All right. Tough crowd. I decided to cut off all but the nation's middle majority of populated areas.

We talked for a bit about war, and I began to feel that I had covered a lot of these topics before—not just in this conversation, but elsewhere. The feeling continued. I already had criteria for these issues. Was my search coming to a close? I still needed to check out the congressional election results, and I still had to calculate and apply the new population criterion. But, for all I knew, maybe I already had too many criteria, enough to eliminate everyone in the United States.

"I think we have a bad connection," Harry said. Actually, I recognized the sound. Someone was hitting the keypad on a phone, and it wasn't in my office. I could hear him fine.

"No, I think we have a bad connection," he said. "Listen." And the keypad was immediately punched again.

Several years ago, while working at a public relations firm, two young entrepreneurs in Connecticut had come to me with a hand-sized device they had invented. When attached to the phone, a button could fake the sound of an incoming call. They called it Gotta Go. I won the business, we got tons of publicity for the product, and the account was a finalist for a big annual PR award. The shindig was held at the United Nations. At the event, Dave, one of the inventors, drink in hand, looked out the window beside me. "You know, I didn't want to tell you this, but we're not really making a lot of money on the product," he said. "Do we really understand what Americans want?" I didn't at the time, but while I was on the phone with Mr. Average, I thought of someone about an hour south of New York City who might.

The numbers on the phone were punched again.

"I think that's a good sign we need to wrap this up," Harry said.

He was right. It was time to let him go, quit following signs, and really see if anyone could perfectly match my J. Average profile. I knew where I needed to head next: Princeton, New Jersey.

# Eleven

# SON OF THE FATHER
# OF THE AVERAGE
# AMERICAN

*Candidates remaining: fewer than 500,000*

*I was in Princeton* to meet the son of the father of the average American.

By taking opinion polling mainstream in the 1930s, George Gallup was the first to give a regular, coherent, and—this is important—consistently accurate voice to the nation's ordinary. His son, George Gallup, Jr., is the longtime chairman of the Gallup Organization and now head of the nonprofit Gallup Institute.

On a pleasant mid-November morning at the Gallup headquarters, executive assistant Marie Swirsky joined me by a large picture window to tell me that the boss had just made it through a long line to receive his flu shot and thus was running late.

No worries. I could use a break before going over things with Gallup. Over the previous day, while on the train and in my Princeton hotel room, I had been busy factoring the Election Day results and other criteria into my ever-narrowing search. I hadn't slept and was anxious to finish the tabulations.

My mind still reeled. I had already discovered quite a bit. Residents of many states had been dismissed. And, mercifully, the population criterion I had been handed by Harry Average did not eliminate the rest of the nation from my search. By focusing on those population areas in the middle majority of the nation, all metropolitan areas with more than 6 million residents—the top six metro areas—and all metro areas with populations under 100,000 were cut (and all nonmetro areas, except they were already gone). The New York City metropolis, the largest in the nation, had disappeared, taking the remainder of New York state and large slices of Connecticut and New Jersey with it. The other areas that would be dismissed from my search map were the Washington-Baltimore and Philadelphia metropolises (the other top-six metro areas are Los Angeles, Chicago, and San Francisco).

Examining my maps in my Princeton hotel room, I had made an even bigger discovery. The only places that could remain in any form were pockets of Connecticut, in three metropolitan areas there. Two of the metro areas (Hartford and New London–Norwich) were centered in Connecticut, and one (Boston-Worcester) reached into the state from neighboring Massachusetts. I stayed up all night, mesmerized by the maps. There are more than 250 metropolitan areas in the United States. I had not only grown up in Connecticut, but in *northeastern* Connecticut, which all three of the remaining metro areas had seeped into like spilt milk. It was almost worth crying over: This was not supposed to be how it worked out, and I was not thrilled. I had begun this journey to discover an America I had not seen before, that I had not understood well enough, and here I was, despite all my work, headed straight back home. Even when I ran the numbers again, over and over in the weeks ahead, I kept ending up in the same area. I couldn't argue with the criteria that I had picked up over the many previous months. I'd accepted guidance from the Americans I had met along the road, worked their concerns into my research in what I was sure was a sound, careful way, and I couldn't dispute the conclusions. Although I seriously thought about it, I couldn't get a redo.

*Marie had me wait* on a sofa outside George Gallup's office. On the walls, an assortment of vintage photographs showed pollsters interviewing ordinary Americans. In one, a laundry deliveryman was being interviewed; in another, a policeman.

On my laptop at the Gallup building, I needed to preview the remaining suburban census neighborhoods in Connecticut to see if any were average. As previously discussed, to fit the average description, a census neighborhood needed to hit the same majority statistics—those that were knowable anyway—that had been listed as criteria for the Average American. For example, most of the residents of the census neighborhood would have to be age eighteen through fifty-three, and most of the residents needed to be in the same home as five years previously.

I had a database, in DVD form, produced by the Census Bureau, that statistically profiled all the census neighborhoods in the United States. With the Connecticut tracts running west to east, each successive page revealed a tract number and its demographics. When a tract matched the Average American statistics, everything from age to income to home value, I would hit an icon that read "Show on Map." This would unveil a map of the neighborhood itself. Once I had the location, I could do some follow-up research to determine whether the neighborhood hit my search's non-census majorities, such as being within 2 miles of a public park and having at least one church. But so far, there were no perfect matches.

With just over twenty census neighborhoods left from more than 65,000 in the United States and more than 800 in Connecticut, I found a possible match. Tract 09-015-8005.

On my computer, I hit the "Show on Map" icon. A colorful computerized map appeared. I took a closer look. I recognized a couple of street names, then spotted the town name: I needed to run the program again. The census neighborhood was in Windham, a suburb of Hartford, and one town south of where I grew up.

"Find anything interesting?" came a chipper voice from behind the sofa a couple of minutes later. Although the voice sounded like that of a young adult, bending slightly forward toward the computerized map was seventy-four-year-old George Gallup, Jr. A tall man with white hair, he had the same type of thick eyebrows, blue eyes, and facial features that stood out in a portrait of his father that had appeared on the cover of *Time* magazine six decades earlier.

*The first thing you notice* walking into Gallup's office is an enormous black and white photograph hanging behind his desk. The picture shows a farmer being interviewed by a Gallup pollster.

As I would later realize, the early milestones in the life of Gallup's late dad, the son of a farmer, can perhaps best be plotted with the rise in peanut butter's popularity. Gallup was born in Iowa in 1901, the year of the first known peanut-butter-and-jelly sandwich (its recipe was first published that year). He started his career at a St. Louis advertising agency in 1922, the year that peanut butter first hit store shelves; finished his education at the University of Iowa in 1928, the year that, as far as is known, peanut butter and chocolate were first eaten together; and in 1935, the year chunky peanut butter was introduced, started a polling business. This business would collect thousands of answers about American viewpoints over the years that would run the gamut from serious issues of the day, such as opinions on military activities and political campaigns, to, in one 2005 report, the merits of peanut butter versus shrimp as America's "most romantic" meal. His first formal poll question may have been posed while he was an editor of the student newspaper in college, to determine who was the prettiest girl on campus. The poll winner, Ophelia Smith Miller, became Gallup's wife.

Glancing at the picture over his desk, their son said, "It reminds me of how much more powerful it is to poll people in person. Face-to-face interaction is always preferable."

In 1935, the senior Gallup convinced many newspapers to run a weekly feature of in-person national poll results. The column was titled "America Speaks!" and highlighted results that were tabulated and supplied by Gallup's new business in Princeton. The day the first "America Speaks!" column ran, the *Washington Post* promoted it by flying a blimp over the city with the news. Gallup was able to land newspaper contracts by promising to reimburse the publishers for their investment in the column if, leading up to the 1936 election, he failed to predict who would be elected president. His chief competition at the time was a magazine called *Literary Digest.* The magazine was going all out to predict the election, mailing 10 million ballots to Americans who were on the magazine's mailing list and listed in phone directories or on automobile registration lists. Nearly 2.5 million of the ballots were filled out and returned. Gallup's team surveyed only 5,000 Americans, but all in person.

After examining his results, Gallup announced that Franklin D. Roosevelt would win. *Literary Digest* announced that Republican challenger Alf Landon would carry 57 percent of the vote. Roosevelt won handily. *Literary Digest* was thoroughly embarrassed and, in what some believed to be a related move, soon after went out of business. Gallup became a media darling, and polling was finally understood to be an accurate, interesting barometer of average American attitudes. After Gallup correctly chose the winner of the next two presidential elections, *Time* magazine dubbed him "the Babe Ruth of the polling profession."

It was Gallup's belief that his scientific work had led to "the redemption of the common man." His son explained that there was more to his father's success than just the face-to-face method. "What made him successful right from the start is that he understood representative sampling and probability theory," Gallup, Jr., said. Instead of simply interviewing a group of people in 1936, Gallup, Sr., had made sure he had an appropriate representation of the country, the right mixture of, say, upper-income males, lower-income females, and so on.

The 1936 election took place in the middle of the Great Depression, and those contacted by *Literary Digest* were predominantly wealthy Americans who could afford such luxuries as magazines, automobiles, and telephones during that time, and who generally leaned Republican. Gallup had shown that accuracy wasn't about the volume of Americans surveyed, but about who was asked. Indeed, today when a poll result paints the average American as crude in some way, it often lacks representative sampling. There are many online surveys that claim "America" has, say, an addiction to beer and/or porn. These polls are regularly solicited from niche websites aimed at certain young males, where the audience is already interested in the subject.

"My dad saw the average American as representative of the majority," Gallup said. "And to be representative of the majority, you need to have a balance that is reflective of the entire country. That majority American is someone I respect enormously."

His dad, almost five decades after he founded the Gallup Poll, had said, "We have found the collective judgment of the people to be extraordinarily sound, especially on issues which come within the scope of the typical person's experience. Often the people are actually ahead of their elected leaders in accepting innovations and radical changes."

*The one census neighborhood* in Connecticut lingered in my mind. I was pretty sure that two McDonald's restaurants were still in the area. I would have to check it out against some other criteria, but it seemed to have potential. If not, there were only a couple dozen more neighborhoods left to examine.

Gallup wanted to know how my search was progressing. I had contacted him before I ever hit the road, thinking that maybe I should visit before I really got started, but he had said my search sounded like a personal quest and asked that I stop by his office only when I felt that it was coming to a close.

In his office, we reviewed my travels and findings. I told him that on my computer, I only needed to shuttle through some remaining neighborhoods in eastern Connecticut, and that the Average American could very well be there.

"I wouldn't be surprised," Gallup said. "I was in that part of the state for a week back in the seventies. Voting demographics in one area there matched the nation as a whole." He said he had done his work there in tandem with the editor of a morning newspaper, the

*Norwich Bulletin.* I knew the paper, the largest daily in eastern Connecticut. I had worked as a reporter there during the only two summers that I had returned to the state during college.

I told Gallup I was actually a bit disappointed to be on the verge of ending up in the far reaches of Connecticut. Somehow I had convinced myself that I would discover a new landscape, not a familiar one, a place so perfectly average that it would even feel exceptional, surreal, filled with treasures of averageness.

"To me, well, it seems like a spiritual journey," Gallup said. Here we go again. "And on spiritual journeys, you find kindred spirits. Trust that you are on the right track." As he reminded me, Gallup had long managed to reconcile the spiritual and the scientific in a way that may surprise—and has even outraged—some people.

Leading up to the 2004 election, an ad critical of Gallup had been placed in the *New York Times* and other media outlets by MoveOn.org, a liberal political action committee unhappy with a Gallup poll of likely voters that had presidential incumbent George W. Bush comfortably ahead of Democrat John Kerry. The ad "outed" Gallup for being an evangelical Christian and displayed a quote from him about how "the most profound purpose of polls is to see how people are responding to God." Gallup had become devout at age nine—he says that is when he first felt the power of God hit him—and later had dreams of being an Episcopalian priest. One summer in college, he had worked as a volunteer Bible teacher and baseball coach at an African American Episcopalian church in Galveston, Texas. He had received his degree in religion from Princeton and has directed many international studies of religious beliefs, or, as he has called it, the inner life.

"I believe the voice of people and the voice of God are one," Gallup told me. "My dad didn't believe that. He was a rational Christian. He once said you could prove God statistically. He felt that God had to be the anti-chance," that there was a greater probability of God's existence than not.

If, as Socrates said to an Athens jury, someone who does not examine his existence to measure its goodness has a life "not worth living," maybe Gallup is happy that the Gallup Poll helps fill this role. "A poll is people, and people, by and large, are good," Gallup explained. "Every time I hear a politician say that he doesn't listen to the polls, I interpret that as his saying, 'I don't listen to people.'"

Said Gallup, "We hear about the common person not having made a mark on society. Or someone who is but a ripple in the ocean of humanity. But by whose standards are they marginalized? They do have great influence and experience great satisfaction through personal experiences. The way they raise children, for example. That gives them a sense of meaning and purpose. They have sacrificed time on other activities to mold our future. Such average gifts may not attract a lot of attention, but does that mean they are not worthy? In many respects, maybe they are even more worthy than those who receive attention. They should not lack self-esteem because of feeling part of the aggregate. No matter how truly ordinary we may be, each of us will always have a clear individuality."

And part of that individuality, he explained a few minutes later, may include occasionally keeping mum. "I would venture that most Americans have at least one secret," Gallup said. In 1999, one poll determined that 63 percent of American adults had kept secrets from their parents when they were teenagers, and even among married couples, the number keeping secrets from their spouse is high. A 2001 survey reported that 40 percent of spouses were in this category. Did I stand a chance of finding out all the information I wanted to about the Average American? And would the status of the Average American stay intact if he held some kind of secret during my investigative process and it was later revealed? I took Gallup's broad smile as agreement.

So who is the most average American Gallup has ever met?

He paused. "As you can see, I've never thought of that question before," he apologized. "My grandmother; my dad's mom," he said a few seconds later. "She was religious. She worshipped FDR. She had high values and was a great mother and a great homemaker. She overcame personal hardships, but still did things right. She was a painter; an artist. She loved animals. She was positive. Her name was Nattie. She died fifty years ago."

It was Gallup, Jr.'s, other grandmother, Olga Babcock Miller—the mother of the prettiest girl at the University of Iowa—who inspired his dad's interest in polling. Miller was running to become Iowa's secretary of state, and Gallup saw surveying as a way for her to target potential voters during the campaign. With Gallup's help, Miller became the first female to hold the office, although she ran as a Democrat in a Republican-heavy state.

Since the 1936 presidential election, the Gallup Poll has served as an especially revealing time capsule of American beliefs, and female-related poll results are indeed among the most telling. In 1938, although the nation was wallowing in the Depression, the poll found that 78 percent of the country was opposed to a married woman working if she had a husband capable of supporting her. A year later, 63 percent of Americans said it was indecent for women to wear shorts in public, whereas most Americans believed that it was acceptable for a man to wear a topless bathing suit on the street. In 1957, Gallup found that 50 percent of Americans thought it inappropriate for a woman to drink alcohol in a public place, such as a restaurant or bar.

Such gender bias is perhaps best dramatized in a 1947 film titled *Magic Town*. Jimmy Stewart plays Rip Smith, a hard-driving Manhattan businessman who is losing business because of his obsession with trying to find one community in America where the demographic makeup perfectly matches the nation. He calls it his "mathematical miracle" theory. His colleagues have other names for it.

"Why don't you give up?" one coworker scoffs. "Stop chasing rainbows."

Rip Smith finds his miracle in a place called Grandview. By interviewing the residents there, Smith is able to successfully determine the national feeling on any and every subject imaginable. All goes smoothly until word gets out that Smith is a pollster and that the town is perfectly average. Many Americans move to Grandview, elated to live in the nation's microcosm. The balance of opinion in Grandview starts to shift, and one day Smith reports that 79 percent of the residents say they would vote for a woman president. The Grandview poll is so preposterous that a newspaper headline screams, "Result Ridiculous." A radio announcer reports that the Grandview poll is "so completely out of tune." In the movie, Gallup reveals a national poll that is nearly the opposite, which destroys Smith's business.

In 1936, a Gallup poll determined that fewer than 35 percent of Americans would vote for a female president. By 1990, Gallup determined the national percentage had hit 80 percent. By 2000, the percentage had topped 90.

"I think polls are just beginning to tap the great wisdom and potential of the average person, his common good," George Gallup, Jr., said.

Bud Roper, after Gallup, Jr., the best-known twenty-first-century pollster, once expressed his outrage that some pollsters dismissed their respondents as "stupid oafs." Also the son of a founding father of polling—starting in the 1930s, his dad Elmo was probably second in industry stature only to George Gallup—Bud Roper once declared, "I'm a big defender of the average American."

Roper died in 2003 and left behind the Roper Center for Public Research, which his father founded in 1947 and of which Roper became chairman. The center, located on the main campus of the University of Connecticut, is the largest public opinion archive in existence. Roper would often take the 150-mile drive from his New York City home to the UConn campus to teach a course in public polling.

The University of Connecticut is also home to the Center for Population Research. Five months before my visit with Gallup, the center had released a study on Connecticut and concluded that, taken as a whole, the state was a demographic mosaic that could not be deemed "ordinary." "The average Connecticut does not exist," said Wayne Villemez, the center's director. This is often the case with states, whose far-flung residents may have less in common with each other than with out-of-state residents in nearby communities. Of course, this fact is often ignored, as the news media continues to be obsessed by the blue state/red state discussion. "It is rather overdone, isn't it?" Gallup offered.

Gallup and I went for a ride through Princeton, a sprawling university town, in his beat-up van, which showed more than 100,000 miles on the odometer. Gallup asked me about where I grew up. UConn was as good an answer as any. My mom and dad, now both retired, had been UConn employees for much of their working lives. I went to a high school that was part of the UConn system, located on the edge of the university campus. Less than 10 miles away is the northern border of the Windham tract that had popped up on my computer about an hour and a half earlier. Outside the census neighborhood, but still in Windham, my three younger brothers had been born in the community hospital, and I had worked down the hill at the town's Dairy Queen.

I had only managed to return home to the area on occasion, about once or twice a year, for the most part. Sadly, I realized, I had not even managed to return home to see my three younger brothers, varsity athletes in high school, for any of their competitions.

"Maybe God is saying you need to go home," George said.

He dropped me off at the Princeton train depot and I thanked him for his support. He worried that my wait for the train to Manhattan was too long, but I told him I was okay sitting in the stationhouse with my computer. While waiting for the train, I finished going through the remainder of the Connecticut tracts, and only one, in the aptly named Plainfield, in the same northeastern Connecticut county where Windham is located, turned out to be a preliminary match. It was part of the Norwich–New London metropolitan area, a region of about 300,000 residents.

Removed from the thick population densities and the many stereotypes of the New York and Boston metropolitan areas they fall between, Plainfield and Windham are two of the twenty-seven towns that make up the part of the state known as the Quiet Corner. On a nighttime satellite map of the Boston to Washington, D.C., metropolitan corridor, the Quiet Corner is easily located; it is the only region that is not lit up like a Christmas tree. Windham is the largest town in the Quiet Corner, with a population of about 23,000. Plainfield has about 8,000 fewer residents.

The Latin words of the Connecticut flag translate to "The Lord who sent us here still watches over us." But when people think of the state, they routinely think of something more secular, the "Gold Coast" residents, those in its southwestern corner, many of whom live in vast luxury and commute to Manhattan to earn fat paychecks. The novel *The Stepford Wives,* and the two movies based on it, portray a creepily idyllic suburbia set in that part of Connecticut. The (literally) fabricated perfection of the fictional town's residents has given America the quintessential unpleasant image of an upscale, conformist bedroom community—a vibe recreated by the current hit television series *Desperate Housewives.* The Quiet Corner is different. As the UConn population study noted, eight established towns in the Gold Coast area sport a combined median household income of $155,655. When Census 2000 was conducted, the Windham and Plainfield tracts each had household incomes within $2,800 of the national median of $41,994.

The Gold Coast, though, is only a small part of the region that is the source of most of what Americans have heard about Connecticut—the western side of the Connecticut River, which cuts the state in half. The world's first written constitution, the model for the U.S. Constitution, was devised there. The west side is where Eli Whitney invented the cotton gin and where P. T. Barnum started the three-ring circus. It is the birthplace of the hamburger, the lollipop, the can opener, the revolver, the sewing machine, and the postage meter, among other everyday American offerings. The world's largest conglomerate (General Electric), a college attended by the last three presidents (Yale), and the nation's most profitable cable television network (ESPN) are there, as is Hartford, the state capital and the nation's insurance center. There are seventy-nine private golf clubs in Connecticut. Seventy-five are in the western half.

The eastern side of the state has its attractions too. The world's first nuclear submarine was from Groton (where a U.S. submarine base is now in danger of closing); the U.S. Coast Guard Academy is in New London; the Mystic Seaport and the Mystic Aquarium are nearby; and the two largest Indian casino resorts on the East Coast, which combined employ about 60,000 people, are also east of the Connecticut River. In Preston, Utopia, the largest movie-studio and theme park outside California has been approved for construction near dairyland. But all these attractions are outside the rustic hills of the Quiet Corner. It's almost as if prioritizing fame is the antithesis of northeastern Connecticut. The area's longtime favorite son, Nathan Hale, a Coventry schoolteacher, became famous because of his undercover work (in 1776, he became the nation's first executed spy, and his last words—"I only regret that I have but one life to give for my country"—have rallied legions of American troops ever since). The UConn men's and women's basketball teams won the NCAA championship in 2004, but a year later, a rule was in place that explicitly forbade UConn coaches and other administrators from automatically classifying themselves as "celebrities" (a state status that would have allowed them to freely profit from endorsements).

Although Connecticut is the most urban of the New England states, two-thirds of its land remains open. Windham and Plainfield, former rural outposts, have, like much of the state, been transformed into suburbia and are closer to Boston and Providence than to New York City. Between 1990 and 2000, twenty-eight of the state's rural towns officially became suburban. Now, Plainfield officials are proposing the construction of a 140,000-seat NASCAR facility.

*The northbound train* finally arrived in Princeton. Four months later, and eight weeks before my self-imposed end-of-April deadline, I took another train north, out of New York City.

With me was the church newsletter my wife had picked up six weeks earlier after Mass a block from our apartment. "As one lives the life of God's grace, it becomes increasingly apparent that what passes for ordinary and commonplace is full of romance and mystery," Father George Rutler, the pastor of the Church of Our Savior, had written in his letter to parishioners. I wondered if I could find the same.

Early in *Magic Town*, Rip Smith decides that to best blend into the most average community in America, he will disguise himself there as a traveling functionary for a Hartford insurance company. "The moment Columbus first sighted land must have been something like this," Smith declares when he gets off the train in Grandview.

As I spotted the Hartford stationhouse from my seat on the train, I thought about my family members. One was waiting for me, and the others had volunteered to share their Connecticut homes with me as I searched for the Average American a short drive from where I was raised. I would finally be home for more than a day.

# Twelve

# THE AVERAGE AMERICAN

*Candidates remaining: fewer than 2,000*

*N*ine years after Mark Twain moved into a showy Victorian mansion in Hartford, Connecticut—the home where he penned *The Adventures of Tom Sawyer* and *The Adventures of Huckleberry Finn,* among other classics—he wrote, "Human nature cannot be studied in cities except at a disadvantage—a village is the place. There you can know your man inside and out—in a city you but know his crust; and his crust is usually a lie."

To continue my journey to know my man—or woman—inside and out, on the day after I arrived in Hartford, deep in a snowstorm that had already blanketed the area, I drove to the village of Windham Center, located about thirty miles from the capital. Set amongst rolling hills, its village green, surrounded by vintage clapboard homes, a post office, a library, a steepled church, and a former inn and tavern, was a vision in white. Snow had been brushed off a large sandwich board advertising a Cub Scout fundraising dinner at the village firehouse just across the street. And as I would start to learn at the dinner—where I sat at a table with one man in overalls and another in a button-down shirt—the locals would mostly suggest that a love for family is the greatest commonality in their lives.

If that sounds pedestrian, there's good reason: The villages of Windham Center and North Windham, and the vast majority of South Windham located in Hartford suburbia, do—as I had begun to suspect earlier—constitute the most statistically average community in America.

Of the two census neighborhoods that had remained as candidates for the nation's most statistically average community, the one within the town of Plainfield could not compete with the Windham villages, the tract that, for my own purposes, I had begun to call "Averageville." Of all the census demographics that were applied, Averageville was closer to the national middle more than 70 percent of the time—for example, with average household size (2.52 people for Averageville, 2.59 for the nation), percentage of residents with at least a high-school degree (80.9 percent, 80.4 percent), those born in the state where they reside (58.3 percent, 60 percent), permanent unattached homes (64.7 percent, 60.3 percent), owner-occupied homes (70.1 percent, 66.2 percent), and those who speak only English at home (79.4 percent, 82.1 percent).

Averageville's annual median household income was only $2,256 over the national standard, and its per capita income $1,634 under. Its annual median family income was $187 over the national mark, and its average commuting time 72 seconds under. Its median home value was $2,600 over, its residents with one or more vehicles 3 percent under, its number of married adults 2 percent over, its number of residents with social-security income 1 percent under, and its average age three years older. Nationally, 69.1 percent of the population is non-Hispanic white, compared to 75.9 percent in Averageville.

The area's nonmajority statistics are similar. Hispanics and blacks, the two most prominent minority groups, each make up more than 10 percent of the population in America and Averageville. Nine out of 100 U.S. families live in poverty, compared to 10 out of every 100 in Averageville. In both the nation and Averageville, those who have attended high school but never graduated make up 12 percent of the population. Nationally, 13 out of every 100 residents are military veterans, compared to 14 out of every 100 in Averageville. After houses, the most common residences in the United States are apartments and mobile homes. In both America and Averageville, they make up between 35 and 40 percent of all homes.

Averageville is a roughly 4-by-6-mile area that actually—I continued to be rattled by this—borders the tract where I grew up. I went to Apollo's, the longtime pizza joint across from the railroad tracks in South Windham. There, I spoke with a Greek woman named Marianna who ran the restaurant with her husband. They had moved to South Windham from their homeland ten years earlier. "We were thinking of calling it Demetri, our son's name," she said, "but I think people here, they like to know things stay the same."

If that's true, they can't always get what they want. In North Windham, on a long street with an aging private airport, a bowling alley, and a public golf course, there is now a public bus route, a Wal-Mart Supercenter, a Sears hardware store, a number of fast-food restaurants, and strip malls with the usual mixture of national chain stores and more unfamiliarly named businesses. In back of the Wal-Mart, Home Depot was preparing to start construction on six and a half acres. The store was approved after guarantees that runoff would not contaminate a nearby swamp of white cedar trees. On the western side of the village, the same busy road now turns to freeway.

There were signs often associated with more rural America. In Averageville, I spotted "Let's Support the Troops" placards on no fewer than forty front lawns, flags honoring late NASCAR driver Dale Earnhardt on three more, and a Dale, Jr., flag on another. There was a pistol and rifle range nearby.

And there were signs often associated with more urban America. Spanish-language posters appeared at various public places in Averageville, such as the H&R Block storefront and at La Inglesia del Sagrado Corazon de Jesus, a Catholic church where Mass is said in Spanish. Elsewhere in the town of Windham, but outside of Averageville, there were plenty of announcements in other languages. I spotted the first ones at a Polish deli and at St. Mary's, a Catholic church that still hosts a weekly French-speaking Mass.

In her modest home on Lovers Lane in Averageville, a French descendant named Therese Kegler-Gervais—a retiree who used to teach math at the school associated with St. Mary's—told me that whoever came up with the idea of changing the name of french fries to freedom fries is out of touch with the mainstream. Indeed, the notion that America dislikes the French was disproved when a 2005 Gallup poll found that the majority of Americans say they have "a favorable view" of France. In Averageville, the most noticeable historical marker is about a Frenchman. In 1780, General Rochambeau, head of the French army, led 6,000 French soldiers down what is now Plains Road in Windham Center. The troops spent the night on the banks of the village's Shetucket River before continuing on to join George Washington's Continental Army.

Averageville has often been seen as a place that one passes by on the way to somewhere else. And it rests in the shadow of people and places that have been. Many homes in the Windham tract displayed flags supporting University of Connecticut athletics. The school's main campus is in Mansfield, which borders Averageville to the north and is known as the first place in America, in 1774, to sign a declaration of freedom from the British.

Bordering the eastern side of the average community is the tiny town of Scotland, the birthplace and childhood home of Samuel Huntington. Many historians have considered Huntington the first true president of the United States. The son of a farmer and one of the signers of the Declaration of Independence, he was president of the Continental Congress when the first constitution of the United States—the Articles of Confederation—was adopted. In 1980, Connecticut's only Ku Klux Klan rally in decades was staged on private land in Scotland. According to an AP report at the time, the anti-Klan protesters roughly equaled the number of Klan ralliers. (Don't try to paint Scotland as red or blue. In 2004, the town's vote counts for George W. Bush and John Kerry were identical: Exactly 430 votes were cast for each candidate.)

Bordering most of south Averageville is the town of Lebanon, where Rochambeau and his troops set up their winter camp before joining Washington's forces, and where the two generals met to go over battle plans. Bordering the west side, and separated by the Natchaug River, is the city of Willimantic, where the local public high school stands. Back in 1880, one of the city's factories—at the time, the largest single-story mill in the world—was the first textile manufacturing plant to be built with electric lighting, helping to usher in the age of multiple shifts and changing the lives of manual laborers forever. The city is still flush with Victorian houses, and according to a local promotional flyer, it is second only to San Francisco in the number that are privately owned. It is home to Eastern Connecticut State University, which started as the first normal school in the state.

In 2002, the *Hartford Courant,* intrigued by the incongruity between Willimantic's "ostensibly small-town charm" and many heroin arrests in the city, did a series on drug usage there. It estimated that there were between 200 and 300 drug addicts in the city, without mentioning whether the estimate was for all addicts or just those using heroin. A year later, Dan Rather came to Willimantic to introduce a CBS News primetime story that was based on the *Courant* report: "If you drive through the streets, you might think you're in almost any state in the country; if life's been good to you, you might even think about buying an elegant Victorian house and raising a family, far from the troubles and trauma of a big city." The rest of the piece was upsetting to many locals. Not mentioned was the compassion of Willimantic—namely, the fact that there are many drug treatment centers located in the city. Addicts routinely come to the area for help, and those that relapse often end up doing so in Willimantic. The drug usage is rightfully a concern, but also unreported in the media coverage was the fact that if the city's number of drug addicts was 200 to 300, it would—at 2 percent of the population—match the national average. In 2005, the Relocation Crime Lab Index reported that Willimantic's average crime rate is just below the U.S. mark.

The city of Willimantic still has its own police, fire, and other municipal services, separate from the three villages of Windham. In 1983, Willimantic technically became a borough of the town of Windham, but it is not part of Averageville.

Like many other places in the United States that search for ways to distinguish themselves by touting something either "above average" or ridiculous, the town of Windham has long gone with the latter. In the summer of 1754, Windham Center residents were well aware that a French and Indian war was on the verge of breaking out. Just past midnight one evening, residents were awakened from their sleep by a symphony of agonizing sounds. Many thought the noise was of Indians attacking. Others were convinced that Judgment Day was at hand. As the noise increased, many ran scared and naked from their homes. Some fell to their knees and prayed. It was sheer panic. As daylight arrived, the true source of the uproar became evident. A drought had left a Windham Center pond nearly dry, and armies of extremely thirsty bullfrogs had been croaking in desperation as they looked for a new water source. Today, a frog is on the town seal, and giant frog sculptures rest on columns spanning the largest bridge in Willimantic.

Averageville—Census 2000 population: 6,612—still has many natural water features and more acreage of nature than developed areas. Indeed, the community still draws many hunters and fishers (licenses $20 and $14, respectively, at town hall). It wasn't long ago that Averageville's land was fully classified as rural. Today, its working farms are all but gone, and its manufacturing plants, which had produced such products as thread and vacuums, largely abandoned, having lost most of the jobs to foreign labor.

I arrived the first week of March with two months to find the Average American before my five-year deadline hit. I started by examining the Census Bureau's official Windham tract map and eliminating all the areas outside the requisite urban zone. Other Averageville areas—apartment communities, mobile-home parks, anywhere too far from the nearest McDonald's, etc.—were also gone.

I next put my feet on the ground and started to hit the village streets, counting more than 500 eligible average American homes. To start winnowing down from this number, I needed to do some lurking about; it was not always easy, for example, to determine if a home had a porch, deck, patio, or balcony. I had decided to go for broke, disqualifying people based on any one mismatch to my list. If they couldn't hit the criteria before I made it past the outer gates of their lives, they should not be considered average. So, any address on a state road was gone. No garage or carport, ditto. And so on. To find out if one home had an external extension, I climbed up a fence in a public park, with binoculars in hand. I thought I was out of view, but when I looked behind me to climb back down, three boys with baseball gloves were staring at me with quizzical looks.

Before I finalized a list of candidates and their addresses, I wanted to secure as much official public information as possible. Town records were helpful in confirming things such as property value, home acreage, and the number and names of registered voters in each home. I was also reading the *Chronicle,* the local paper, as intensely as if I were going to be tested on its contents, to see if any helpful information about residents might pop up.

I was down to about 200 homes on March 15 when I read a front-page *Chronicle* story accompanied by two color photos about a Windham Center resident who had seen an image of the Virgin Mary in his blue bar of Dial soap. "I ran the soap under the faucet and just happened to look down when it immediately struck me. I was looking at the Virgin Mary," said Bob Dancosse. The man said he was not a practicing Christian. I checked my list. His home had already been removed anyway. However, a story in the paper five days earlier had delivered a potential impediment to my search. Because of a couple of burglaries in Willimantic, a police lieutenant had advised area residents: "Be very wary of anybody coming to your door, or if you see anyone at your neighbor's door, report it immediately." I was on the verge of knocking on strangers' doors and wanted to continue to keep my search low key. Attention from the police would not be cool.

Four weeks after my arrival in Averageville, I was finally ready to start knocking. My search map was down to ninety-four eligible houses, with the name of at least one adult resident in each. I prepared to contact everyone on the list. I recognized one of the names, a Windham Center resident, from a *Chronicle* article. Rosa Tirado had won the 2005 Cupid Award, the top community honor in Willimantic, the old mill city. Tirado, who has been a foster parent for twenty-three children, is a kindergarten teacher at Sweeney, a Willimantic elementary school in a residential neighborhood. The school has a big sign out front that reads "Everybody is Somebody at Sweeney." Three years earlier, Tirado had been honored as the top teacher in the Windham school system.

I decided to meet Tirado at her school, so after the final bell, I joined her in her classroom. As would become my standard approach for getting things started with J. Average candidates, I noted simply that I was doing a research project and was interested in seeing if anyone in a certain statistically average part of Windham was in fact "average." In my hand, having taken Mr. Q's place—he had earned the right to retire—was my final list of J. Average criteria, which I had spent more than a year discovering and which had led me to Averageville.

Tirado, a jolly, dark-haired woman with glasses, was cooperative but modest. "If I had my say I wouldn't be recognized at all," she said in a thick Puerto Rican accent. "I don't know if we should be honored for what we like to do. I think that's recognition enough. I love my kids here and my foster kids."

After I asked her where she displayed her awards, she fished a certificate out of the bottom of a drawer. "I guess I can't get upset, that they want to give out awards," Rosa said. "They mean well."

An eleven-year-old girl with kinky black hair entered the classroom, politely introduced herself to me, then gave Rosa a big hug. She wished Rosa a happy birthday.

"She's a foster child; my supervisor is her foster mom," Rosa explained later. "A wonderful child, but she needs a lot of love. It looks like someone in New Jersey may be adopting her, but she is sad because all her sisters are here. And one of the sisters had a baby and she loves to hold that baby. New Jersey sounds like a new start for her, but she doesn't want to leave those she loves."

As was my preference, I was finding out through casual conversation with Rosa if she hit the criteria on my list, and not by administering a formal checklist. I asked Rosa about the girl's birthday comment. Rosa said she was turning sixty-one, a little too old to fit the criteria. Several other facts, including her being born in Puerto Rico, were not matches to my profile for the Average American.

I showed Rosa my list of eligible homes and some of the adults I had listed as living there. "I like it," she said. "Not just Anglos on there." Like the nation, Willimantic has more Hispanics than any other minority race or ethnicity, and that percentage, also like the nation, is heading toward a majority. And Windham has more Latino residents than any town or city in eastern Connecticut. Rosa regularly teaches classes in Spanish and said that, unlike the elementary schools in the Windham villages, Sweeney had a Latino population making up half or more of the student body.

In addition, Windham has a rich eastern Connecticut Indian history that is now reflected, in an odd, glitzy way, in the Foxwoods and Mohegan Sun megacasinos, located within a forty-five-minute drive of Averageville. The first resort is owned by a Pequot Indian tribe and the latter by the Mohegans. In the early 1600s, a Pequot named Uncas founded the Mohegan tribe and became its chief. His land came to include the parcel where Windham now lies.

In 1675, Uncas's family willed the Windham parcel to twelve of the Englishmen who had helped the Mohegans in intertribal battle. John Cates, a white man, and Joe Ginne, a black man, Windham's first nonnative settlers, resided in Windham's first home seven years later—in Windham Center, or Hither-place, as it was called in its early days. Some believe Cates had fled England to avoid religious persecution under the reign of Charles II. Upon his death, his will bequeathed 200 acres to the poor people of the town, and Ginne to the town's pastor.

John and Lynn Butler, a mixed-race couple in Windham Center, were on my list of remaining Average American candidates to visit. Walking near their house I noticed that the top half of their front door was missing. "Some people around here are prejudiced, and I'm not talking about John['s race]," said Lynn, a blonde in a white T-shirt and jeans. "I just don't think some neighbors are as forgiving as they should be when it comes to our past." Both said they were recovering drug addicts. "We had a lot of people over here in past years for activities we now understand are wrong. But I don't think our neighbors, for the most part, have changed their minds. There are mainly older people on this street and they need to understand we share many of the same beliefs that they do."

Unbeknownst to the couple, one of their older neighbors, whom I had interviewed during a pause from raking her yard, had said I should probably stay away from the house with the half-door. "They're not really the type of people who will talk with you," she had said. However, the couple spoke for more than an hour, sharing their life stories. John, a tall man, even read to me from one of the poems he'd been writing, a warning against drug use titled "Oh My God, The High."

"I think we're as spiritual as anyone else around here," Lynn confided.

Does she attend church?

"Every day, right here," she said. "I used to be an atheist, but now, God is my best friend. If we believe that God is always with us, then why can't our home also be our church? We're thinking of putting a sign on the front yard that says 'God Lives Here.' Maybe that's what we need to show for our neighbors to treat us as equals."

"On second thought, that may just add to their fright," John cracked.

The Butlers failed to hit many Average American criteria. Lynn was unemployed, for example. She said it was difficult for her to find work. She is average in that respect. In 2005, a Pew Research poll found that 60 percent of Americans believe that jobs are difficult to find in their community.

I could not find much that was unaverage about Averageville. When I asked residents what makes the three Windham villages atypical for America, the most popular guess among homeowners was that their property-tax rate was probably higher. Since 2000, their property tax had been at either 2 or 3 percent of property value, whereas some studies have placed the national average at either 1 or 2 percent. The residents' state income taxes and sales taxes were more in line with national averages: Most Connecticut workers pay a state income tax of 4.5 percent, about the same as the national average, and Connecticut's 6 percent sales tax falls into the 5 to 6 percent figure that has been the national average since 1991.

Other Averageville residents pointed out that North Windham, Windham Center, and South Windham rely on their volunteer fire departments and on state police for their everyday protection. One state police unit patrols from an area in North Windham, but Frank Mauro, a retiree who volunteers at the St. Joseph's Living Center senior home near his Windham Center home, said, "I was getting a security system installed and I wanted to know what the average response rate was here. I found out it was between ten and twenty minutes. That seems rather high to me." The national average is about thirteen minutes.

Mauro, a former music teacher, and his wife, a retired insurance agent, were both on my list. I dashed to the local radio station when I heard him being interviewed live one morning on a program that often interviewed nearby just-folks. Mauro was talking about volunteering to help vision-impaired citizens. After I introduced myself, he invited me to his home.

"I think I'm average and I think that is a compliment," Mauro said at his meticulously kept ranch house on one of the several roads that I needed to visit that had common first names—such as Alice, Earl, and Henry. The Mauros had already flunked some of my profile questions, but Frank had promised to introduce me to a couple next door who were on my list.

Although Allan White had been a neighbor for years, Mauro said that he couldn't put his finger on what the man did for a living. "Wow," Mauro said, "I know him pretty well. I guess we always have many other things to talk about." I told Mauro that this kind of familiarity, without talking about your career first and foremost, was all but unheard of where I lived in New York City.

White saw Mauro coming over to his property, also perfectly tidy. The snow had melted, and White could sense Mauro needed some help. "Frank, I saw some mole holes on your lawn," said White, a computer programmer as it turned out. "You know all you need is peanut butter?" Frank didn't know. "Just put it on a mousetrap," White said. "Worked like a charm for me." His comment prompted me to think of a house gift I could offer the Average American—that is, if I could find him. Peanut butter would suffice. Mr. Q had told me long ago that on average, Americans consume three pounds of peanut butter per year, and that most Americans prefer smooth over chunky. Three pounds of smooth would do it. If they preferred chunky, they could use it to whack moles.

White, sporting slacks and a white dress shirt and looking like a vintage Caucasian suburban sitcom dad, did not pass the Average American test. However, he talked about graduating from Windham High in 1968, in the class of the first Hispanic ever to graduate from the school, now considerably Latino. "Isnoel Rios," White said. "Wonderful guy." Isnoel became Dr. Rios, an educator at UConn who retired in 2004.

Longtime Windham High English teacher Bill Skoog, not an Average American candidate, was someone I would still call a person of interest. Windham High encourages students to "demonstrate a sense of community," and under Skoog's guidance, and in response to the *Hartford Courant*'s story on the drug arrests in Willimantic, which the paper had given the title "Heroin Town," the students came out with a book titled *Hero in Town*. It was a collection of about seventy-five stories of local everyday people who inspired the students—parents, police officers, teachers, volunteers, a secretary at a doctor's office, a judge, a social worker, and on and on. "I just told them that news can be about ordinary lives," Skoog said. Wrote student Destiny Raymond in the book, "I see a caring community. I see people I know, hard workers and loving families."

However, the hard work of the students would eventually be overshadowed. The book, published in the spring of 2003, included a salute to Willimantic resident Billy Sullivan, a student at Windham High—and, as it would happen, a sufferer of a severe mood disorder—who had written to George W. Bush and received a letter back. "By striving for excellence in your endeavors, you reflect the spirit of America," the president wrote. In the summer of 2003, the mother of Sullivan's girlfriend told Sullivan she didn't want him to move in with her daughter. That August, the mother was shot dead in New Hampshire. In July 2005, Sullivan would be found guilty of murdering her.

"We always hear about the fringes, not those in the middle," said Jessica Lemire, a Windham High grad and now an administrative worker at Windham Community Memorial Hospital—and another candidate on my list. I walked down her long driveway in North Windham and she welcomed me into her home. In a side room, her young son and daughter bopped their heads to music from a rock station.

"I went to Windham High from Catholic school before high school," Lemire said. "And I heard horrible things about drugs and fights there. But I saw one fight in four years and it was deserving. I've been offered pot once, but have never used it. You hear a lot about the good and the bad, but what about the others? The ones whose parents taught them right? The ones with the best morals? They can be invisible. I had one close friend in high school and said hi to everyone. But I was not part of the popular crowd. I was just there, is how I see it. But my husband and I both feel we're happy here. You know, in a way, maybe the average person you're looking for is really the most satisfied person."

Unfortunately, Lemire would not make the Average American cut. Neither would Karin Gaucher, a teacher at St. Mary–St. Joseph, the Catholic elementary school in Willimantic that Lemire had attended. "I treasure the values we teach here every day," Gaucher said in her classroom as we sat on chairs designed for six-year-olds. A sign on the wall read "Kids are Special." Gaucher was cochair of a just-completed—and successful—ten-year reaccreditation process. "We had to write a mission statement," Gaucher said. "I particularly love one part of it—JOY. As all the kids now know, it stands for putting Jesus first, then others, and then yourselves. We enjoy the diversity we have around us—for instance, I teach a lot with the Jewish holidays in class—but I believe that children who learn about JOY and the morals that stem from it have a pretty terrific start in their lives."

Not far away was the one building that serves as the most visible beacon throughout Windham: St. Joseph's, the ornate Catholic church completed by Irish laborers in 1874. The huge steeple—recently replaced after being destroyed by a hurricane in 1938—dominates the Windham skyline. Its bell ringing is the most reliable sound in town. I had stopped by the church a couple of Saturdays previously. To my surprise, Willis West, who had been the pastor of a church about fifteen miles away where I had been confirmed, and where I had attended weekly services while finishing high school, was conducting a baptism. Before I left for college, Father West had stopped me after Mass and asked if there was anything he could answer for me. He even asked about whether I was okay with money. I said no thanks to both offers. I knew I would be out of there shortly, so the fewer bonds the better. At St. Joseph's, a woman informed me that West was a monsignor and the church's pastor. I exchanged a quick hello with him and accepted his offer to stop by sometime to chat.

Although I was making progress connecting with many of those on my list, I still had a lot of door-knocking ahead. On the last day of March, the final South Windham home was crossed from my list without anyone fitting into my proverbial glass slipper. On April Fool's Day, an elderly woman answered my knock and demanded, "This is a joke, right?" A sensible enough question. The same afternoon, Maureen Overcash, a teacher at the public elementary school next to St. Joseph's, had clicked through much of my J. Average criteria, then tripped up on such qualifications as not having a pet and having two houses. So her husband was out too.

April Fool's Day seemed to be a good day for J. Average barbs. The AP wire ran a story about a survey created by a public relations professional, where respondents had to name the most foolish person in America from a preselected list. The Average American finished third, behind Michael Jackson, who was on trial for child abuse, and convicted wife murderer Scott Peterson. That day, at the Windham Theater Guild playhouse, the farce *Run for Your Wife!* debuted, in which a wife says that her husband cannot possibly have thwarted a crime because he is ordinary. At that point, finding the Average American was not a joke to me. I would have settled for any type of Average American, no matter how negative, if only the person existed.

I continued reaching out to people on my list. In her glass-enclosed office on Main Street—a.k.a. Route 66—a curly haired insurance agent, Diane Laveway, like many other residents who would be eliminated, was strictly complimentary when I asked about life in the Averageville tract. "What I love about where we are is that we are so close to everything," she said. "Boston, Providence, Hartford, the casinos, rural, city, in between." The Massachusetts, Rhode Island, and Connecticut capitals are each less than 100 miles away.

How about any commonalities of those in the three Windham villages?

"Hardworking," she said, pausing. "Yes, hardworking."

Her sentiment echoed the 1948 motion picture *Pitfall,* in which Dick Powell played an insurance company employee. "You're John Forbes, average American, backbone of the country," his wife reminds him.

"But I don't want to be an average American, backbone of the country," he replies. "I want someone else to be a backbone and hold me up."

Roger Nadeau is fine with being a backbone. The president of the Willimantic Little League and a maintenance supervisor for a power plant, he spends most of his working hours outdoors. My wife was in town from New York for a long weekend to assist in my search, and on Monday, April 11, we spotted the husky former Navy engineer tidying up his side yard at an address on my list. He invited us to chat with him on his deck, where his wife, Cheryl, a school cafeteria worker, joined us.

"Average American I perceive as a positive because I see it as a majority, but on political lines I feel it's a minority because too many Americans are complainers and not doers," Roger said. He and his wife are each registered as unaffiliated voters. "I look at Town Council and other political bodies and they are not true representatives of the majority. There needs to be as good a cross-section as possible. A black, a white, Hispanic, low-income person, middle-income person, a preacher, how's that for a start?"

"You know, there was a lot of complaining about Wal-Mart going up here," Roger noted later. "But it creates good jobs for low-income families. I'd like to think that is a majority opinion. Some people seem to complain about how Wal-Mart and other jobs are not perfect, but I think most workers everywhere would say the same. I don't always like the way I'm treated on my job, but you need to respect the paycheck. I just worked 143 hours in two weeks—eighteen-, nineteen-hour days. It's not like I could say 'I'm tired; I'm running machinery.'" There had been a major outage, and Roger had needed to fix a downed engine. "They utilized me and my coworkers instead of hiring in people like they normally do because they're in a budget crunch," Roger explained. "We can sit there and argue, but when we lose our jobs, where would that leave us?" Offered Cheryl, "I see people complaining about the most trivial things in this country. I want to say, 'Just shut up and look around. Your problems are not exactly life and death.'"

Ultimately, both Nadeaus struck out on some of the criteria on the first page of my four-page Average American profile. Even though I was applying only majority criteria, looking again at my list I wondered whether I had raised the bar too high for the most average American. To review, starting back with my visit to the Census Bureau sixteen months earlier, I needed to find someone—in *this* community—who met 140 criteria, and who had also met them for the majority of the previous five years.

Up through the day that Myklar the Ordinary had suggested I look for signs, I had collected sixteen criteria: U.S. or D.C. citizen, lives in same home as five years previously, resident of native state, resides in nation's most average community, family is "extremely" or "very" important, high-school graduate, in paid labor force or working toward it, has at least one married couple in home, has offspring, regularly in bed before midnight, believes in God, is Christian, is respectful of others' religions, attends church at least once a month, religion is "very important" in own life, and is respectful of all races.

By the time I'd arrived at the starting line of the Kansas marathon, I had collected thirty more: annual moviegoer, lives in owner-occupied home, resides in one house (a "one-unit, detached"), has direct access to one or two motor vehicles, home has garage or carport, has driver's license, has two to four people residing in home, regularly wears seat belt, household has discretionary income, is in full-time paid labor force *or* retired from it, has at least one pet, is not trying to be nationally known, is satisfied with the way things are going in personal life, supports current abortion laws—but believes the act of abortion is wrong—and supports the stricter enforcement of environmental regulations, describes self as very or fairly happy, believes money can't buy happiness, has home valued between $100,000 and $300,000, participates in recycling, has fired a gun, believes in the right to bear arms, is against public use of semiautomatic weapons, is in favor of registration or waiting lists for gun owners, believes gambling is an acceptable entertainment option, has gambled with money in at least one organized game of chance in the past year, household has a craft or hobby, donates money to charity annually, gives time to charity annually, and has a net worth between $30,000 and $300,000.

While in Kansas, my total number of J. Average criteria would grow nicely, thanks to these twelve additions: lives where there is at least 0.1 inches of snow annually, and where the average annual temperature is between 45 and 65 degrees, is between eighteen and fifty-three years old, spends most of time indoors, gets moderate exercise weekly, has health insurance, walks under own power, weighs 135 to 205 pounds, lives in urbanized and suburban America, resides on zero to two acres, and has a private lawn. Hawaiians led me to these new criteria: supports the U.S. troops, drinks soda, drinks coffee regularly or occasionally, has an electric coffeemaker in the home, eats bread weekly, believes music can bring family closer together, has stereo in the home, wears glasses and/or contacts to "correct his vision," has all five senses, can read English, can speak English fluently, his community mirrors racial/ethnic make-up of the nation, life is "impacted" by drugs or alcohol, opposes legalization of marijuana for recreational use, supports the use of pot for medicinal use, has visited the ocean, lives within 100 miles of the ocean, and lives in the Eastern-most time zones.

As a result of my time with presidential candidate Average Joe Schriner, I had these criteria: has consumed alcohol, considers homosexuality an acceptable alternative lifestyle, has color television, has cable service, has a DVD and/or VCR, commonly watches television daily, household's per capita income is between $15,000 and $75,000, primary weekday destination is within 5 miles of home, primary mode of transportation is the privately owned motor vehicle, home has a porch and/or deck and/or balcony and/or patio, has outdoor grill at home, eats meat (red and white), has one to three registered voters in household, lives on a local road, household files federal income-tax return, household files state income-tax return, pays sales tax in state, eats ice cream at least once a month, lives within 2 miles of a public park, and uses recreational facilities annually.

Down the stretch, I had these qualifications: chief local politician is a Democrat, local governing council is mostly Democratic, reads local newspaper daily, has read or has started to read at least one book within the past year, uses landline phone, uses mobile phone on a regular basis, home is within range of cell service, believes friends are "extremely" or "very" important, home has a paved parking area to his garage or carport, favorite way to spend the evening is in the home, home is between ten and fifty years old, home has between four and six living-purpose rooms, grew up within 50 miles of current home, has a kitchen, a clothes washer, a clothes dryer, an automatic dishwasher, at least one full bathroom, brushes teeth daily, visits the dentist annually, showers daily, has a Christmas tree every year, has a credit card, ATM card, and household credit-card debt, uses the Internet, has played video or computer games over the past year, is a football fan, is a baseball fan, political viewpoints are three, four, or five on a scale of one to seven, owns jeans, has done better financially than parents, has at least one living parent, and has at least one living sibling, represented by at least one Democratic U.S. senator and a Republican U.S. House representative, takes annual vacation time, has listed phone number, eats at McDonald's annually, lives within 3 miles of a McDonald's, within twenty minutes of a Wal-Mart, shops at Wal-Mart annually, is between 5 feet 3 inches and 5 feet 10-1/2 inches in height, and lives in the middle majority of the nation's populated areas.

I had been determining whether Averageville residents matched these criteria by going in whatever order was most efficient. For example, if they looked to be over fifty-three, I would start with age. With Roger Nadeau, the Willimantic Little League president, I had thrown some curveballs, as I usually did to ensure that no one could simply answer yes-or-no questions with a yes, in case they were purposely trying to match my profile.

Up the street from the Nadeaus, my wife and I buttonholed a young trucker named Paul, who was placing his garbage on the curb for pickup. His wife rolled down her window as she wheeled into the driveway a few minutes later. "They say they are swingers and want to know if we're interested," Paul lied with a straight face. Alas, the couple would become the last residents of North Windham to be crossed off my list. "He's president of the Little League?" Paul asked with surprise when I mentioned my discussion with Nadeau. "Good, thanks. I'm going to go talk with him. Our daughter is interested in getting into T-ball."

Paul was happy, but I was feeling stressed. So far, only one household had failed to cooperate with me—and a friendly resident who knew the inhabitants explained to me that they would fail to match at least a couple of my criteria—but only twenty-six homes in Windham Center remained on my list and I did not have any Average American matches. At homes, workplaces, and elsewhere, I had spoken with retirees, students, stay-at-home moms, private school teachers, university employees, a phone-company technician, the wife of a National Guardsman who had served in Iraq and was now in Germany, an officer of a local soccer league, a FedEx employee, a performance clown named Razzie, a sporting goods salesman, a second-shift JC Penny manager, a former Willimantic postmaster, and assorted other locals. Everyone was underqualified to be J. Average. I saw a sign near the Willimantic city square that read "Cooperative Oil Company—We're Not Your Ordinary Company." I thought of my search: I'd had plenty of cooperation, but no ideal ordinariness. I soldiered on.

On the first Wednesday of June in 1882, an item in the Windham newspaper noted, "'By Jumbo' is the new phrase which is supplanting 'By jingo' among the street urchins." On the second Wednesday in April 2005, I was down to fifteen homes and was about to experience my own by-Jumbo moment. On a breezy afternoon under fair skies, I visited Windham Tech, a state vocational high school located in Willimantic. A man pushing a broom outside the main office graciously asked if he could be of help.

*D*uring *my senior year* of high school in the late 1970s, the students knew our custodian simply as Zooman, a nickname that seemed appropriate for the person responsible for cleaning up our messes. On the annual locker clean-out day, many students would not place their trash in nearby receptacles, but hurl it nonchalantly into the corridor. Janitors and other custodial workers may be the ultimate ignored, seemingly invisible, average Americans. They simply go about their jobs, in most cases as others continue to work and live life around them, often without so much as an exchange of words. And there are many such individuals; on Labor Day in 2004, the Census Bureau listed "janitors/building cleaners" as one of the ten most common jobs in the United States, with 2 million nationwide.

In high school, my class silk-screened T-shirts of Zooman's face, convincingly framed with his dark mop of hair and thick mustache. Zooman's mug appeared over a tagline that read "Keeper of the Zoo." The shirts were one of the items sold to raise money for a class trip. I bought one. I thought it was funny, a janitor as a somebody.

*A*t *Windham Tech,* I introduced myself to the man with the broom and said I was looking for a maintenance worker named Robert Burns. I'd been told he worked there. A school official overheard us and walked me down a couple of hallways to a windowless office in the back of a large storage room with many used computers.

Zooman recognized me as soon as I mentioned my name.

He was the same Robert Burns on my list.

He looked me in the eye, put his left hand on my right shoulder, and firmly shook my hand.

When I had shown my list of finalists to some people in Mansfield, where I had attended high school, I was reminded that Bob Burns was the name of a custodial worker who had been at my old school for a few years. Zooman? One said that the old Bob Burns was now working at Windham Tech. I wasn't sure he was the same Robert Burns as the one on my list until I found him, however.

Zooman's hair was now short and flecked white. The mustache was gone. He wore glasses. He had a lazy right eye, although I did not recall noticing it when I had last seen him, more than a quarter of a century earlier. He smiled broadly and began to reminisce.

Zooman remembered a promise I had once made, one that I'd forgotten years ago. One time, when I was wearing the shirt with his mug—evidently for gym class—I had promised to wear it under my school jersey in my first college cross-country race. While Bob spoke with me at Windham Tech, he even remembered the name of the university I was heading to.

The fact is, I did not wear his face on my chest in any race after I left high school. I was off to another world, and no custodian or any other everyday person was going to stop me from reaching extraordinary heights and dreams.

Zooman's title had changed: He had become the building maintenance supervisor at Windham Tech. So had my perspective. On his desk, he had a horizontal three-part picture frame with head shots of his children—two sons and a daughter. I asked about them and he proudly talked about each one. His two eldest lived in the area. David was an attorney, married to his high-school sweetheart, and the father of a baby girl. Nicole had graduated with a degree in human relations and was a private juvenile caseworker. She was married to a man who had grown up on Connecticut's Gold Coast. Bob said his younger son, Jared, had been a swimmer at Windham High and had helped set a school relay record in his final competition. Jared had recently graduated from the Air Force Academy in Colorado and was planning a fall wedding to a young woman from Ohio. He was in training at an Air Force base in Pensacola, Florida. Explained Bob, "He's in the back seat—the guy who's going to make sure you have all the armament you need." Bob mentioned that his wife had recently retired from an out-of-town rural-development job for the U.S. Department of Agriculture, where she had started as a secretary years earlier. Zooman was married to Sue and was already a father when I had last seen him, but I had no idea of such details in his life then.

Bob, also a graduate of Windham Tech, had a baseball field to tend to for an afternoon game, and other chores, and was looking forward to a pizza date that evening with David and his grand-daughter. "I'd love to chat some more," he said, adding that he had plans for the next couple of nights but could spend more time to-gether on Friday. He invited me to his home. I was happy with the offer. I had some questions to ask him and his wife.

*Friday, April 15, tax day,* was a perfect afternoon for pilots taking off and landing at the Windham Airport. Near the end of a cul-de-sac a couple of miles to the south, the blue skies complemented a perfect American scene at the Burnses' single-story red house with white trim. The stars and stripes flew from a flagpole in the front yard. On the garage door, a novelty sign read "U.S. Air Force Park-ing Only." A red Intrigue and a white Sierra truck were parked out-side. The latter sported a yellow magnetic "Support Our Troops" ribbon on the back panel. Hanging to the left of the front door was a small model of a white picket fence. It read "Welcome."

Including Bob's residence, I had fourteen homes remaining in my search. One of them was a gray house across the street. Most of the twelve residences on the road had similar floor plans, and all but one, Bob's home included, had been built in the early to late 1960s. Based on the latest town assessment, from 2001, the values of the road's twelve properties covered a thin spectrum from $105,200 to $123,840, and within that same range was the national median value posted the same year by the Census Bureau. The road's devel-oper had gotten construction help from Bob Burns's uncle, a well-driller. "I was told he may have had the first rotary pneumatic drill in the state," Bob would later explain. "He was pretty valuable."

Beyond a long wooden fence, the Burnses' well was nicely camouflaged. Bob is among the 59 percent of Americans, according to Gallup, who have a garden or a lawn "that needs to be taken care of." In the front yard was a rose bush Bob had planted in memory of his Italian American mother-in-law, Rose.

Rose's daughter Sue answered my knock at the front door. Both she and her husband have dark features—including dark hair, as do most Americans—and she spoke shyly, as she had upon meeting Bob in 1972, while she was working as a server at an area Kentucky Fried Chicken. Their first date was to a Mansfield movie theater to see *The French Connection*—appropriately, as they would learn that French is the one heritage that they know they share. At the time, Bob, also of Irish and Scottish blood, was the proud owner of a new AMC Hornet, as he has always, consciously, only purchased American-made vehicles. He was paying for it by working as a $3.25-an-hour custodial worker at UConn, a job that mainly consisted of jumping off the back of a truck and filling burlap bags with trash. Bob and Sue, who are in their early fifties, had both grown up in Willimantic, and had each received their final diploma in high school. Their second date was to the drag races, and their third to a rock concert at UConn. Within two months, Bob had presented a pre-engagement ring to Sue that had a diamond chip and an inscription that read "LOVE." He proposed marriage during a sunset at the lake where he had spent many of his boyhood days fishing. They married in 1973, and they lived in their first home, a tiny cottage near the lake, through the birth of their second child.

I joined the Burnses at a dining table in their main room, from where I could see a cluttered room through an open door. The former bedroom of their younger son, it is now a home office with a computer, plus an authentic casino slot machine from Japan that Bob's kids had given to him for Christmas. Including their bedroom, their total number of rooms gave them the same number as the average American. And like most American homes, the house did not have a separate dining room, but did have a refrigerator-freezer, a stove, heat, air conditioning, and a microwave oven.

Above the television, a doll collection lined a plain shelf. Just below was a model of a P-51 Mustang, a World War II plane that Bob said reminded him of his son's training aircraft. Above the staircase leading downstairs were a long line of family wedding photos dating back, seamlessly, to 1901. Many other photos of family members were displayed around the room. Standing on a shelf in the entertainment center was an empty photo frame with a sticky note that read "family." Sue had already prepared it for a photo of their second grandchild, as their daughter was expecting.

Laying flat on a desk in the computer room was a photo of their son Jared, standing taller than George W. Bush as the two men shook hands a year earlier at the Air Force Academy graduation ceremony. The president had delivered the commencement address, and Jared had received his diploma. "No matter what we say about the president sometimes, that was a proud moment," said Sue, who, like her husband and most party-affiliated voters, is a registered Democrat. Incidentally, one of the two speech characteristics I would notice from Bob—his occasional swapping of *owe* for *ah,* as when he told his wife, "I'll speak with Nicole about her travel plans tomorrah"—was reminiscent of the president, who has been known to publicly utter such deviations as "thourah" for "thorough." (Bob also has a proclivity for saying, "I says," as in "So I says to him, 'Yeah, I know, my nephew is serving in the Middle East.'")

It seemed that the Burnses could talk all night about family. "Sue asked me if I wanted anything for my birthday," said Bob, whose birthday was less than a week away. "I really don't. She said maybe some fishing stuff, and I can see that. But for the most part, I have everything I need. I've got three terrific children and a great wife."

As was my routine in town, I had said that I was on a search to find some people who fit statistical averages, to understand more about the average American. "You know, you talk about being average," Bob said. "I think average Americans are people who work hard but not too much where they can't put their family first." This family-before-work attitude may be why a 2001 ABC News poll found that 72 percent of Americans did not believe they worked "too hard."

"I've always thought I was an average person," Bob said. "With Sue, I've always tried to provide enough for our children, so that their lives can be a little bit better than our own. I see an average person as someone making a decent living in a good community, and I am fortunate to have that. . . . I have a job that lets me be part of the community, and I can't see having it any other way." I would later find that the Burnses, like 76 percent of Americans, are satisfied with "the way things are going" in their local community (versus only 46 percent who say the same thing about the United States).

Said Sue, "I think being average means you are in good company. . . . I think about the foundation our children have. They understand the meaning of hard work. They all worked for this local businessman growing up [at a recently closed roadside ice-cream stand in Windham called Uncle Ken's], and he always said they were hard workers. It's comforting 'cause we know they will pass the same on to their children." And with their kids out of the house, and their understanding of how important it is for military students miles from home not to get lonely during holiday breaks, the small bedroom in the basement had been offered to the Coast Guard Academy in southeastern Connecticut in case a cadet or two needed a guest room.

Bob and Sue seemed happy. "Bob definitely gets that, people saying he's an upbeat guy," said Sue. "One of my girlfriend's kids said she even asked her dad, 'Why can't you be happy like Bob is all the time?'" Three months earlier, a *Time* magazine study on happiness had found that 79 percent of Americans described themselves as optimists, and 80 percent said they generally wake up happy, findings I would later learn describe the Burnses. However, like most Americans, Bob had not always had cause in his life for such uninterrupted happiness. For one thing, his right eye, the result of a congenital cataract he'd had since birth, had required three surgeries when he was young. As a result, he had missed a lot of classwork, and by high school, he said, "I was just an average student; math, that was the death of me" (at Windham Tech, he would float between the two academically middle groups in the school).

He had great vision in his left eye, 20/15, but his weak right eye had kept him from excelling at contact sports. Nonetheless, in high school he had earned a spot on his freshman basketball team, only to quit because of a blow he suffered to his face that convinced him not to risk his eyesight. Cataracts, a clouding of the eye lens that can lead to serious blurred vision, are the nation's leading cause of blindness and may even be an ordinary lifetime experience. According to a report issued by Pennsylvania's Altoona Hospital, "by age 75, about 70 percent of all Americans have cataracts."

"All in all, I was frustrated I was never really considered a good athlete," Bob said. To help make up for it as an adult, he had started playing softball and taking it seriously, staying out late with teammates, happy to be an accepted jock. Sue, reminding him of his responsibility to family, eventually helped convince him to put an end to that. He now regularly exercises alone.

A small black dog, a Lhasa apso Bob said he and Sue often take for walks, wandered over to my side of the table. My list of Average American criteria pretty much etched into my brain, I had already recognized from our conversation that regular moderate exercise and having a pet were but two of the many prerequisites. Sue's recent retirement, in March, was the only mismatch I could think of so far. I decided it was time to start knocking things off my checklist, although by now in Averageville that had frustrated me each time. Because I had dropped candidates in some cases if they did not match even one criterion, I had pretty much resigned myself to the notion that I would not come up with a clear "winner" and so would need to reinterview a lot of residents to gauge how closely they could come to matching the rest of the profile, even if it took me past April. (If anyone was to move away after that five-year deadline, I was confident, now that I had their names, that I could still find them).

Sue would miss a handful of criteria, but for Bob, the hits just kept on coming—even when I tried to steer him away from matches. Was he a pro basketball fan? Not really, but he volunteered that he was a passionate fan of UConn sports and a fan of both the Green

Bay Packers (he chose them at age thirteen because he liked their green and yellow jerseys) and the Boston Red Sox.

There was no way he could have known the answers. He had at least one living sibling—both sisters. He had a deck—built it himself. He had mentioned a hobby—fishing, which 58 percent of Americans have experienced. He was a book reader—he was in the middle of *God's Other Son,* an old novel by national radio personality Don Imus—and a newspaper reader, with subscriptions to the local paper and, for the weekends, the *Hartford Courant.* "I can miss a day," Sue said of the newspaper, "but Bob has withdrawals if the paperboy doesn't deliver it. [On those days] he always heads straight to the store to pick it up."

Bob matched more than ninety criteria perfectly, and I had less than half my criteria remaining. I had some seriously mixed emotions. On the one hand, I had my first serious Average American contender; even though I had routinely mixed up the order of the criteria I applied depending on how my conversations went, no one else had successfully knocked off so many questions without a mismatch. I thought, well, he wasn't a woman; although I'd planned to use female gender only as a tiebreaker, it was at least one sign that he was not invincible. But why did I want to think he couldn't match my list?

The answer, I would figure out, was simple. Zooman, like Windham, was not the hidden treasure I had hoped to find. I had already known about this man before I had even set out on my search, and what's so exceptional about something already familiar?

Maybe, I would later consider, I had not really learned as much on the road as I had thought. Why had I been looking for someone unknown and unusual, when my journey was about averageness? And why shouldn't Average American finalists and their surroundings be familiar? I was familiar with these folks—this is the area where I was from. And I was familiar with the profile—I had studied it for months: It was the same profile I had been applying all over the three Windham villages.

Bob Burns, who puts his political viewpoints in the middle of a seven-point scale, is 5 feet 8 inches and, give or take a few, 185 pounds—three more J. Average matches. During a tour of the house, I would count four telephones; the average American has a minimum of three. Although I hadn't put this item on the list, it would still be of interest, much like when I later learned that Bob's shoe size is 10-1/2, the exact same as the average American man.

At the Burnses' home, a weird feeling inside me convinced me to put further questioning on hold. I wanted to stay objective, not root for or against Zooman. I could easily finish my investigation later. I asked Bob and Sue about a couple across the street that was still on my list, John and Sue Decker. It was getting late, but we called their home. Sue Decker, an administrative assistant at the Willimantic Police Department, politely said that she would prefer to talk the next day. I called back the next afternoon and she offered that she was free if I wanted to stop by her place that Tuesday evening, three days later. She liked my idea of the Burnses joining us if they could.

We actually met at the Burnses' house first, for some pizza and conversation, while the Deckers' eleven-year-old son, Kyle, skateboarded with a friend across the street. Sue Decker, who was sporting a bright lime-colored blouse, is a bubbly blonde whose hairstyle and pleasant giggling reminded me of the actress Goldie Hawn. We eventually moved to her home, to a dining table next to a stack of schoolbooks and homework assignments that Kyle had placed there. Kyle was skateboarding instead of playing basketball because the hoop out front had been accidentally hooked and snapped clean by a town snowplow a month before. His mom expressed her frustration that during two visits she had made to the town's first selectman's office, she had been told that there was no money in any budget to repair her destroyed property. "All that's left is a stump," she said, "and that's a real hazard, especially if anyone walks by barefoot."

I thought about the notion that the average American can't fight town hall. I had explained what I was up to and how I'd ended up in their community. Over the previous three and a half days I had contacted every remaining household on my list, with no matches. Said

Decker, "When I think of average, I think of these people who marry, they have three or four kids, the mom gets to stay home and not work and the dad has a great job. . . . And I think they live in a big beautiful house and they go on vacations and all that. I'm not quite there." She didn't make as much as Bob—I would learn that his annual salary is considerably shy of six figures—but she was closer to the national average. I asked her if there was anything that was *not* average about her two neighbors. "No, not really."

"Oh, Christmastime," Decker said, finally thinking of something. "We don't do a lot of decorating, but Bob, he has all sorts of outdoor Christmas stuff. He lights up the street."

"I like the holidays," Bob confessed.

"Yeah, one of the reasons we don't park in the garage," his wife cracked. "A few boxes of holiday stuff in there." She said that Bob had been given a commendation by the town on two separate occasions for his cheerful Christmas displays.

Decker's husband was out with friends. He is a UConn landscaper—the exact same position that Bob's dad had held for most of his working life. The two couples have been neighbors for years. When Decker's eldest son, now moved away, was at Windham High School, he had walked across the street and asked the Burnses' daughter if she would be his date for the prom. She said yes. Another time, when one of the Burnses' sons and some friends, dressed in camouflage, were playing paintball in the yard at night with some big guns, Sue Decker had caught a glimpse of them hiding behind the bushes and called the police, unsure of whether terrorists had come to attack her dead-end street. "Doesn't sound so bright, does it?" Decker asked me.

"They should have warned you, and you were better safe than sorry," Sue Burns answered.

"She wasn't alone," Bob said to me. "A hunter came out of the woods wondering the same thing."

We talked about the area, and all three said that the regular-people spirit of the area is most evident on the Fourth of July, at a veritable Average People on Parade. On that date for the previous

nineteen years, a town parade had been open for everyone to participate in without even a need to apply—anyone could walk, drive,
bike, or otherwise advance down the middle of Main Street, where
they were, either alone or in groups, encouraged to celebrate freedom. "You find yourself interacting with people you otherwise
wouldn't get to know better, and that is why it's special," said Bob,
adding that he was planning to drive his truck in the twentieth
annual event with, as is parade custom, marching-band music
cranked up.

"With the growing minority population, there is a division in
some people's mind," his wife noted.

"But that all goes away during the parade," Decker added. "You
should come." I said I'd try and asked about their acceptance of all
races, one of my search criteria and a test they all passed. Sue Burns,
like her husband a non-Hispanic white, noted that her daughter was
married to a Hispanic man.

When I asked about religion, I learned that Sue Decker's son was
attending a Catholic school. Both families, it turned out, were regu-
lars at St. Joseph's, the church where my former pastor presides. Did
they know Monsignor West?

"He married us," Sue Decker said. "Do you want to see the
videotape?"

"We were married at St. Joseph's, too," Bob said. "And both of
our kids' weddings were there." Bob said his faith is a key part of his
life, indeed, like most Americans, as indicated by a 2004 *Newsweek*
poll, he believes the Bible is literally true, and he mentioned that in
his first job out of high school, before he worked at UConn, he was
the janitor for St. Thomas Aquinus, a church on the university campus. I had received my First Holy Communion at St. Thomas, and it
was the church that my family had attended when I was in junior
high. Unbeknownst to me until my chat in the Decker home, Bob
was working at the church at that time.

I was starting to think it all made sense, in a way. As much as I
had been concerned that Averageville was too familiar to me, and
that the Average American could be as well, why shouldn't his
church DNA be familiar too?

The possibility soon became reality.

Although he was not aware of it at the time, Bob Burns—Zooman, *Zooman*—went on to hit every last Average American criterion, the only person I had met to do so. He was the only American who could hit all 140 Average American criteria. And, as I was observing, he was hitting more averages that weren't even on my list.

It seemed too unbelievable really, the odds that I would end up where I did. Who would believe it?

Bob was the most average American.

For my discussion at the Deckers' house, I had even snuck one last criterion into my list, asking whether any of them preferred chunky or plain peanut butter. Bob went with plain, the majority choice.

He had well earned his three pounds of peanut butter, but for two and a half months, I kept my mouth shut. I would recheck the numbers and follow up on any that sounded suspicious, even run a background check for any major anomalies—I had become quite obsessive about the search—and with Bob, I would need to secretly find a way of gauging whether he was uninterested in generating any national attention, the last qualification.

My heartbeat quickened as I thanked Sue Decker—she had made a gallant run at being J. Average, hitting more than a hundred of the criteria—and then I walked with the Burnses across the street and into their front yard. I gave Bob my phone numbers and e-mail address and said he could call me if he wanted to know how he had fared in my search. I decided that if he did not call me anxious to know how he did, my final criterion would be met. I would give him until July 4, when I would return for the town's parade.

*The next day,* I needed to fulfill an earlier promise. I visited St. Joseph's to chat with Monsignor West.

When West had come to the church a couple decades ago, it was in terrible shape. The windows were broken, the altar a mess, and the church was so cash poor that West couldn't afford to heat the main room. Masses had to be held in the basement, where there was spot heating.

"The bells would not ring, because bricks would pop out. The foundation would not support it," explained West, who had been in the middle of working on a divorce decree in his restored rectory when I stopped by. "The bishop told me he needed me to go to a church that was one of the poorest in the diocese, but one of the richest in faith. One person in the diocese told me, 'God help you, God help you.' First thing, I started a novena, because I had a feeling that the church could get back to normal. Kevin, that was the goal.

"On Christmas Day, 1988, that's when I knew we were back to normal," West said. "That day, the bells rang again."

I shared with my former pastor that my quest to find the most average American had taken me to the tract across the river. I said that the Average American would most probably be a member of his church.

West didn't ask for any names. Instead, he spoke of the type of person he believed it to be. "The average American," he said, "is someone who has a great love for who and where they are. A love of country, faith and morals, that's what I see. I see those who have earned what they have. It hasn't just been handed to them."

I had learned a lot. But I was still amazed at my being where I was, for the reasons that I was, and who I had found. It seemed so unbelievable.

"Not if you believe," West offered.


*From Monsignor West's office window,* we could see down the street to the movie-theater parking lot where participants in the Fourth of July parade would line up. Many weeks later, that's where I would spot Bob Burns decorating his truck with a sort of American safari theme. At a family barbecue a couple of days earlier, his older sister had presented to him a tan pith helmet—the hat commonly associated with safaris—that had been their dad's.

Bob was wearing the helmet, with a small U.S. flag stuck to its front. Fastened to the vehicle were a few plastic blow-up and plush animals and no fewer than two dozen more flags. A large Uncle Sam doll faced outward from a side window. Zooman was wearing black boots, olive cargo shorts and a matching vest, tinted prescription glasses, and the pith helmet.

There were four generations of Burnses in and around the truck, and despite a technical glitch—Bob was trying to get some external speakers in his truck bed to work—a lot of smiles. In the back of the pickup, his wife was holding their grandchild, a two-year-old with an enormous smile. Listening attentively to the girl's dad was Bob's mother. She still lived in Willimantic, where she had worked for years in the stamping and clinching department of Electro-Motive, a train-parts manufacturer whose Willimantic operations, now gone, were a short walk from the Burnses' home. Bob was—no surprise here—the middle child of the family.

I headed to the end of the parade route, a block down from the Dairy Queen, where in April I had discovered that a coworker of mine there many years ago was now the boss. From a group of parade watchers, a woman shouted my name. I turned, and walking toward me to chat was Rosa Tirado.

About half an hour later, a group of drama students from E.O. Smith, my high-school alma mater, marched by wearing shirts proclaiming *Anything Goes,* the name of the play the students were in rehearsals for. It could have just as easily been the parade theme. A rowdy, happy day, what makes the annual Windham Fourth interesting is community residents' open sharing of opinions in the midst of the patriotic—but almost anarchic—event. Emphasizing the point: Marching directly in front of the town's first selectman throughout the entire parade was a man dressed in red, white, and blue who held up a large sign calling for his impeachment. (No, it was not John Decker airing his family's basketball-hoop grievances).

About forty minutes later, Zooman, marching outside his truck, which was driven by his son, made his way down Main Street. His vest was unzipped, just enough to expose a hint of what was on the gray T-shirt he was wearing underneath. It was the "Keeper of the Zoo" shirt from those many years ago at E.O. Smith.

"That's so great you got a chance to see our parade," Bob said when I found him at the finishing area. "So what did you think?"

Having had two months to reflect on my search, I had thought a lot, not necessarily about the parade. For one, about what I had missed by avoiding average experiences for so long. Observing Bob enjoying time with his generations of family members, I was reminded of how much his life had given him. I thought about something Bob had told me at his dinner table. "I could have chased after bigger money," he had noted of his career choice, which started after his planned carpentry career never took off. "Sue knows there was one way, if I wanted to get involved with some shady people and give up normal hours, I could have gotten it, too. But I think we have always understood that if you are parents, it's more about giving of your time than flaunting any money or luxuries. I try to live by that rule. I will never apologize for not making more money." With his daughter, who would grow up to be a competitive cheerleader, he remembered not only taking her to dance classes but learning dance steps. He and Sue had become team parents for her high-school squad. He is still a chaperone for a post–Little League international baseball exchange program in which his younger son participated. "I'd like to think I don't just *say* I love them, but that I *show* them that I do," he had added. "They are our luxuries."

Bob had consciously given up the chance to be above average so that he wouldn't miss out on being average. I recognized the same of my parents. During my long search in Averageville, I had spent more time with them than in many past years combined. Although retired, they were active helping others. My mom was doing volunteer work at the Windham hospital, and my dad for Habitat for Humanity in Willimantic. (They are both the sort of modest people who will probably wish I didn't even say this much about them, so I'll stop.)

I thought about how I had come around to not only accepting, but embracing, the reality that Zooman was the Average American. But after I left Bob with his family, I knew my journey was not over.

*Just past two thirty* on that Independence Day, the birds were singing when I knocked on Bob's front door and held behind my back a gift bag with three pounds of smooth peanut butter. Near the door, a sign in a small flower garden had a passage from Ecclesiastes, popularized by the Byrds when Bob and Sue Burns were schoolkids: "To every thing there is a season and a time to every purpose under heaven."

Bob answered the door. I said I wanted to see what decorations he had dug out of the garage for display on the Fourth of July. "Sure," he said, and pointed out two signs. On the garage was a cloth banner with a red, white, and blue heart-shaped flag that featured the opening lyrics of "My Country 'Tis of Thee." Nearby, there was a vertical red and white banner depicting the Statue of Liberty, with the words "GOD BLESS AMERICA." He invited me through the house and out the back door to say hi to Sue, and we joined her at a glass-top table on their backyard deck. Facing the left side of their quarter-acre property from my chair, I could see a small tomato garden. Beyond that, a long line of similar backyard decks led to the main road. Bordering the Burnses' back yard straight beyond the deck were woods, which led to the property of St. Joseph's Living Center.

I gave a little speech, about how, as the Bible and the Byrds may have been trying to tell us, the world is full of all kinds of individuals. We are all different. I said that when it comes to being the most average person in America, well, that means one is distinctive and "different," too. I talked about what I had learned on my journey, including the realization that although I had started out scared of being ordinary, that was probably because deep down, I had been afraid that I already was. I said that the Average American didn't need to chase glory because he already had glory in his own life, that I greatly admired the Average American, and that I was happy with where my search had taken me. I said that although others may have ended up in other places if they had made the same journey, I was convinced that there would be those who would have found the same man that I had. I said that the Average American is Bob Burns.

He swallowed hard.

"What an honor," he said softly.

It took a while for the news to sink in for him, so for the next five hours, through an improvised grilled-hamburger dinner on his deck, I focused on a broader subject, asking him and Sue about life. At one point, Bob talked about his love of fishing from a riverbank in the community. I got a primer on baiting and stocking schedules, but there was something deeper on his mind.

"I just put my line in the water and it's an amazing feeling," he shared. "If I have any problems or troubles, I just look at the water, and picture them running away with the currents. Then I think about all the good things in my life."

Maybe we could go fishing together some time.

"I usually go by myself," Bob said. "But if you really want to."

What an honor, I said.

# A Note on Methodology

*Below are the guidelines* applied in my search for the most average American, some of which were presented in more detail earlier in the book:

- My original search pool consisted of all residents of the fifty states and Washington, D.C., as this is the primary American population covered by the U.S. Census. I then narrowed the search to residents who are U.S. citizens, as to be an "American" is most often understood to mean that one is a citizen of the United States.

- I decided that I would be led to future criteria only by people I met during my journey—and who I felt were part of that journey. They needed to volunteer, in words or action, criteria or categories that were important to them in some way. I believe this decision was especially significant as it ensured that I would closely listen to and observe everyday Americans and, as a result, gain a better understanding of what truly resonates in their lives—the overriding purpose of my travels. Other research methods would not have granted me these insights, allowed "average" Americans to participate in the process, nor enabled me to accept their guidance in the way that I wanted—both for personal (why I hit the road) and professional (the credibility of the search) reasons.

- As I traveled, I continued to add to my collection of statistical averages—a.k.a. Mr. Q—that aided in finalizing many criteria. I routinely conducted further research on most categories to make sure that the criteria were supported by credible statistics from government agencies, polling firms, research organizations, news media, and/or other reliable sources. (See the chapter notes for more information on sources.)

- Many of the professional studies about "the average American" that I came across during my search actually referred to the average *adult*. I used such findings only if there was good reason to believe that both the total national population and the total U.S. citizen population were reflected in the majority.

- All but two of the final criteria defined a majority statistic, that is, some characteristic of more than half of the national population. The two other criteria stated the most average American needed to reside in the nation's most average community and that community also needed to reflect the racial/ethnic makeup of the country.

- The average community had to match the same majority statistics that were applied to the Average American. For example, like the Average American, the majority of residents of the most average community would need to have a high-school diploma. Many of the majority statistics describing the Average American were not available or could not be determined on the community level (for example, the level of happiness of a certain community's residents), and therefore were not used in the community criteria.

- Throughout the search, I applied only statistics that were *affirmative* (and in the majority) as criteria, as people had to "earn" their average status. For example, candidates could be advanced for having flown on an airplane or having had a routine physical over the past year (affirmative statistics that capture the majority of Americans, and, as it turned out, the Average American). Conversely, statistics that expressed *inaction* could not be applied as majority statistics. Continuing the above examples, candidates could not advance for *never* having flown to Seattle or for *not* having drugs prescribed to them in a physician's office over the past year (although these groups are in the majority, the statistics refer to inactivity). In addition, two or more minority groups could only be combined to form a majority if together they formed a like category. For example, those

Americans who believe family is important (as opposed to those who do not believe family is important) are in the majority. If the two most-populated minority groups were seamless, they could form a smaller majority. So those who said that family is "extremely" or "very" important (side-by-side answers on the scale) were the two greatest responses overall and created a seamless majority.

- For reasons explained earlier in the book, I decided that the Average American would have to have fulfilled the requirements for at least five years, starting in April 2000, the month on which Census 2000 is based. In keeping with the spirit of the search, each criterion needed to be in place for the majority of the five years, and at the end of the five years, and similarly, the Average American needed to match the criterion both for the majority of the five years and at the end of the five years. For example, Census 2000 determined that 60 percent of the U.S. population was born in the state in which they now reside, and there is good reason to believe that this percentage was in place for the majority of the five years after Census 2000 and at the end of those five years.

- Each search criterion that was a statistical majority was based on a *mean* number whenever possible. "Mean," the traditional statistical term for an average, is the number arrived at after adding up all the numbers in a group and dividing the sum by the number of items. For example, if a group consists of seven people aged 30, 30, 30, 35, 40, 40, and 55, the mean average age of the group is 37.14. Because many people also understand the *median* number to be average, each statistical majority applied during the search also captured the *median* number, if it was known. The median is the point at which there is the same number of individuals above and below. In the above example of ages, 35 is the median.

- If I had a precise average number that would allow me to do so, I determined a "middle majority" to serve as the criterion. I calculated this by starting at the average number and working out evenly and repeatedly in both directions to the nearest single numbers (or to the nearest known increments) until the majority, over 50 percent of the population, was captured. For example, it is just as correct to say that most of the U.S. population is under 40 as it is to say that it is over 30, but for a balanced measurement, I started at 36 (the national mean and median age) and worked out in whole numbers in both directions, then stopped when the majority of the population was captured—making the majority threshold from age 18 through age 53.

- If an average fraction between zero and one could actually describe someone and was known—the average number of inches of dew appearing daily in someone's community, for example— I could make the middle majority between zero and a higher number. However, because zero could not advance someone, the person would be required to have, in the preceding example, at least a trace of daily dew. For those criteria where having something with a fraction less than one was not possible, I would need to stop at one when working out from the average number, and continue in the other direction to capture the majority.

- As U.S. citizens make up more than 93 percent of the total national population, if the "middle majority" was known for either the national population or the national citizen population, and not the other, I accepted that it was the same for both, unless there was good reason to believe otherwise.

- Although I applied the most credible statistics I could find for each criterion, I certainly do not claim that they are perfect. As the Census Bureau notes, "In any large-scale statistical operation, such as Census 2000, human and processing errors occur." If a statistic was released as a majority number, and if I used the statistic rather than dismissing it as biased or potentially inaccurate in some way, it was accepted without change. I did not factor in a margin of error.

- For the census tract information, I utilized the most updated and comprehensive census computer program available—LandView 6, released by the Census Bureau in 2004. The metropolitan-area boundaries and populations applied in the search were those determined by the Census Bureau.

The numbers of candidates remaining—the tallies that appeared at the top of each chapter—were my estimated totals from the search.

Some statistics used during the search were replaced in the book with updated information. All the original conclusions still apply.

Finally, if the way I went about looking for the nation's most average American, or my final conclusion, has any deficiencies or errors, whether they be scientific, interpretative, or of any other sort, these deficiencies are unintentional and my sole responsibility. As I have reflected upon my journey, it is my belief that if I had it all to do over again, I would end up in the exact same place, with the exact same Average American.

# *Notes*

ABBREVIATIONS

C2    Census 2000
CB    U.S. Census Bureau

## AUTHOR'S NOTE

xii    "can expect to spend forty-eight hours": Fetto, John, "Mall Rats," *American Demographics*, March 1, 2002.

## CHAPTER 1: "ALL THAT IS GREAT, GOOD OR BEAUTIFUL"

2    "'great, good or beautiful'": cited in Stigler, Stephen M., *The History of Statistics*, Belknap Press of Harvard University Press, 1986, p. 171.

2    "fat, dumb, and ugly": Among those who have publicly used the phrase to describe the average American: in a humor book, Strupp, Peter, *Fat, Dumb, and Ugly: The Decline of the Average American*, Simon & Schuster, 2004.

7    "a high-school diploma": analysis of CB demographics.

8    "America is often described as NASCAR Nation": Among the outlets that have publicly used the phrase: *National Review*, November 10, 2003, in a cover story of that name, and *The Daily Show* (Comedy Central), July 26, 2005, by host Jon Stewart to introduce a taped piece.

8    "54.1 percent to be precise": C2.

9    "100 million Americans": C2.

## CHAPTER 2: "OBSCURITY IS FOREVER"

12   "'They are the ones of our middle class'": Whyte, William H., *The Organization Man*, Simon & Schuster, 1956.

14   "to a panel discussion": "Snapshots: Documenting the American Family," May 8, 2003, Tribeca Performing Arts Center, New York City.

17   "J. Average would need to hold": 49 percent believe family is "extremely important" and 47 percent believe family is "very important," Gallup, 2003.

## CHAPTER 3: THE MIDDLE WAY

19   "'strip life down'": cited in editor's synopsis of Wilder, Thornton, *Our Town: A Play in Three Acts,* Perennial Classics, 1998.

20   "sixth most sunny": *Dallas Morning News*, June 23, 2004, cites the National Weather Service.

20   "'other industries or occupations'": Lipka, Mitch, "A populist cry to keep 'Garden' in Garden State," *Philadelphia Inquirer*, November 17, 2004.

20   "'critical community issues'": National Civic League press release, "White House Ceremony Today Honors All-America Cities," July 31, 2002.

20   "named Battle Mountain": Weingarten, Gene, "Why Not the Worst?" *Washington Post Magazine*, December 2, 2001.

21   "paid a St. Louis PR firm" / "'call us the most average'": Vogrin, Bill, "Peoria Looking for Respect in Bid for Better Image," Associated Press, August 6, 1987.

21   "survey of cities": Lohr, Steve, "Forget Peoria: It's Now, 'Will It Play in Tulsa?'" *New York Times*, July 1, 1992.

21   "Wichita Falls, Texas, metropolitan area": Fine, Jon, "A Visit to America's Most Average City," AdAge.com, November 26, 2001.

21   "'I think we're something else'": Hanna, Bill, "Wichita Falls, Texas, finds new title more than middling good," *Fort Worth Star-Telegram*, December 7, 2001.

22   "'most young people are well balanced'": "The Corporation of the District of Saanich: Youth Development Strategy," 2003.

22    "randomly plucked from the files": Geographic Names and Information System, United States Geological Survey.

25    "'the landscape of the soul'": Rivenburg, Roy, "Is Boredom Bad?" *Los Angeles Times*, February 22, 2003.

26    "covered in depth": Johnson, Steven, *Everything Bad Is Good for You*, Riverhead Books, 2005.

27    "'dumbing down or compromising'": Surowiecki, James, *The Wisdom of Crowds*, Doubleday, 2004, p. 35.

28    "books per public-school student": both figures from National Center for Education Statistics.

30    "most Americans are either in school": C2.

30    "headed by a married couple": CB.

31    "26 percent of Americans who live alone": CB.

31    "in bed": 74 percent of Americans are regularly in bed before midnight, National Sleep Foundation, study conducted by WB&A, 2001.

31    "million night-shift workers": Epstein, Victor, "Night crews inhabit different world," *Omaha World-Herald*, October 23, 2001, cites "Circadian Technologies Inc., a night-shift management consulting firm."

## CHAPTER 4: ORDINARY MAGIC

35*n*  "Speaking of Martin, his 2003 novel": Martin, Steve, *The Pleasure of My Company*, Hyperion, 2003. Another fictional account of a singular most average American comes from author Judy Budnitz, in "Average Joe," a short story published in her book *Flying Leap*, Picador USA, 1998.

36    "'the religious aspect of the country'": de Tocqueville, Alexis, *Democracy in America*, various editions, 1835–1840.

36    "would believe in God": 92 percent, Quinnipiac University Polling Institute, 2003.

38    "primary faith is Christian": 159,506,000 out of 207,980,000 adults, 2001, "Statistical Abstract of the United States: 2003," U.S. Census Bureau, 2003.

38    "respect others' religions": 37 percent are "very positive toward other faith traditions" and 50 percent are "tolerant of other religious points of view," Gallup, 2003.

38     "proclaim America a Christian nation": Quindlen, Anna, "The Spirit of the Season," *Time*, January 3, 2005, p. 139.

38     "could not place Protestants": Price, Joyce Howard, "U.S. Protestant population seen losing majority status," *Washington Times*, July 21, 2004.

39     "attend church services at least once a month": 58 percent, Gallup, 2003.

39     "religion is a 'very important' aspect of his or her life": 61 percent, Gallup, November 2003.

41     "'no longer liberates, but debilitates'": Schwartz, Barry, *The Paradox of Choice*, Ecco, 2004, p. 2.

### CHAPTER 5: YOUR NAME IN LIGHTS

52     "Robert McKee declared": McKee, Robert, *Story*, Regan Books, 1997.

52n     "In 2004, Dr. Alan Wilson and his colleagues": Schwartz, John, "Just Average, and Therein Lay His Greatness," *New York Times*, November 16, 2004.

53     "marquee borrowed from": Scott, A. O., "That Mythic American Hero: The Regular Guy," *New York Times*, December 8, 2002.

53n     "Regarding Paul Giamatti": Booth, William, "Your Truly Average Leading Man," *Washington Post*, October 28, 2004.

55     "J. Average lives in a traditional house": C2.

55     "a 'one-unit, detached'": C2.

55     "one or two motor vehicles": C2.

55     "have a garage or carport": 64,547,000 out of 106,261,000 housing units, "Statistical Abstract of the United States: 2003," U.S. Census Bureau, 2003.

55     "living in a home of two, three, or four persons": CB data analysis (2003 American Housing Survey, from Census Bureau: two-person homes, 34.424 million; three-person homes, 17.326 million; four-person homes, 15.319 million).

57     "The only income group in the minority": Russell, Cheryl, "Most Households Have Fun Money to Spend," *American Consumers*, December 1999.

61     "at least one pet": Kogan, Rick, "Best in World," *Chicago Tribune Magazine*, March 31, 2002.

62    "'cavorting desperately, endlessly, before us'": de Zengotita, Thomas, "Attack of the Superzeroes," *Harper's*, December 2004.

63    "Las Vegas has become the most popular tourist city in America": Stein, Joel, "The Strip is Back," *Time,* July 26, 2004.

63    "'more upscale and younger'": Grover, Ronald, "How Will TV Survive Its Own Reality Show," *BusinessWeek*, October 11, 2004.

67    "found unhappiness common": O'Neill, Jessie H., *The Golden Ghetto: The Psychology of Affluence*, Hazelton, 1997.


## CHAPTER 6: GUNS, GAMBLING, AND GIVING IT AWAY

72    "who recycles at least on occasion": 88 percent, Roper, 1997.

74    "Americans say gambling is 'an acceptable entertainment option for themselves or others'": Peter D. Hart Research Associates, 2003.


## CHAPTER 7: SOMEWHERE OVER THE RAINBOW

85    "had risen 369 percent": Jones, Del, "Saucony CEO puts his foot down on loyalty," *USA Today*, October 18, 2004.

85    "'average Americans and their hopes, fears, and values'": cited in Yardley, Jonathan, "The Mouse That Roared," *Washington Post*, January 18, 1998.

85n   "after a thirteen-year study/'anatomical sense'": Wilford, John Noble, "Running Extra Mile Sets Humans Apart in Primates' World," *New York Times*, November 18, 2004.

95    "'with people you like'": Burling, Stacey, "We're so flaky about snow," *Philadelphia Inquirer*, December 5, 2002.

95    "annual average falls in the 45- to 65-degree range": analysis of NOAA data.

96    "I found that this makes the majority of Americans aged eighteen through fifty-three": CB.

97    "a July 2003 front-page story on the report": McClintock, Pamela, *Daily Variety*, July 22, 2003.

97    "'buying the same brand'": Greene, Kelly, "Marketing surprise: Older consumers buy stuff, too," *Baltimore Sun* (via *Wall Street Journal*), April 12, 2004.

97  "Well, the Average American can name all Three Stooges"/"When he takes a shower": Winter, Christine, *Sun-Sentinel*, "And the survey says . . . ," August 27, 2000.

97  "he sometimes pees": Brown, Terry, "Tick One Box Only," *Herald Sun*, December 1, 2001.

97  "but never sings": Grimes, David, "America's bathrooms are busy," *Sarasota Herald-Tribune*, April 15, 2001, cites survey conducted by National Association of Continence.

98  "The Average American would spend most of his time indoors": 18 hours spent indoors for every hour spent outdoors, Raymond F. Dawson, director, Texas Institute for the Indoor Environment, Department of Civil Engineering, University of Texas at Austin, "Indoor Environmental Science and Engineering" presentation, Environment in the Balance conference, San Diego, California, 2003.

99  "smooth over chunky peanut butter": Snapshot, *USA Today*, March 8, 1999.

104  "'And get heavier'": Bjerga, Alan, "Is the U.S. government's farm policy making you fat?" *Wichita Eagle*, November 28, 2004.

108  "'the home church of Jesus Christ'": Hayden, Dolores, *Building Suburbia: Green Fields and Urban Growth, 1820–2000*, Pantheon, 2003.

109  "NBC News singled out in 1964": The calculation was for *David Brinkley's Journal:* "Election Year in Averagetown."

109  "James Cain chose the Los Angeles suburb of Glendale": *Los Angeles Times*, December 28, 2003.

114  "'the real source of his power'": *New York Times*, March 29, 1969.

## CHAPTER 8: GOING COASTAL

122  "J. Average needed to have a stereo": 75 percent in 2001, "Statistical Abstract of the United States: 2003," U.S. Census Bureau, 2003.

123  "A landmark 2003 study": cited by Wade, Nicholas, and Wilford, John Noble, "New World Ancestors Lose 12,000 Years," *New York Times*, July 25, 2003.

126  "'The bar has gone up'": Morton, Carol Cruzan, "Harvard Public Health Now" newsletter, February 7, 2003.

128  "'impacted' by drugs or alcohol": Peter D. Hart Research Associates, 2004.

131 "how far most of the population lives from the ocean": Grassle, J. Frederick, director of marine and coastal sciences, Rutgers University, presentation to U.S. House subcommittees, Washington, D.C., July 12, 2001. And Bouchier, David, "Want Less Traffic? Try Nebraska," *New York Times*, April 23, 2000.

## CHAPTER 9: FANFARE FOR THE COMMON MAN

133 "'mowed the lawn with my cousin'": Hoffer, Richard, "The importance of being Barry," *Sports Illustrated*, May 24, 1993.

133 "'Hey, I'm an ordinary, average guy'": Allan Hug, a spokesman for Americans For Better Choice, cited as source of quote in "Ditka: Second Thoughts Until the Day I Die," WGMG-TV (www.local6.com), July 14, 2004.

133 "deodorant at the supermarket": Elfman, Doug, "Average Dude," *Las Vegas Review-Journal*, April 23, 2004.

134 "'the triumph of the average man'": Keller, Bill, "The Radical Presidency of George W. Bush," *New York Times Magazine*, January 26, 2003.

134 "'he puts on that barn jacket'": Dowd, Maureen, "Pride and Prejudice," *New York Times*, March 18, 2004.

134 "was not what Kerry said at the rally": Pesca, Mike, "Fumble on the Kerry," *Slate*, September 28, 2004.

138 "'The stigma of being gay'": Mehren, Elizabeth, "Acceptance of Gays Rises Among New Generation," *Los Angeles Times*, April 11, 2004.

139 "The last time a particular television program": *The World Almanac and Book of Facts*, World Almanac Books, 2005, p. 313.

140 "the American colonies already had a higher per capita income": Barone, Michael, "A Place Like No Other," *U.S. News & World Report*, June 28/July 5, 2004.

142 "Most workers in America have a maximum commute of 5 miles": "Today Is 'Bike to Work Day,'" *Arizona Daily Sun*, May 26, 2004.

142 "24.3 minutes": CB, American Community Survey 2003.

143 "about three in four U.S. homes": Bragg, Roy, "Got beef? You're not alone," *San Antonio Express-News*, February 14, 2004, cites 77 percent from National Cattleman's Beef Association.

146 "'We are not a mass marketer'": Bianco, Anthony, "The Vanishing Mass Market," *BusinessWeek*, July 12, 2004.

148 "J. Average would need to consume ice cream at least once a month": 78 percent of Americans eat ice cream at least once a month, PR Newswire, July 7, 2004, press release announcing results of Harris Interactive survey for Dairy Queen.

148 "live within 2 miles of a public park": 75 percent, National Recreation and Park Association, 2003. More than 75 percent use local parks and recreation facilities.

## CHAPTER 10: AVERAGE AMERICAN VOTER

150 "in an Olean newspaper story": Eberth, John T., "Northrup, Bean are political newcomers, but not novices," [Olean-Bradford-Wellsville] *Times Herald*, October 22, 2004.

151 "The nonprofit Recovery, Inc.": Low quote from Recovery website.

154 "politician is Democratic": "We're the teechers [sic] round hear," *Economist*, November 22, 2003.

154 "there are over 15 million more registered Democrats": about 72 million registered Democrats and about 55 million registered Republicans, Neuharth, Al, "Why politics is fun from the catbirds' seats," *USA Today*, January 23, 2004.

155 "more than half of all Americans use mobile phones": Rodgers, Will, "Always Roaming," *Tampa Tribune*, May 26, 2003.

155 "the average American is within five years of his best friend's age": Yost, Barbara, "Face it, we need each other," *Arizona Republic*, May 6, 2004, cites *American Demographics* as source.

157 "where they spent the most time growing up": Opinion Research Corporation, 2004.

157 "Christmas tree annually": 80 percent, Ohio University E.W. Scripps School of Journalism, 2002.

164 "'means a good job and financial security'": Bartlett, Bruce, "American Dream Momentum," National Review Online, October 18, 2004.

164 "at least one living parent": based on AARP findings for the senior population.

164 "at least one living sibling": 95 percent of all American adults under

sixty-five, Crispell, Diane, "The Sibling Syndrome," *American Demographics*, August 1996.

169　"Wal-Mart saved Americans a total of about $20 billion": Bianco, Anthony, and Zellner, Wendy, "Is Wal-Mart Too Powerful," *BusinessWeek*, October 6, 2003.

169　"twenty-minute drive of a Wal-Mart": from *St. Louis Business Journal*, November 14, 1997. This is conservative given the growth of Wal-Mart (which would not release an approximate figure). However, the Average American ended up living well within this twenty-minute mark: indeed, about a five-minute door-to-door drive from residence to store.

### CHAPTER 11: SON OF THE FATHER OF THE AVERAGE AMERICAN

177　"flying a blimp over the city": Moore, David W., *The Superpollsters*, Four Walls Eight Windows, 1995, pp. 31–32.

182　"'The average Connecticut does not exist'": quote from "Study fails to find 'average' Connecticut town," Associated Press, 2004.

184　"seventy-nine private golf clubs in Connecticut": analysis of listings on ctgolfer.com.

185　"With me was the church newsletter": January 16, 2005, for Sunday services at the Church of Our Savior, New York City. The newsletter also noted something not so ordinary: "President George W. Bush has invited one of our faithful, William McGurn, to be his chief speechwriter."

### CHAPTER 12: THE AVERAGE AMERICAN

191　"a local promotional flyer": "Come to Historic Willimantic," distributed by the Windham Region Chamber of Commerce.

191　"heroin arrests": Gordon, Tracy, "Heroin Town," *The Hartford Courant*, October 2002.

193　"'I ran the soap under the faucet'": "Local man finds faith in a bar of soap," Daly, Gail Ellen, *Chronicle,* March 15, 2005.

193　"from a [Willimantic] *Chronicle* article": Lake, Heather, "Newest Cupid stunned by honor," [Willimantic] *Chronicle*, February 15, 2005.

200 "a story about a survey": "Most Foolish American survey crowns Michael Jackson as biggest fool," *Seattle Post-Intelligencer* (via Associated Press), April 1, 2005.

200 "the farce": performed in town at the Burton Leavitt Theatre on Main Street.

203 "at least 0.1 inches of snow annually": analysis of NOAA data.

203 "can read English": C2.

203 "can speak English fluently": C2.

203 "has visited the ocean": Ocean Conservancy.

203 "has cable service": 68.0 percent in 2001, "Statistical Abstract of the United States: 2003," U.S. Census Bureau, 2003.

204 "home has a porch and/or deck and/or balcony and/or patio": "Statistical Abstract of the United States: 2003," U.S. Census Bureau, 2003.

204 "has read or has started to read at least one book within the past year": 81 percent, Gallup, 2002.

204 "home has between four and six living-purpose rooms": CB.

204 "visits the dentist annually": Centers for Disease Control and Prevention.

204 "has a credit card": Sautters, Denise, "Living beyond their means," Copley News Service, May 4, 2004.

204 "ATM card": 69.8 percent in 2001, "Statistical Abstract of the United States: 2003," U.S. Census Bureau, 2003, p. 750.

204 "has played video or computer games over the past year": Peter D. Hart and Associates, 2000.

204 "football fan": Gallup, 2001.

204 "a baseball fan": Gallup, 2001.

204 "political viewpoints": National Election Studies, 2000.

204 "has listed phone number": Survey Sampling International, 2002 (72 percent of Americans).

204 "eats at McDonald's": Schlosser, Eric, *Fast Food Nation*, Houghton Mifflin, 2001.

204 "live within 3 miles of a McDonald's": Allen, Scott, "The Greening of McDonald's": *Boston Globe*, January 24, 2000.

204 "lives in the middle majority of the nation's populated areas": CB metropolitan-area data analysis.

## A NOTE ON METHODOLOGY

224   "having flown on an airplane": 90 percent of Americans have flown, a threefold increase over the past three decades, Forbes.com, September 15, 2003.

Some poll data was accessed from the on-line database of the Roper Center for Public Opinion Research.

For more notes, please visit www.theaverageamerican.com. On the site, you will also find further and recommended reading, a bibliography, and other news related to *The Average American*.

# Acknowledgments

*I appreciate immensely* the guidance I received from Rebecca Klemm, the president of Klemm Analysis Group, a statistics firm in Washington, D.C. As I first began this project, Rebecca helped me better understand national demographics and provided valuable reassurance that my quest to find the most average American was scientifically sound. Also at the very beginning, La Neice Collins and Lisa Walden provided research assistance and were a joy to work with. I would also like to acknowledge and thank Alison Carlson for starting me down the path that led me to the would-be client mentioned in the book's prelude.

I enjoyed turning my experience into a book in large part because it allowed me to work closely with two remarkable professionals—my editor David Patterson and my agent Jennifer Joel. To each of them, I am forever grateful for their expertise and kindness. Peter Osnos, the book's publisher, provided tremendous support for which I am deeply grateful.

In addition to the many people—some average Americans and some not-so-average Americans—mentioned earlier in the book, I would like to recognize those who helped me to get to the end of the road and to get the job done: Bonnie Card, Henry Chanin, Lorraine Chanin, Meryl Coratelo, Cathie Horn, Peter Leeds, Wayne Norman, Neal O'Keefe, Todd O'Keefe, Sue O'Keefe, Shaughn O'Keefe, George Parker, and Bev York.

For their assistance during the writing process, I would like to acknowledge Jaime Leifer, Robert Kimzey, James Martin, Clive Priddle, Melissa Raymond, Alyssa Sheinmel, Katie Sigelman, and Katherine Streckfus. I thank—most of all—my wife Kathy, my inspiration beyond words.

---

# Index

of *The* Average American, 213–214
height as, 1–2, 170–171, 204,
213–214
weight as, 101–104, 112, 213–214
*Pitfall,* 201
Place names, averageness of, 22
Plato, 121
*The Pleasure of My Company*
(Martin), 35
Pledge of Allegiance, 36
Politics. *See also* Presidency, American
Average American Party in,
150–151, 153, 158, 160–161
average Americans' beliefs about,
23–24, 27, 64, 204, 210, 213
*The* Average American and, 210,
213
averageness in, 6–7, 134–135
*Bowling Alone* on, 158
Builders Party in, 161
celebrities and, 167
centrism in, 158–160
children and, 166–167
culture war in, 158
democracy in, 6–7
Democratic Party in, 144–145, 158,
166–167, 204
elections in, 134–136, 146, 148,
149–150, 154–155, 157–158,
160–161
Green Party in, 161
House of Representatives in, 145,
153, 204
Libertarian Party in, 161
local, 153–154, 160–161
mudslinging in, 149–150
*The Myth of a Polarized Nation* on,
158
in New York, 149–150, 155,
157–158, 160–161
news media and, 154, 158–159, 182
Noonan on, 134
O'Neill, Tip, on, 154
opinion polls in, 158–159, 177,
179, 181

partisanship in, 144–145, 158
Peace and Justice Party in, 161
in Pennsylvania, 135–136
Populism in, 111
presidential candidacies in,
134–136, 146, 154, 177, 179
redistricting in, 144
religion and, 39, 137–138
representation in, 145, 153, 204
Republican Party in, 144–145, 158,
166–167, 177, 204
running and, 86
Senators in, 145, 153, 204
Socialist Workers Party in, 161
state, 181
strategies in, 146–147
television influencing, 154
voter registration and, 143, 145,
154, 193, 204
voter turnout in, 160, 163
women in, 181–182
Populism, 111
Presidency, American
of Bush, George W., 113, 134, 136,
138, 144, 146, 154, 159, 179
candidacies for, 134–136, 146, 154,
177, 179
of Eisenhower, 36, 112–114
of FDR, 46, 82, 145, 166, 177, 180
of Ford, 39
of Hoover, 134
of Jefferson, 3, 6–7, 144
Kerry running for, 134–136, 154,
179
of Lincoln, 105
of Nixon, 145
opinion polls on, 159, 177, 179
of Reagan, 134, 139
of women, 182
*The Progress Paradox* (Easterbrook),
65–66
Protestantism, 34, 36, 38, 41–42,
62–63
PTA. *See* Parent-Teachers Association
Public opinion polls. *See* Opinion polls

# DATE DUE

| | | | |
|---|---|---|---|
| | | | |
| | | | |
| | | | |
| | | | |
| | | | |
| | | | |
| | | | |
| | | | |
| | | | |
| | | | |
| | | | |
| | | | |
| | | | |
| | | | |
| | | | |
| | | | |
| | | | |
| | | | |
| | | | |

GAYLORD | | | PRINTED IN U.S.A.